CREEPY **ANALYTICS**

This wonderful, insightful, timely, and inspiring book is a must-read for anyone seeking to grasp the essential risks and rewards of studying the human experience in the workplace. *Creepy Analytics* serves as a thoroughly researched and skillfully written guide for business leaders, CHROs, and HR analytics professionals who aspire to harness the promise and potential of people data and analytics—ethically and responsibly.

—Al Adamsen
Founder and CEO, People Analytics and Future of Work

This excellent book, by one of the leading voices in HR analytics, highlights the dangerous gap between what we *could* and *should* know about people through data and AI, and provides smart ethical recommendations for avoiding legal troubles.

—Tomas Chamorro-Premuzic
Professor, University College London and Columbia University;
author of *I, Human: AI, Automation, and the
Quest to Reclaim What Makes Us Unique*

HR analytics represents the new data-driven methods for change. In this book, Falletta is the George Carlin of HR, speaking truth to power, while providing a practical process that ensures our commitment to remaining evidence-based and ethical.

—Beth Feild
Director and Head, Organization Development, Xerox

Falletta has built a handbook for ethical practices throughout the HR analytics cycle. This book is chock-full of useful direction for addressing important HR analytics questions in organizations in an effective and ethical way. Leaders, managers, HR professionals, HR analytics practitioners, and students will all find this volume valuable!

—Alexis Fink
VP, People Analytics and Workforce Strategy, Meta;
President, Society for Industrial and
Organizational Psychology

Falletta has done a masterful job addressing some of the most important ethical issues for workforce analytics which are often cast by the wayside. This book provides an important perspective that all leaders and practitioners working in the space should read.

—Alec Levenson
Senior Research Scientist, Center for Effective Organizations,
Marshall School of Business, University of Southern California

Without a framework, such as the one introduced in this new book, it is difficult to stay firmly grounded when generating HR analytical insights and making ethical decisions given the shifting legal landscape, the evolving workplace, as well as the arrival of increasingly powerful artificial intelligence platforms. In this book, Falletta provides a compass for this brave new journey.

—Rebecca Ray
EVP, Human Capital, The Conference Board

Falletta in *Creepy Analytics* makes a compelling case for the HR analytics community to stop, step back, and evaluate the value and the proper position of their work. As a CHRO, I now want my team to read this together and to plot our analytics strategy against it.

—Bill Strahan
EVP, Human Resources, Comcast

CREEPY
ANALYTICS

Avoid Crossing the Line and Establish Ethical HR
Analytics for Smarter Workforce Decisions

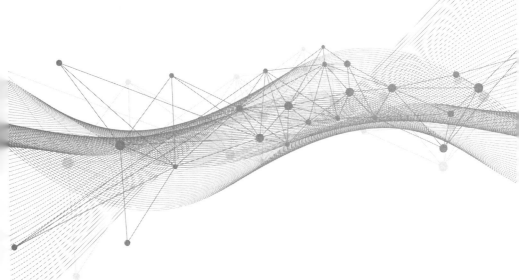

SALVATORE V. FALLETTA

1 2 3 4 5 6 7 8 9   LCR   29 28 27 26 25 24

ISBN   978-1-265-13267-5
MHID   1-265-13267-4

e-ISBN   978-1-265-13361-0
e-MHID   1-265-13361-1

This publication is designed to provide accurate and authoritative information in regard to the subject matter covered. It is sold with the understanding that neither the author nor the publisher is engaged in rendering legal, accounting, securities trading, or other professional services. If legal advice or other expert assistance is required, the services of a competent professional person should be sought.
    —*From a Declaration of Principles Jointly Adopted by a Committee of the American Bar Association and a Committee of Publishers and Associations*

McGraw Hill books are available at special quantity discounts to use as premiums and sales promotions or for use in corporate training programs. To contact a representative, please visit the Contact Us pages at www.mhprofessional.com.

McGraw Hill is committed to making our products accessible to all learners. To learn more about the available support and accommodations we offer, please contact us at accessibility@mheducation.com. We also participate in the Access Text Network (www .accesstext.org), and ATN members may submit requests through ATN.

CONTENTS

PART I

The Promise and Peril
of HR Analytics

PART II

The HR Analytics Cycle

ACKNOWLEDGMENTS

This ambitious undertaking received support from numerous individuals, and although it would be challenging to mention them all, I would like to express my heartfelt gratitude. First and foremost, I am immensely thankful to my family for their unwavering support and patience throughout the entire research and writing process. I am especially grateful to my wonderful wife and partner, Wendy Combs; my daughter, Sabrina Falletta; and my sons, Brandon Falletta and Logan Falletta. I would also like to honor the memory of my late mother, Hope Falletta, and extend my love and appreciation to my father, Salvatore Falletta, as well as my father and mother-in-law, Richard (RJ) and Suzanne Combs.

In addition, I want to extend special recognition to individuals who played significant roles in this endeavor. My sincere thanks go to the editorial team: Pattie Amoroso, Christopher Brown, Donya Dickerson, Maureen Harper, Michele Matrisciani, and Jonathan Sperling at McGraw Hill, as well as the layout design and copyediting team: Steve Straus and Alison Shurtz, whose guidance and support have been invaluable. I am also grateful to Nicole Lacasse for her exceptional work in creating the models, frameworks, and figures in this book.

Furthermore, I would like to acknowledge the support and friendship of my good friends, colleagues, mentors, and supporters. Kevin and Dena Niksich, hailing from the great state of Georgia, kept me grounded with their outdoor adventures, mountain climbing and hiking, and ultrarunning. Kimberly and Austin Cone, my fantastic neighbors, have been a constant source of inspiration and companionship. Anna McCurdy provided invaluable compassion, counseling, and coaching to support my post-pandemic psychological well-being. Ade McCormack, a brilliant colleague whose expertise encompasses leadership, digital disruption, and helping organizations adapt to an "increasingly unknowable world," has provided both wit and inspiration on this journey. I am grateful to Rajashi Ghosh, my former colleague and departmental chair at Drexel University, who is now at Teachers College at Columbia University, for her friendship, mentorship, and support. I would also like to express my gratitude to my teacher and mentor, Dr. George A. Baker III, Professor Emeritus, North Carolina State University, who unfortunately passed away during the course of the research for this book, but whose influence and teachings will always remain with me.

Additionally, I extend special thanks to Peter Romero, People Analytics Lead at the University of Cambridge's Psychometrics Centre, and his colleagues Akiyo Tsuchimoto and Hiraku Nakanishi at the Institution for a Global Society, as well as Haruka Asai at Tamura Corporation for graciously contributing a case study for this book.

Lastly, I would like to extend my heartfelt appreciation to the individuals who shared their insights during interviews for this book. Special thanks go to Chris Butler and Richard Rosenow from One Model, and Nicholas Garbis from Ford Motor Company. Additionally, I am grateful to the many HR leaders, experts, and HR analytics practitioners who provided encouragement and support, as well as those who reviewed the manuscript and provided feedback and endorsements, including Al Adamsen, Amy Armitage, Tomas Chamorro-Premuzic, Pasquale Davide de Palma, Robin Erickson, Beth Feild, Alexis Fink, Jessica Kriegel, Alec Levenson, Amit Mohindra, Kevin Oakes, Rebecca Ray, and Bill Strahan.

INTRODUCTION

Most people work just hard enough not to get fired
and get paid just enough money not to quit.

—George Carlin

In the wake of global talent shortages, the great resignation, and the "quiet quitting" phenomenon, as well as the ongoing transformational and technological trends, the promise and potential for HR analytics have never been greater for the HR profession and the organizations we serve. HR analytics has a long and rich history of adding value to businesses. Over the years, it has evolved from its humble beginnings in HR research and measurement to encompass a broader range of data sources, methods, practices, AI-powered technologies, and analytical tools. Leading organizations are indeed leveraging advanced HR analytics to glean critical insights that inform workforce decision-making.

Throughout the past decade, several excellent books have been written on the topic of HR analytics, also known as talent analytics, human capital analytics, people analytics, or workforce analytics. For instance, Alec Levenson's book *Strategic Analytics* is an exceptional resource that advocates for an enterprise approach to analytics to ensure alignment with the strategic objectives of organizations.[1] Another outstanding book is *The Power of People* by Nigel Guenole, Jonathan Ferrar, and Sheri Feinzig, which makes a compelling case for broader label for the field, namely "workforce analytics," considering the composition and characteristics of today's workforce (including employees, contract workers, gig workers, and others).[2] Recently, Jonathan Ferrar and David Green have authored a comprehensive and practical book titled *Excellence in People Analytics*.[3] This book not only includes several case studies but also serves as a blueprint for the HR analytics community, emphasizing the importance of establishing an overall governance and operating model.

However, despite the excellent resources available and good intentions of the HR analytics community, there has been a gradual erosion of workplace privacy and ethics, alongside a "datafication" and "quantified employee" agenda that undermines the potential benefits of HR analytics. While many in the HR analytics community argue that "big data" doesn't mean Big Brother, numerous workplace technologies, practices, and stories have garnered negative attention. Therefore, our profession needs an evidence-based and ethical approach to developing HR analytics capabilities that cultivates an ethical mindset and establishes an ethical ecosystem throughout an organization's HR analytics journey.

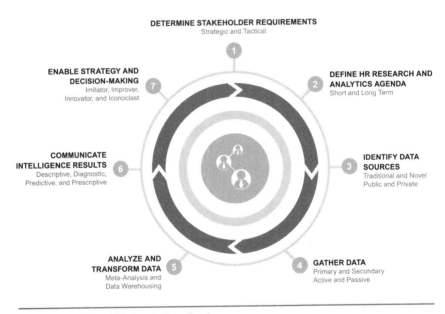

DETERMINE STAKEHOLDER REQUIREMENTS
Strategic and Tactical
1

ENABLE STRATEGY AND
DECISION-MAKING
Imitator, Improver,
Innovator, and Iconoclast
7

DEFINE HR RESEARCH AND
ANALYTICS AGENDA
Short and Long Term
2

COMMUNICATE
INTELLIGENCE RESULTS
Descriptive, Diagnostic,
Predictive, and Prescriptive
6

IDENTIFY DATA
SOURCES
Traditional and Novel
Public and Private
3

ANALYZE AND
TRANSFORM DATA
Meta-Analysis and
Data Warehousing
5

GATHER DATA
Primary and Secondary
Active and Passive
4

Figure I.1   The HR Analytics Cycle

In 2008, I introduced a seven-step process approach for building HR analytics capabilities, known as the HR analytics cycle (Figure I.1).[4] Throughout the years, we have adapted the HR analytics cycle to incorporate current trends, tools, and techniques, with a particular emphasis on four key areas: (1) evidence-based management, (2) HR research and experimentation,

(3) ethical practice, and (4) strategy and execution. Considering these areas, HR analytics can be defined as a proactive and systematic process for ethically gathering, analyzing, communicating, and using evidence-based HR research and analytical insights to enable smarter workforce decisions and help organizations achieve their strategic objectives.

This book, *Creepy Analytics: Avoid Crossing the Line and Establish Ethical HR Analytics for Smarter Workforce Decisions*, presents a retooled HR analytics cycle that prioritizes evidence-based and ethical practices. While the main title, *Creepy Analytics*, may imply a singular focus on dubious HR analytics practices and a new-Luddism indictment of digital HR and AI-powered technologies, the primary objective of this book is to provide a practical guide to implementing HR analytics ethically and responsibly while raising the bar to be more evidence-based.

Creepy Analytics will be helpful to several different audiences, including:

- HR analytics leaders
- HR analytics practitioners
- HR analysts
- Chief HR officers
- Social, behavioral, and organizational scientists
- HR professionals
- Talent management leaders
- HR architects and strategists
- Workforce planning specialists
- HR center of expertise (CoE) leaders who are accountable for HR analytics and strategy work
- External consultants who specialize in HR analytics, strategy, and talent management
- Data scientists who specialize in HR analytics
- Behavioral economists
- Human capital management (HCM) technologists

In Part I, I introduce and discuss the promise and peril of HR analytics. Chapter 1 provides an overview of the promise and potential of analytics in the context of HR, including a definition of HR analytics and the multitude of monikers used to describe the practice. This chapter also offers historical context, acknowledging the pioneers who laid the foundation for HR analytics long before the emergence of big data and the data science revolution. Chapter 2 delves into the potential pitfalls of

HR analytics, considering datafication, technological advancements (such as black box AI-powered platforms), the "Future of Work," and what I refer to as the "quantified employee agenda." Chapter 3 further explores the paradox and peril of HR analytics, focusing on a range of practices, technologies, and data sources that exist within ethical gray areas, some of which have been deemed questionable to downright creepy. Chapter 4 introduces the concept of evidence-based management, highlighting its connection to HR analytics, workforce decisions, and the adoption of HR practices. This chapter emphasizes the significance of cultivating an ethical mindset and establishing an ethical ecosystem, and it introduces a framework for ethical outcomes at each step of the HR analytics cycle.

Part II provides a comprehensive explanation of the seven-step HR analytics cycle:

Step 1: Determine Stakeholder Requirements (Chapter 5)

Step 2: Define HR Analytics and Research Agenda (Chapter 6)

Step 3: Identify Data Sources (Chapter 7)

Step 4: Gather Data (Chapter 8)

Step 5: Analyze and Transform Data (Chapter 9)

Step 6: Communicate Intelligence Results (Chapter 10)

Step 7: Enable Strategy and Decision-Making (Chapter 11)

At the end of each chapter, ethical practice guidelines and tips are outlined for each step of the HR analytics cycle. These practice tips aim to promote the ethical outcomes mentioned earlier and to guide the development of HR analytics capabilities without crossing the creepy line.

In Part III, guidelines for starting and scaling the HR analytics CoE are discussed in Chapter 12. This includes recommendations on how to structure and position the HR analytics function for success, as well as the role, competencies, and characteristics of the HR analytics leader and the composition of the broader HR analytics team. Chapter 13 highlights three case studies using the HR analytics cycle as a framework. These case studies demonstrate practical applications of HR analytics in real-world scenarios. In the Conclusion, I share some thoughts regarding the future of evidence-based and ethical HR analytics, deliver a clarion call to the HR analytics community, and offer some distinct perspectives as to whether we will ultimately have a bright or a dark future.

PART I

The Promise and Peril of HR Analytics

CHAPTER 1

Monikers, Meaning, and Misleading Origin Story

*Right now, I'm having amnesia and déjà vu at the
same time . . . I think I've forgotten this before.*

—Steven Wright

The human resource (HR) profession is abuzz with talk among scholars, practitioners, thought leaders, and technology vendors of the
promise and potential of HR analytics—or what is synonymously
referred to as talent, human capital, people, or workforce analytics. Despite
the hype and flurry of interest in HR analytics, there is little agreement on
the monikers and meaning used to label and describe the practice. Moreover, there is little clarity on the HR analytics origin story. Some insist that
HR analytics is a new, revolutionary discipline, while others characterize
HR analytics as evolutionary capability and practice.

This chapter provides an overview of the terms used to refer to analytics in the context of human resources and explores the meaning of HR
analytics based on definitions from both academic and popular sources. A
more inclusive definition for HR analytics is presented, which emphasizes
the importance of evidence-based management, the broader role of HR

research and experimentation, ethical considerations, and HR analytics' role in strategy and execution. This chapter also offers historical context and recognition to those who paved the way for HR analytics long before the rise of the "big data" and data science revolution, and the plethora of SaaS-based platforms and data visualization tools that followed.

Multiple Monikers

Before delving into the meaning of HR analytics, it may be helpful to describe the multitude of terms used to label the practice. Although there is a general consensus around the overall value and impact of HR analytics, there are both nuance and definitive distinctions between the labels.[1] For example, the following monikers are frequently used across the HR community:

* Human capital analytics
* Talent analytics
* Workforce analytics
* People analytics
* HR analytics

In general, HR professionals use these monikers interchangeably, while others in the HR analytics community tend to align themselves more or less with a specific moniker. Although seemingly synonymous, each moniker differs with respect to purpose, underlying values, and the competencies and capabilities needed to carry out HR analytics work. These subtle differences also suggest how HR analytics should be structured and organized, and where it should reside in the organization in terms of ownership, leadership, and accountability.[2]

Human Capital Analytics

"Human capital analytics" was one of the earlier terms used to describe the HR analytics movement and associated activities and work. Although infrequently used today, this moniker is still favored among those advocating for human capital reporting standards and in the management consulting industry intent on demonstrating the economic value, impact, and return on investment (ROI) of HR programs, practices, and processes. However, few organizations use this moniker today to describe their HR analytics capabilities in terms of measuring the intangible value of human capital and delivering evidence-based and ethical analytical insights that enable HR strategy and smarter workforce decisions.

Talent Analytics

In the context of talent management and the war for talent, "talent analytics" is another popular moniker. However, this particular term has lost some of its luster within certain sectors and industries (e.g., government, highly unionized organizations) given its narrower and perhaps exclusive focus on the acquisition, development, and retention of high-potential talent. High-potential talent refers to "individuals with the talent (innate characteristics and learned skills), ability, and desire to rise to and succeed in a more senior role."[3] Outside of the United States, throughout Europe and much of Asia, "the term *talent* is reserved for only the highest performing employees."[4] As such, talent analytics does not necessarily represent the broader workforce nor consider the organization as a whole in terms of organizational behavior and effectiveness. Nonetheless, some organizations continue to use "talent analytics" or "talent intelligence" to describe their HR analytics capabilities, particularly when it resides within the workforce planning, talent acquisition, and/or talent management function.

People Analytics

"People analytics" is arguably the most popular moniker in use today to describe HR analytics. In their book *Excellence in People Analytics*, Jonathan Ferrar and David Green contend that "people analytics is not about HR. People analytics is about the business."[5] Indeed, people analytics is about adding business value and gleaning critical workforce insights for smarter workforce decisions, assuming it is performed ethically and responsibly. When it comes to the "people analytics" moniker itself, who could argue with it? It seems friendly enough and connotes a set of underlying humanistic values as compared to sterile, dehumanizing terms such as "human resources" or "workforce." Notwithstanding, the term "people analytics" suggests the analysis of data on people outside of the context of work and the workplace, which signifies a lack of boundaries for the practice when you consider privacy and ethics.

Workforce Analytics

"Workforce analytics" is a more inclusive moniker that is gaining momentum within the broader HR analytics community. In their book *The Power of People*, Nigel Guenole, Jonthan Ferrar, and Sheri Feinzig contend that "people analytics" is too ambiguous and does not represent the entire workforce when we consider the "rise of machines" in the workplace.[6] For example, the composition and characteristics of today's workforce are evolving to include employees, contract workers, gig workers, and others. In addition, the term "workforce analytics" emphasizes the importance of demonstrating the value and impact of the entire workforce, and not just the HR function.[7] Moreover, the "Future of Work" is ushering in new advancements in technology such as artificial intelligence (AI), automation, and robotics—a nonhuman workforce. Further, "workforce analytics" unambiguously asserts some boundaries whereby the focus is squarely within the context of work and the workplace. Therefore, a strong case can be made for "workforce analytics" as a more inclusive, yet focused moniker that best characterizes the field.

HR Analytics

In this book, the preferred moniker used is "HR analytics," despite the growing popularity of "people analytics" and the valid arguments for the "workforce analytics" label. The decision to use "HR analytics" is based on several principled reasons. First, "HR analytics" has been an established term in the field for two decades since it was introduced by Edward Lawler, Alec Levenson, and John Boudreau in their *Human Resource Planning* article titled "HR Metrics and Analytics: Use and Impact."[8] Second, "HR analytics" has a longer and more robust history, spanning over a century in terms of HR research and measurement activities, whereas "people analytics" has a more recent origin, as explained in the section "Misleading Origin Story" later in this chapter. Third, the label "people analytics" can easily lead to ethical concerns and blur the line between work and personal life if excessive data collection and analysis occur on people outside of the workplace. Lastly, scholars have recently pushed for the standardized use of "HR analytics" as a term for research purposes.[9]

It is generally agreed that HR analytics is a team sport and collaborative effort involving practitioners from various disciplines, such as industrial and organizational psychology, human resources and organizational behavior, management, behavioral economics, statistics, business intelligence, data science, mathematics, computer science, computer engineering, and others. Some argue that HR analytics should be placed under an enterprise-wide business intelligence function and report to line management outside of HR.[10] This has led to the hiring of business intelligence, data science, and technology professionals to lead the HR analytics capabilities and function. However, it takes a social, behavioral, and organizational scientist with an HR background to effectively lead the function and accurately and ethically interpret the insights derived from HR analytics in the context of individual, group, and organizational behavior.[11] As such, the HR analytics function should remain within the HR function and report directly to the chief HR officer (CHRO) to ensure its strategic legitimacy, influence, and impact. (This will be discussed in depth in Chapter 12.)

As the HR analytics community becomes more aware of the potential paradoxes and pitfalls of the discipline, the "HR analytics" label will likely come full circle as the preferred term in scholarly research and practice, as it was first introduced two decades ago (Figure 1.1).

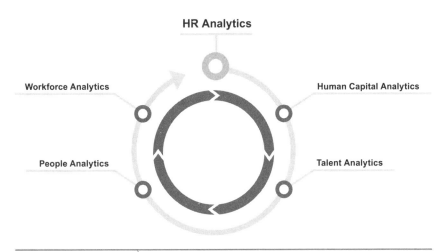

Figure 1.1   HR Analytics Comes Full Circle

The Meaning of HR Analytics

HR analytics means different things to different people. For some, HR analytics simply refers to descriptive HR metrics and reporting, while for others it means sophisticated predictive modeling procedures.[12] More recently, HR analytics has shifted and supposedly matured from analyzing data derived from highly structured and traditional data sources to mining and modeling data from unstructured and novel data sources.[13] In the largest study to date—namely the HR Analytics Project—I conducted a survey and explored the meaning of HR analytics with those who perform HR research and analytics work in 220 Fortune 1000 firms.[14] Respondents were asked to rank order several statements that characterize the meaning of HR analytics. The results are as follows (in rank order):

1. Making better workforce decisions by using the best available scientific evidence and organizational facts with respect to evidence-based HR.
2. Moving beyond descriptive HR metrics (i.e., lagging indicators—something that has already occurred) to predictive HR metrics (i.e., leading indicators—something that may occur in the future).
3. Segmenting the workforce and using statistical analyses and predictive modeling procedures to identify key drivers (i.e., factors and variables) and cause-and-effect relationships that enable and inhibit important business outcomes.
4. Using advanced statistical analyses, predictive modeling procedures, and human capital investment analysis to forecast and extrapolate "what-if" scenarios for decision-making.
5. Standard tracking, reporting, and benchmarking of HR metrics.
6. Ad hoc querying, drill-down, and reporting of HR metrics and indicators through an HRIS and/or HR dashboard, scorecard, and reporting tool.
7. Operations research and management science methods for HR optimization (i.e., What's the best that can happen if we do XYZ or what is the optimal solution for a specific human capital problem?).

In addition to the multitude of monikers and descriptors used to characterize HR analytics, several competing definitions have emerged in the academic literature (see Table 1.1). Some of these definitions refer to metrics, external benchmarks, decision-making, and value creation, while others emphasize the role of technology, advanced statistical analysis, and data visualization. As mentioned earlier, scholars have distinguished between HR metrics and HR analytics.[15] More recently, an evidence-based review using an integrative synthesis approach revealed that HR analytics goes beyond HR metrics and uses a more sophisticated analytical toolset to inform HR strategy and evidence-based decision-making.[16]

Table 1.1 Academic Definitions of HR Analytics

"HR analytics (is a process) . . . to understand the impact of HR practices and policies on organizational performance. Statistical techniques and experimental approaches can be used to tease out the causal relationship between particular HR practices and such performance metrics as customer satisfaction, sales per employee, and, of course, the profitability of particular business activities."[17]

"HR intelligence is a proactive and systematic process for gathering, analyzing, communicating, and using insightful people research and analytics results to help organizations achieve their strategic objectives."[18]

"HR analytics is an evidence-based approach for making better decisions on the people side of the business; it consists of an array of tools and technologies, ranging from simple reporting of HR metrics all the way up to predictive modeling."[19]

"HR analytics [is defined] as demonstrating the direct impact of people data on important business outcomes."[20]

"A HR practice enabled by information technology that uses descriptive, visual, and statistical analyses of data related to HR processes, human capital, organizational performance, and external economic benchmarks to establish business impact and enable data-driven decision-making."[21]

"HR analytics is the systematic identification and quantification of the people-drivers of business outcomes, with the purpose of making better decisions."[22]

"People analytics is an area of HRM practice, research and innovation concerned with the use of information technologies, descriptive and predictive data analytics and visualization tools for generating actionable insights about workforce dynamics, human capital, and individual and team performance that can be used strategically to optimize organizational effectiveness, efficiency and outcomes, and improve employee experience."[23]

"HR analytics are the statistical measures that can show connections, correlations and even causality between HR metrics and other business measures."[24]

"Any analyses done individually or at the role level and is the domain of what is traditionally considered workforce analytics. Specific topics include motivation, employee engagement, competencies, leadership development, training, compensation, and more. In addition, any analysis that seeks to explain business processes through the lens of individual differences falls into this category."[25]

(continued)

Table 1.1 Academic Definitions of HR Analytics *(continued)*

"Workforce analytics refers to the processes involved with understanding, quantifying, managing, and improving the role of talent in the execution of strategy and the creation of value. It includes not only a focus on metrics (e.g., what do we need to measure about our workforce?), but also analytics (e.g., how do we manage and improve the metrics we deem to be critical for business success?)."[26]

"Workforce analytics is a process—one that is continuously advanced by improving problem-solving through sound measurement, appropriate research models, systematic data analysis, and technology to support organizational decision-making."[27]

"HR analytics is a set of principles and methods that address a strategic business concern that encompasses collecting, analyzing, and reporting data to improve people-related decisions."[28]

"HR/people analytics can be broadly categorized as the various use of big data, cloud computing and machine learning for informing HR decisions."[29]

"[HR] analytics is about drawing the right conclusions from data. It includes statistics and research design, and then goes beyond them to include skill in identifying and articulating key issues, gathering and using appropriate data within and outside HR function, setting the appropriate balance between statistical rigor and practical relevance, and building analytical competencies throughout the organization. Analytics transforms HR logic and measures into rigorous, relevant insight."[30]

Moreover, numerous definitions of HR analytics can be found in popular sources such as books, reports, white papers, and on various websites and blogs. The definitions included in Table 1.1 are from the academic literature. However, there are also several credible definitions from various trade sources such as books and professional associations (see Table 1.2).

Table 1.2   Trade Definitions of HR Analytics

"[HR] analytics is a mental framework, a logical progression first and a set of statistical tools second."[31]

"HR analytics refers to the application of a methodology and integrated process for improving the quality of people-related decisions for the purpose of improving individual and/or organizational performance."[32]

"[HR] analytics [is] the discovery of meaningful patterns of data to understand the drivers of performance."[33]

"People analytics is a combination of human resource management, finance, and data analytics."[34]

"Workforce analytics uses statistical models and other techniques to analyze worker-related data, allowing leaders to improve the effectiveness of people-related decision-making and human resources strategy."[35]

"Predictive HR analytics [is] the systematic application of predictive modeling using inferential statistics to existing HR people-related data in order to inform judgments about possible causal factors driving key HR related performance indicators."[36]

"People analytics [is] the integration of disparate data sources from inside and outside the enterprise that are required to answer and act upon forward-looking business questions related to the human capital assets of an organization."[37]

"Workforce analytics [is] the discovery, interpretation, and communication of meaningful patterns in workforce-related data to inform decision-making and improve performance."[38]

"People analytics is about analyzing data about people to solve business problems. It's sometimes called HR analytics or workforce analytics."[39]

"People analytics consists simply of applying evidence to management decisions about people."[40]

"People analytics is the analysis of employee and workforce data to reveal insights and provide recommendations to improve business outcomes."[41]

Curiously Missing

HR analytics is a nascent discipline in terms of the academic literature, and these definitions reflect the authors' disciplinary backgrounds and serve to mark the boundaries of the field. With few exceptions, however, these definitions curiously lack attention to, or focus on, the following:

1. **Evidence-based management:** Making smarter workforce decisions through the conscientious, explicit, and judicious use of the best available evidence from multiple sources—including the use of scientific research findings.
2. **HR research and experimentation:** The broader role of internal HR research or external partnership research conducted in the context of social, behavioral, and organizational sciences.
3. **Ethical practice:** Ethically gathering and using HR data and insights.
4. **Strategy and execution:** Helping organizations achieve their strategic objectives.

Defining HR Analytics

Leading organizations are now expanding their HR research and analytics practices to include a wider range of data sources and approaches beyond simple metrics, scorecards, and reporting. However, respected experts argue that this expansion can lead to a lack of strategic focus, with too much emphasis on data mining and not enough on model building and testing. To address this issue, HR analytics should concentrate on generating new data and deeper insights that align with and support the overall business strategy and execution, using quantitative and qualitative approaches.[42]

Strategically aligned HR analytics projects that involve active HR research and experimentation to collect new data and test specific hypotheses play a crucial role in enabling strategy and decision-making. However, organizations should not limit their HR analytics capabilities and priorities to a small number of projects that cater solely to the needs of powerful stakeholders. Instead, the HR analytics agenda should include innovative and potentially disruptive projects and leverage evidence-based sources of information, such as scientific research findings, when making strategic choices. More importantly, organizations need to consider the ethical implications of HR analytics. Ultimately, insights derived from a wide range of HR research and analytics should inform an organization's HR strategy and workforce decisions. This approach involves HR analytics projects that may not always be strategically aligned or sanctioned by stakeholders.

With the goal of incorporating evidence-based management, a broader role for HR research and experimentation, ethical practice, and strategy and execution, the following definition is presented.

HR analytics is a proactive and systematic process for ethically gathering, analyzing, communicating, and using evidence-based HR research and analytical insights to enable smarter workforce decisions and help organizations achieve their strategic objectives.

Misleading Origin Story

There are several books and articles that summarize the origin story of HR analytics. Like all storytelling, the veracity of the story matters. One popular yet misleading story is that HR analytics, specifically "people analytics," all began at Google in 2007. Unfortunately, when it comes down to it, the HR profession, in general, and the HR analytics community, in particular, suffer from a form of generational amnesia. To be fair, this tends to happen whenever a seemingly new and innovative concept or idea enters the fray. Indeed, the HR profession has always been enamored with shiny new objects, provocative ideas, and next practices, even if they are not always new at all. But is HR analytics different? The short answer is no!

First, let's go back to the Google story. In 2006, Google hired Laszlo Bock as their SVP for people operations, and the company has done some amazing work in the HR analytics space. In fact, they built their entire people operations function with a data-driven approach in mind.[43] In 2007, Google retained a top-notch executive search firm, Russell Reynolds, to search for their first director of people analytics. I know this because I was among the candidates screened and interviewed for the job that same year. In the end, Google hired Prasad Setty to lead the people analytics team, and under Bock and Setty's leadership, their HR analytics maturity and capabilities mushroomed, moving from descriptive analysis to predictive analytics and actionable insights.[44]

Google was likely the first to use the "people analytics" label to describe their HR analytics team and capabilities, as they were using the "people operations" moniker to describe their overall HR function. Surely, Google played a vital role in shaping and popularizing people analytics as we understand it today, but the myriad of methods and practices that make up people or HR analytics work did not originate at Google. In fact, HR analytics has a long and rich history that spans over 100 years.[45] Numerous breakthroughs, discoveries, and HR research and measurement practices led to the emergence of HR analytics. For example:

- Measuring individual differences and intelligence[46]
- Social psychology[47]
- Industrial psychology and efficiency[48]
- Scientific management[49]
- Applied psychology[50]
- Social intelligence[51]
- Psychological types and personality[52]
- Attitude measurement techniques[53]
- The Hawthorne Studies[54]
- Action research[55]
- Personnel/employee/talent selection[56]
- Assessment centers[57]
- Workforce forecasting and analysis[58]
- Data-driven methods for change[59]
- Human capital measurement and metrics[60]
- Employee and organizational surveys[61]
- HR benchmarking[62]
- Evaluation/ROI[63]
- Scorecards[64]
- Evidence-based practice[65]
- HR decision science[66]
- HR intelligence (broader HR research, measurement, and analytics practices in the context of competitive intelligence and HR strategy)[67]

These same HR research and measurement practices are still widely used today and will continue to be integral to HR analytics work far into the future. As George Orwell famously wrote, "Each generation imagines itself to be more intelligent than the one that went before it and wiser than the one that comes after it. This is an illusion, and one should recognize it as such, but one ought also to stick to one's own worldview, even at the price of seeming old-fashioned: for that worldview springs out of experiences that the younger generation has not had, and to abandon it is to kill one's intellectual roots."[68] Therefore, we must not forget the social, behavioral, and organizational scientists, as well as the HR measurement pioneers who paved the way long before the "big data" and "analytics" monikers and the data science revolution came into vogue.

Pioneers such as Douglas Bray, a renowned industrial and organizational psychologist, led the HR research function at AT&T for almost three decades from 1956 to 1983.[69] Other notable industrial and organizational psychologists, including Allen Kraut, Allan Church, and Lise Saari, either led or were part of the personnel/workforce research groups at IBM throughout the 1980s and 1990s. During this time, several other long-standing advocates paved the way for HR research, measurement, assessment, surveys, and analysis work, such as William Macey, Benjamin Schneider, William Schiemann, and Jack Wiley, to name a few.

Jac Fitz-enz, an esteemed expert on strategic HR measurement, paved the way for the HR metrics and benchmarking movement in the late 1970s and early 1980s.[70] He went on to establish the Saratoga Institute in 1977, which was eventually acquired by PwC, and the Workforce Intelligence Institute in the mid-2000s. In 1992, Robert Kaplan and David Norton introduced the Balanced Scorecard concept, and less than a decade later, Brian Becker, Mark Huselid, and Dave Ulrich developed the HR Scorecard[71] as a strategic HR measurement system to help organizations measure, manage, and communicate the strategic role of the HR function through key performance indicators (KPIs) and metrics.

In 2000, Rob Briner, a well-known organizational psychologist, introduced the concept of evidence-based practice to the human resource management community.[72] Briner observed that organizational leaders and managers often ignore scholarly research findings and tend to rely on popular business books and management fads and trends when making critical workforce decisions and adopting HR programs and practices.

In 2001, while serving as the head of global HR research and analytics at Intel, I conducted the first benchmarking study to identify broader HR research, measurement, and analytics activities across the high-technology industry (e.g., Dell, IBM, Microsoft, and SAP). As part of the study, I conceptualized and coined the term "HR intelligence," which represents broader HR research and analytics in the context of competitive intelligence and HR strategy. In 2004, I introduced a systematic approach to establishing an HR intelligence agenda and a set of core capabilities. Moreover, I have been a strong advocate for combining HR intelligence (analytics) with HR strategy and planning,[73] a perspective I maintain throughout this book.

During this time, John Boudreau and Peter Ramstad called for a HR decision science approach, where organizations strategically analyze their data and information to make better decisions regarding their key talent.[74] Additionally, Jeffrey Pfeffer and Robert Sutton popularized the concept of evidence-based management in 2006.[75] They argued that science and empirical evidence should drive key business decisions, strategic choices, and the adoption of critical management practices, rather than hunches, trends, fads, and the total nonsense peddled by the consulting industry and popular press.

Since then, many books and articles have emerged on the topic of analytics in general and HR analytics in particular. For instance, in 2007, Thomas Davenport and Jeanne Harris, in their book *Competing on Analytics: The New Science of Winning*, argued that leading organizations are building strategic capabilities and competitive advantage through data-driven intelligence and insight with advanced analytics.[76] In 2008, Wayne Cascio and John Boudreau authored a book on decision science and HR measurement, *Investing in People: Financial Impact of Human Resource Initiatives*.[77] In 2010, the first books specifically including HR analytics in their titles were *The New HR Analytics* by Jac Fitz-enz and *The HR Analytics Handbook* by Laurie Bassi, Rob Carpenter, and Dan McMurrer, which featured the seven-step HR analytics cycle discussed in this book.[78] That same year, a *Harvard Business Review* article entitled "Competing on Talent Analytics" was published and widely read within the HR analytics community.[79]

For over a decade now, numerous books and articles have been written and published on the topic of HR analytics. However, with a few exceptions, the authors of these publications have conveniently overlooked or perhaps forgotten HR analytics' true origin story. To be fair, HR analytics can mean different things to different people. For some, it is merely an extension of HR metrics and reporting with, perhaps, the "power to predict." For others, HR analytics involves the application of business analytics or business intelligence that entails mining and modeling big data using powerful data warehousing, aggregation, reporting, and visualization tools. Nonetheless, some experienced practitioners acknowledge the historical roots of HR analytics and advocate for a broad approach that encompasses everything mentioned above and more, including active HR research and experimentation, metrics and reporting, psychometric testing, advanced analytics, evidence-based management, and other workforce data analysis activities.[80] (Chapter 7 describes a comprehensive list of HR analytics data sources and practices.) Therefore, if we consider the wider context of HR analytics, its true origin story becomes more apparent.

Revolutionary or Evolutionary Capability?

When considering the long and rich history of HR analytics, it becomes clear that numerous predecessors and precursors led to its emergence. The use of data to understand the workforce, drive change, and provide critical insights for strategy and decision-making is not a new concept. What is new is the inclusion of data sources beyond the traditional boundaries of the social, behavioral, and organizational sciences;[81] the availability of advanced technological and analytical resources; and a renewed interest in analytics by senior leaders who are seeking novel ways to leverage data for evidence-based and smarter workforce decisions.

This renewed interest in data-driven leadership, coupled with the data science revolution and the "Future of Work," has propelled the human capital management (HCM) technology industry to new heights. Today, for example, there is a plethora of digital tools related to HR analytics, including SaaS-based platforms, data aggregation and visualization tools, apps, chatbots, AI, and deep or machine learning capabilities. These technological tools and trends are reshaping the means by which HR analytics is performed and the skills needed to do so in the future. Business intelligence professionals, economists, computer engineers, data scientists, mathematicians, statisticians, and HCM technologists have all entered the fray.

However, it is important to remember our past. Proclamations such as "The Geeks Arrive in HR: People Analytics Is Here"[82] are not entirely accurate and arguably perpetuate a false narrative and misleading origin story. The fact is that "geeks" have always been a part of HR. Just ask the social, behavioral, and organizational scientists, HR measurement pioneers, and data-driven HR leaders who are old enough to remember. Therefore, HR analytics should be characterized as an evolutionary rather than a revolutionary capability with a rich history and a promising future.

CHAPTER 2

The Quantified Employee Agenda

No matter the place, no matter the time,
and no matter what you do,
your life has now become an open book.

—Edward Snowden

The promise and potential of HR analytics are exciting, and the possibilities limitless. Increasingly, organizations are developing HR analytics capabilities to promote the success of both the organization and its employees. However, despite the good intentions of the HR analytics community, there has been a gradual erosion of workplace privacy and ethics, alongside a "datafication" and "quantified employee agenda" that jeopardizes the success that can be achieved from HR analytics.

This chapter delves into the paradox and peril of HR analytics in terms of the data science revolution and datafication, technological advancements, and what is known as the "quantified employee agenda." It is worth noting that this chapter is not a gratuitous criticism of the technology industry nor a condemnation of all things AI-powered. Instead, the chapter aims to summarize the transformative and technological trends that are emerging, including the "Future of Work," and to highlight potential pitfalls in adopting new and emerging technologies, including AI, in the context of HR analytics.

The Datafication of Everything

Amid the big data and data science revolution, as well as the rise of the Internet of Things, datafication has become a strategic mandate for organizations in all sectors and industries. Often used interchangeably with big data, datafication is a relatively new technological trend that involves collecting, codifying, and converting virtually every aspect of our lives into data. The term "datafication" was popularized by Viktor Mayer-Schönberger and Kenneth Cukier in their book *Big Data: A Revolution That Will Transform How We Live, Work, and Think*. According to the authors, datafication "refers to taking information about all things under the sun" and "transforming it into a data format to make it quantified."[1] Furthermore, they argue that big data and the "datafication of everything" are sources of new economic value and innovation.

Datafication is already providing numerous benefits to organizations and society, such as monitoring weather patterns, tracking volcanic and seismic activity, improving healthcare, detecting fraud, and tracking student learning outcomes in universities. The value and benefits of datafication are clear in terms of improving product and service quality, innovation, and productivity, among other things. Consequently, more and more organizations are seeking novel ways of transforming human activities into data, allowing them to track, analyze, optimize, personalize, and monetize activities that were previously invisible or largely ignored. We are indeed entering an era of big data, where everything, including our preferences, choices, geolocation, habits, personality, social interactions, and behaviors, is being collected, codified, and converted into data, both inside and outside of the workplace.

The notion of the "datafication of everything" is not as far-fetched as it sounds. Take, for instance, Google's endeavor to scan and digitize every book on the planet. Despite encountering a few legal setbacks, Google successfully scanned over 25 million books.[2] Additionally, there is the "quantified self" movement, in which fitness enthusiasts and technology aficionados strive to measure every aspect of their health, fitness, and well-being through wearable technologies like Fitbit, Jawbone, and Apple Watch. Furthermore, social media platforms collect and monitor data and information from our social relationships and interactions to market products and services to us, which, in turn, influences our behavior. Through advanced analytics and predictive modeling, social media companies can refine and customize the content and advertisements we see. Today, datafication is actively used and is fundamentally changing the way we live and work. According to Mayer-Schönberger and Cukier,[3] "once the world has been 'datafied,' the potential uses of the information are limited only by one's ingenuity." Indeed, the ultimate goal of datafication and the data science revolution is to uncover all potential uses for data and information, and the economic value that can be realized, which, in turn, justifies the datafication of everything.

The Creepy Line

Most of us are now familiar with the infamous quote from Google's former CEO, Eric Schmidt, about how Google goes right up to "the creepy line," but does not cross it. In an interview at the Washington Ideas Forum with the *Atlantic* editor James Bennet, Schmidt stated, "The Google policy on a lot of things is to get right up to the creepy line and not cross it."[4] To be fair, if we consider the larger context of his comment, we realize that he uttered it in jest. In the same interview, Schmidt jokingly responded to a question about implanting microchips in people's brains, saying, "I would argue that implanting something in your brain is beyond the creepy line— at least for the moment, until the technology gets better."[5] Joking aside, when we consider how frequently "the creepy line" quote was used in the press, blogs, and several documentaries, it reflects a general anxiety and fear that exists around datafication, technology, and the creepy analytics practices that many organizations engage in.

Surveillance Society

The ominous implications of datafication and the creepy line go far beyond the unrestrained proliferation of technology and the unfettered collection, codification, and conversion of every aspect of our lives. It is the limitless potential of datafication and the accompanying privacy and ethical concerns that should give us pause. Shoshana Zuboff, in her bestselling book *The Age of Surveillance Capitalism: The Fight for a Human Future at the New Frontier of Power*, argues that many of the world's largest technology companies are collecting an unprecedented amount of data on human experiences to create "prediction products" that can be sold to buyers who want to understand and shape future human behavior.[6] Zuboff refers to this process as "surveillance capitalism," which threatens the concept of free will and our personal and professional freedom. Zuboff contends that surveillance capitalism aims to create a world of ubiquitous computing, where everyone becomes a source of raw behavioral data to be mined and modeled in order to manipulate and control human behavior on a global scale.[7] Therefore, datafication and a datafied worldview have implications not only for basic human rights but also for workers' rights. Although this may sound like Orwellian dystopian hyperbole, there are curious and compelling parallels between Zuboff's concept of surveillance capitalism and the emerging "quantified employee agenda."

The Quantified Employee Agenda

What is the meaning of "quantified employee" in the context of HR analytics, and who or what is driving it? Almost a decade ago, Josh Bersin wrote an insightful article in *Forbes* titled "Quantified Self: Meet the Quantified Employee."[8] He discussed how the human capital management (HCM) technology industry is pushing for a quantified employee agenda in the workplace, which includes employee monitoring and always-on employee listening and sensing platforms, in response to the popular cultural phenomenon of the quantified self. Although Bersin acknowledges the potential privacy and ethical implications of these tools and practices, he argues that they are simply an extension of the trade-offs we make when using various technologies in our personal lives, such as Google and Facebook.

While the notion of the quantified employee has clear benefits for organizations, such as increased employee accountability, productivity, and retention, the benefits for employees themselves are less clear. Furthermore, a quantified workforce is not necessarily a wholly positive development (Figure 2.1). For example, a study conducted by The Conference Board found that employees believe their employers are collecting data about them, sometimes without their knowledge or consent.[9]

Consequently, a quantified employee agenda might adversely affect the very outcomes HR analytics hopes to achieve, such as improving employee morale, engagement, and retention. So what exactly are the benefits for employees?

In the context of the quantified self, individuals use various personal analytics to track their health and fitness levels to optimize their performance and improve their overall well-being, which are all apparent benefits. However, the advantages of a quantified workforce for employees are yet to be determined. Real-time monitoring, data-driven performance coaching and feedback, and AI-powered behavioral nudging are hardly desirable value propositions for employees. Therefore, organizations must clearly articulate the tangible and intangible benefits of a quantified workforce while fostering trust and transparency.

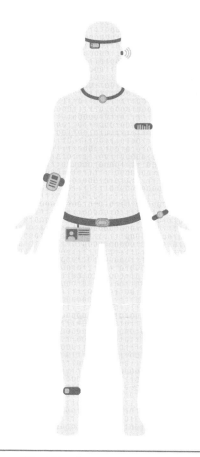

Figure 2.1   The Quantified Employee

The premise of the quantified employee assumes that organizations can persuade employees to willingly participate. As mentioned earlier, trust and transparency are imperative when it comes to privacy and ethics. Without them, organizations are likely to fail in terms of creating a modern-day version of "Digital Taylorism" and dehumanizing the workplace systematically. This is especially true if organizations try to force or coerce employees to comply with the quantified employee agenda. Such actions are the reason employees are hesitant to join, whether it involves the use of employee monitoring tools, sociometric sensors, wearable devices, or creepiest of them all—microchip implants. If the quantified employee agenda is left unchecked, it may undermine the good intentions of the larger HR analytics community and jeopardize the value and impact that ethical HR analytics projects and practices can achieve. Meanwhile, the unbridled proliferation of technology, proprietary algorithms, and black box AI platforms complicates our best intentions and raises images of Big Brother, control, and manipulation in the workplace.

Black Box AI and Algorithms

Over the past decade, the HCM technology industry has introduced numerous SaaS-based and AI-powered platforms to aid organizations in measuring, analyzing, monitoring, tracking, screening, selecting, listening, sensing, quantifying, managing, shaping, nudging, engaging, coaching, and retaining people in the workplace. However, despite all the hype and dangerous half-truths, ethical concerns have arisen regarding the potential abuse and bias of these technological advancements.

For instance, many of these AI-powered platforms use a proprietary algorithm and an unexplainable "black box." A black box refers to an AI system whose processes are not transparent to the end user, meaning the user is unaware of the AI method or algorithm used and how it operates. Black box AI employs a proprietary machine learning algorithm, which produces insights based on a large dataset. The inputs to the black box model are the data points, while the outputs represent the decisions. The outputs of black box AI are generally remarkably accurate due to the complexity of the proprietary algorithms. However, it is unclear whether the predictive claims and assertions made by technology entrepreneurs are supported by science or merely "snake oil."

Arvind Narayanan, an associate professor of computer science at Princeton University, recently presented on "How to Recognize AI Snake Oil" and contends that "much of what is being sold as AI today is snake oil."[10] Many HCM technology companies offering automated and algorithmic candidate assessment and screening, for example, are based on "bogus AI" but still manage to raise hundreds of millions of dollars. Narayanan questions how this happened and why HR professionals seem so gullible.

According to Narayanan, "AI has become an umbrella term for a set of related technologies" that differ significantly in terms of underlying technological sophistication, power, accuracy, validity, and reliability. In other words, the average HR professional or HR analytics practitioner is unable to differentiate between the underlying AI technology that powers Google's Alpha Go, AI-enabled self-driving cars, or AI-powered platforms that claim to predict competence, job performance, culture fit, personality, or the like. Thus, these companies exploit public confusion and the gap between hype and reality by labeling whatever they sell as "AI."[11]

Due to the proprietary nature of algorithms, HCM technology vendors are typically unwilling to share and, in some cases, unable to explain the underlying mechanisms at work. These mechanisms refer to the specific methods, rules, and combinations of variables that lead to a prediction or decision. To compound the issue, the science behind these tools is often shoddy and based on the vendors' internal research rather than academic scholarly literature (evidence-based management is discussed in Chapter 4).

Black box AI is still prevalent today and is the dominant paradigm among technology entrepreneurs and developers. In recent years, advances in AI, machine learning (ML), and deep learning have led to the widespread belief that the most accurate models must be complex and unexplainable. This belief suggests that interpretability must be sacrificed for accuracy and predictive power. In a recent white paper by One Model, Taylor Clark and Nicholas Garbis argue that we live in a "cult of complexity" when it comes to AI and ML. This trend is problematic if we are to realize the full potential of AI and ML in an ethical and responsible manner.[12] Interestingly, research has shown that this belief is often incorrect, and complex black box models are not necessarily more accurate than simple and explainable predictive models.[13]

Black box AI is often touted as a way to eliminate human bias in workforce decision-making. However, the data used to train AI models or ML algorithms can introduce bias into the system. In other words, AI in effect is learning all our worst impulses. Specifically, bias can creep in if the data used to train the algorithm is overrepresented or underrepresented in terms of gender, race, age, sexual orientation, and disability, whether the data is real-world or synthetic. Synthetic data, which is computer-generated data that mathematically and statistically reflects real-world data, can be as good as or even better than real data for training AI systems and predictive models.[14] However, synthetic data may focus on specific patterns and biases in the real world and amplify them. Consequently, synthetic data used to train AI-powered platforms can lead to inaccurate predictions and bad workforce decisions.

Real-world data contains biases too, which became apparent when Amazon's AI-powered platform discriminated against female job applicants. The platform's machine learning algorithm was trained to identify particular keywords in résumés that were mostly submitted by male applicants, leading it to learn that male candidates were more desirable. Despite Amazon's attempts to address this bias, the company eventually abandoned the platform.[15] This scenario illustrates the unintended consequences that can arise from relying solely on algorithms, emphasizing the significance of incorporating a "human-in-the-loop" approach that involves greater human involvement in the entire process. In all fairness, however, humans are not always paragons of unbiased reason and integrity. In fact, we're pretty good at being irrational, unethical, and biased.

In his newly published book, *I, Human: AI, Automation, and the Quest to Reclaim What Makes Us Unique*, Tomas Chamorro-Premuzic reminds us to acknowledge our human nature and recognize that AI, in all its manifestations, reflects our biases, prejudices, and unfair rules. According to Chamorro-Premuzic, these issues become evident as AI learns to emulate our thinking and decision-making. Therefore, he suggests that a combination of AI to help mitigate bias and an "ethical human in the loop" is necessary. However, he also warns that the very bias we are trying to minimize can be "exacerbated when humans lack integrity and expertise."[16]

In the context of HR analytics, both the HR profession and the workforce deserve access to ethical and explainable AI (Figure 2.2), regardless of whether a human is involved in the decision-making process. This type of AI enables us to understand how decisions are made based on the data and algorithms used. Additionally, it is transparent and verifiable, providing evidence of the science and data underlying the platform's algorithms and predictive assertions. Thankfully, there has been a recent movement toward the development of explainable and ethical AI, often referred to as "white box" AI. This has been prompted by the General Data Protection Regulation (GDPR) in the European Union (EU), the proposed AI Act, the California Consumer Privacy Act (CCPA), and the recently proposed legislation in the US Senate—called the Stop Spying Bosses Act—among other recent efforts by government and the private sector. For instance, One Model's cofounder and CEO, Chris Butler, and his team have designed their platform and products with ethical considerations, transparency, and GDPR and AI Act compliance at the forefront.

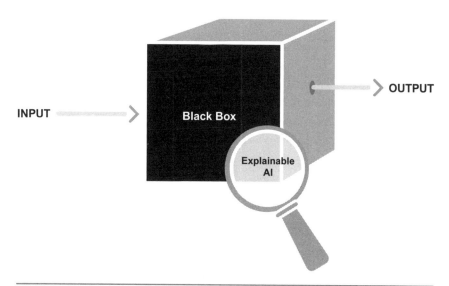

Figure 2.2   HR and the Workforce Deserve Explainable HR

However, "many technology entrepreneurs prioritize delivering their platforms and products at scale," leading to the use of a "one-size-fits-all approach" when it comes to AI/ML, say Butler.[17] This often involves a complicated, proprietary, and unexplainable AI/ML algorithm trained on generic and biased datasets. In contrast, white box AI employs simpler linear models based on an organization's internal data, which can be corrected to mitigate potential bias and improve validity and reliability over time. Interestingly, white box AI models have been found to be just as accurate in certain contexts and situations.[18] Therefore, HR analytics leaders should consider the potential risks and rewards before using tools from HCM technology vendors who are unwilling to provide transparency into their black box AI.

Too Many Models and Curves

In addition to unexplainable AI, HR analytics leaders are constantly bombarded by industry analysts and consultants with a plethora of maturity models and innovation adoption curves (such as innovators, early adopters, early majority, late majority, and laggards). In the early years, these maturity models were practical frameworks used to describe the level of HR analytical capabilities and sophistication in organizations. They were also useful in terms of benchmarking HR analytical maturity within and across industries. However, these models and curves have evolved to become too prescriptive when it comes to technology, tools, and analytical techniques that should be used.

For instance, these models and curves consistently position advanced technologies such as AI/ML platforms, chatbots, wearables, and network intelligence, as well as tools like R, Python, SQL, and data visualization, as inherently better and invariably necessary for HR analytics success. Similarly, they situate unstructured data, novel data sources, passive data-gathering methods, and advanced statistical procedures as superior to structured data, traditional data sources, active data-gathering methods, and other forms of data collection and analysis such as qualitative methods. Essentially, these models and curves are deceptively designed to shame organizations and HR analytics leaders into purchasing more digital products and tools by creating a false sense of urgency. After all, no organization wants to be labeled as a "laggard" or "unsophisticated" in terms of their HR digital stack and analytical maturity.

Enabling smarter workforce decisions and adding value to the business are far more important than obsessing over where an organization stands on a particular HR analytics maturity model or technology adoption curve. This is especially true for small and midsized organizations that cannot afford to procure a full stack of HR digital tools with the latest AI-powered platforms or hire a group of PhD-trained business intelligence professionals, data scientists, or data engineers. Therefore, in many ways, these models and curves serve the interests of the HCM technology industry and perpetuate the quantified employee agenda by placing too much emphasis on always-on passive data-gathering methods and analyzing unstructured data from novel data sources using advanced data science approaches.

HR's Inescapable Attraction to Shiny Gadgets

Industry analysts, consultants, and HCM technologists are not the only ones promoting the quantified employee agenda. The HR profession is also compliant and, perhaps unconsciously, complicit in the datafication of everything related to digital HR. In general, HR professionals are easily beguiled by the latest HCM technologies, tools, and toys to add to their digital HR stack. While it is natural to keep track of new and emerging technological innovations, we should not naively believe that technology alone is the miraculous talisman that can solve all our most pressing business problems. Nevertheless, thousands of HR professionals attend large conferences and events such as the HR Technology Conference and Exposition to peruse the latest technological innovations offered by the industry.

To be fair, these conferences feature a cutting-edge agenda and an impressive lineup of some of the best thought leaders and speakers in the industry. However, they rely heavily on paid sponsors and exhibitors, such as technology and software vendors and HR analytics consultants, who showcase their products and services to an eager audience. Although it is important to envision a digital HR strategy and road map, HR analytics leaders should do their homework before stepping into uncharted territory and chasing the next shiny gadget. Lastly, we should be cognizant that a multibillion-dollar HCM technology industry (technology vendors, IT research and advisory firms, and industry analysts) is constantly shaping and influencing our choices.

The Ends Justifies the Meanness

I am not a Luddite and bear no malice toward the HCM technology, advisory, and consulting industry. The marketplace is home to many outstanding technology vendors such as HRCoffee, One Model, OrgVitals, and QuestionPro Workforce, to name a few. It also includes conscientious thought leaders and consultants like Al Adamsen at People Analytics &

Future of Work, Amit Mohindra at People Analytics Success, and Jonathan Ferrar and David Green at Insight222. These entities help their clients achieve their strategic objectives with HR analytics while being mindful of privacy and ethics.

Within the HCM technology industry, most entrepreneurs initially conceive their technological innovations and applications with the greater good in mind. However, as they scale and grow, the profit motive and potentially ulterior motives may creep into the equation for some, in order to stay ahead of the innovation curve, latest trends, or hype cycle. In a recent conversation with Chris Butler, cofounder and CEO at One Model, he mentioned that "there will always be HCM technology vendors willing to push the boundaries and build technological platforms that cross the creepy line."[19] Nonetheless, it is reassuring to know that some technology entrepreneurs develop socially responsible and ethical technology products, such as explainable, white box AI/ML platforms. One Model, for instance, designed their cloud-based solution with ethics at its core from the outset. Their AI/ML models are transparent, explainable, and more importantly, correctable. Rather than utilizing a proprietary black box, One Model trains their models using their client's data and strongly advocates for a human-in-the-loop approach, aiming to ensure ethical processes and outcomes. Therefore, as hinted at earlier, HR leaders should stay informed but largely ignore the social media chatter and hype before considering new and emerging technologies to add to their digital HR stack.

In today's HCM technology marketplace, where shiny gadgets are abundant, a conscientious and mindful approach is desperately needed. The HCM technology industry carries a social responsibility and moral obligation to carefully consider the types of technologies and tools they create and introduce to the market. This involves the mindful application of AI/ML that benefits both organizations and individual employees. Technology entrepreneurs must foresee potential privacy and ethical implications of their innovations, as well as any unintended consequences, before they enter the market. However, Edward Snowden cautions us that technology and ethics often have few boundaries, stating, "technology doesn't have a Hippocratic oath. So many decisions that have been made by technologists in academia, industry, the military, and government since at least the Industrial Revolution have been made on the basis of 'can we,' not 'should we.' And the intention driving a technology's invention rarely, if ever, limits its application and use."[20] Compounding the issue is the fact that new technologies frequently outpace legislation, despite the HR analytics community's desire to act responsibly concerning privacy and ethics. Consequently, when a new technological innovation or AI platform enters the market, we should demand explainable AI and critically question the science behind the measures and algorithms employed, as well as the claims and predictions made.

HR leaders in collaboration with their organization's IT colleagues should play a significant role in shaping the HCM industry's technology road map and strategy to ensure that technology entrepreneurs neither outpace customer demand nor overreach. Unfortunately, HR leaders and digital HR professionals alike often rely on information sources from independent research and advisory firms, industry analysts, and technology vendors who engage in a questionable "pay to play" game. In this setup, industry analysts are paid by technology vendors to write glowing reviews, while independent research and advisory firms charge organizations a subscription fee for access to their "independent research reports." At the same time, these firms charge technology vendors a fee for advice on how to enhance their products and market position. This dubious practice puts organizations at a serious disadvantage when it comes to procuring new HCM technology products. Therefore, the best solution is to conduct your own research and evaluate the HCM technology market based on your organization's overall needs, with a particular focus on its HR analytics capabilities.

The Future of Work

The "Future of Work" is a popular buzzword that has been driving the quantified employee agenda in the context of HR analytics and digital HR. According to the Society for Human Resource Management (SHRM), it refers to how work, workers, and workplaces will evolve in the upcoming years.[21] The Covid-19 pandemic has accelerated this trend and trajectory, making the future of work a hot topic among industry analysts and HCM technologists. The future of work is now, they say. While technological advancements such as AI, robotics, automation, and augmentation are often associated with the future of work, other factors like remote work and the gig economy are also shaping how work is done, who does it, and from where. SHRM has identified three essential elements to consider: how work is done, who does the work, and when and where work is done.[22]

AI and ML are already playing a significant role in how work is done, and this trend is set to continue. Robotics and automation are no longer futuristic concepts but are already radically changing how work is performed. John Boudreau suggests that even tasks that were once regarded as exclusively human and safe from automation are now being automated. However, instead of solely replacing humans with automation, Boudreau advocates for a more optimal solution that involves a combination of automation and human workers.[23] By using automation and other technologies such as AI and robotics to augment their work, humans can accomplish tasks more efficiently.

When it comes to who does the work, organizations typically rely on full-time and part-time employees, but more recently, they have also turned to contractors, gig workers, and crowdsourcing contributors for specialized or temporary projects. Due to technological advancements and ever-changing skill requirements, leaders are increasingly leveraging workers and skill sets from within and outside of the organization.

In their book *Work Without Jobs: How to Reboot Your Organization's Work Operating System*, Ravin Jesuthasan and John Boudreau argue that organizations need to rethink and reboot their "work operating systems" in terms of how, who, when, and where work is performed. Specifically, they suggest breaking down the notion of jobs into their "component parts" and focusing on individual workers' skills and abilities, as well as the capabilities derived from the application of automation and augmentation.[24]

The future of work also involves where and when work is performed, characterized by colocated workspaces, fluid work schedules, and flexible arrangements such as remote work. While colocated workspaces remain the norm for most organizations, fluid work schedules are on the rise to meet employee and customer needs. Remote work has become increasingly popular, especially since the Covid-19 pandemic, despite some high-profile CEOs and companies insisting on a return to the workplace. Therefore, the future of remote work is bright and likely here to stay.

However, the transformative and technological trends underlying the future of work perpetuate the datafication of everything and the quantified employee agenda described earlier. As we strive to remain ethical and responsible, the HR analytics community must remain vigilant and keenly aware of potentially dubious technologies, data sources, and practices that could undermine our good intentions.

CHAPTER 3

From Shades of Gray to Downright Creepy

Predictive analytics can enable a customized employment value proposition that maximizes mutual benefit for organizations and their talent; but at what point do predictive analytics become too creepy?

—John Boudreau

This chapter continues the discussion on the paradox and peril of HR analytics. It focuses on HR analytics practices that are dubious, ranging from questionable to downright creepy. While some argue that "Big Data doesn't mean 'Big Brother,' "[1] numerous workplace technologies, practices, and stories have made headlines that suggest otherwise. Don Peck's article in the *Atlantic*, "They're Watching You at Work," captures the essence of the issue, stating that "the application of predictive analytics to people's careers—an emerging field sometimes called '(HR) analytics'—is enormously challenging, not to mention ethically fraught. And it can't help but feel a little creepy."[2] Even the Society for Industrial and Organizational Psychology (SIOP) recognizes the creepy nature of some HR analytics practices and recently hosted an expert panel discussion titled "Leveraging Passive Data: From Creepy to Cool."[3] Whether creepy can ever be considered cool is a matter of debate and raises some profound questions for the broader HR analytics community to grapple with. Therefore, this chapter presents numerous examples of questionable and arguably creepy analytics practices reported in both academic literature and popular press.

Analysis of Email and Calendar Data

Email is one of the most widely used forms of workplace communication. However, emails sent or received through employer-provided email accounts are not typically considered private. Legally, employers have the right to monitor emails and calendar information in order to protect proprietary or sensitive information, prevent theft of trade secrets, or detect other malicious activity.[4] Popular workplace applications like Microsoft's Office 365 and Google G Suite have various analytical tools to track and monitor workforce communication and collaboration on a large scale. Employers can even read draft emails in G Suite, so employees should be cautious when drafting emails to their superiors or colleagues.[5]

While tracking email and calendar productivity is not new, analyzing email content and calendar data, including metadata, subject lines, and whether someone copies or blind copies others or accepts or declines meeting invites, can provide rich HR analytical insights. The analysis of email data can reveal information about productivity, treatment of coworkers, willingness to meet and collaborate, patterns of written language, and what those patterns reveal about intelligence, social skills, and behavior.[6] As natural language processing (NPL) tools improve and become more affordable, organizations will be able to automatically search through their workforce's email traffic for phrases or communication patterns that can be linked to measures of success or failure in specific roles.

Datafication of Frivolous Factors

The datafication of personal preferences, characteristics, and behaviors that have little relevance to job performance are all the rage and problematic. For instance, Google has reportedly used elaborate, bespoke surveys that delve into applicants' and employees' attitudes, preferences, and values on seemingly trivial aspects of their personal lives (such as "What magazines do you subscribe to?" and "What pets do you have?") as a proxy measure of personality, intelligence, cultural fit, job performance, and attrition likelihood, among other things, according to an article in the *New York Times*.[7]

Personality Scores Derived from Social Media Profiles

In a recent survey conducted by SIOP, participants were asked to share their opinions on passive data science scenarios, including the utilization of Big Five personality scores, extracted from applicants' social media profiles (including demographics, pictures, activity, and text), as a means to determine the priority of interview invitations. The survey aimed to explore whether this practice was perceived as "creepy or cool." The results were quite revealing, with 77.1 percent of respondents describing the practice as "totally creepy/no way!" Meanwhile, 20 percent expressed "some nervousness" about it, and a mere 2.9 percent found it to be "totally cool/ no concerns."[8]

Proxy Variables and Measures

Proxy variables and their concomitant measures (the methods and tools) are often used in situations where it is difficult or impractical to directly measure a particular variable or outcome of interest. However, despite their supposed predictive utility, proxy measures assume a specific worldview and can lead to erroneous conclusions that can potentially harm individuals and groups.[9] So why are they frequently used in HR analytics? The reasons for this vary, but in essence, proxy measures enable an organization to indirectly measure attitudes, values, motives, personality traits, and other characteristics without the candidate or employee's understanding the actual underlying variable being measured. By design, proxy measures lack transparency and face validity to prevent savvy job candidates from cheating, gaming the survey or test, and/or pretending to be someone other than themselves.

After all, a brilliant psychopath could easily see through a standard personality test. Remember Dr. Hannibal Lecter in the iconic movie

Silence of the Lambs, in which he famously asks Agent Clarice Starling, "Oh, Agent Starling, you think you can dissect me with this blunt little tool?"[10] Likewise, a highly educated and clever job candidate could make short work of a mainstream personality test and essentially pretend to be anyone the hiring organization desires. For instance, reflecting upon the intriguing American action drama series from the late 1990s, *The Pretender,* we encounter Jarod, a young man known as a "Pretender"—a genius imposter capable of swiftly acquiring the intricate skill sets necessary to impersonate professionals in various fields.[11]

Oh, the joys of proxy measures—the perfect tool for weeding out the pretenders and psychopaths, regardless of how brilliant and talented they may be. Who needs diversity when you can just stick with the same old boring, "normal" personalities, right? Except, of course, for the C-suite, where a cult of personality is more than welcome. But let's not forget about the unintended consequences of using proxy measures instead of valid and reliable measurement scales. Who knows, you might just weed out the next Steve Jobs by mistake.

Hometown as a Proxy and Predictor of Attrition

In certain cases, a job candidate's place of birth or hometown in which they were raised can be a somewhat reliable indicator of their likelihood of leaving the job.[12] For instance, applicants who hail from large cities are more prone to quitting their job compared to those from small towns. It seems to make intuitive sense. Employees from major metropolitan areas like New York City or the San Francisco Bay Area (Silicon Valley) know that the world is their career oyster. Conversely, those from small farming communities in the Midwest are more likely to think twice before leaving their current employer. If we combine the previous example with Google's bespoke survey and an employee's birthplace as an accurate predictor of employee turnover, the thinking may be that people from small towns who love dogs are more loyal than cat enthusiasts raised in an urban jungle. Alternatively, it could be argued that individuals who favor *People* magazine are better leaders than those who read *Scientific American.* Nevertheless, is it appropriate to base workforce decisions on frivolous factors and proxies that may or may not be explicitly related to a desired or undesired outcome?

Wellness Programs and Portals

Employers are increasingly worried about rising healthcare costs, and many have responded by implementing wellness programs to promote healthier lifestyles among employees. Health insurance providers often offer discounts to employers who encourage participation in wellness programs and use wellness portals. Employers may offer incentives such as reduced healthcare costs to encourage participation, but critics argue that voluntary wellness programs have not been effective enough and that employers may resort to punitive measures such as penalizing employees with unhealthy lifestyles and chronic health conditions.[13]

The ethical implications of forcing participation or penalizing certain employees for healthcare costs are debatable. Critics point out that wellness programs may give employers too much control over their employees' lives and could disproportionately impact protected employee groups. However, wellness programs can be beneficial to both employers and employees if implemented correctly. Healthy employees are likely to be more productive, so doing nothing is not a viable option.[14] The key is to create a well-intentioned program that benefits both the organization and individuals without infringing on their rights.

Health Risk Monitoring and Nudging

Predictive healthcare analytics is a burgeoning field that has implications for HR analytics and workforce decisions. According to a *Wall Street Journal* article, some employers are using outside firms to monitor and predict the health risks of employees.[15] For instance, companies are partnering with third-party wellness firms to gather and analyze employee data in order to determine which workers are at risk for certain health conditions, such as Type 2 diabetes. Consequently, these employees receive personalized messages that encourage them to visit a doctor or enroll in a weight-loss program.

Although employers typically do not receive individual data, these third-party "wellness firms" provide aggregate data on the number of employees who are at risk for a particular condition. However, to what extent should employers use this data about their employees' health conditions, habits, prescription drug use, and other similar information, even if their intentions are good with respect to health and wellness? Some employees may find this behavioral health nudging intrusive and irritating, even if it is meant to be for their own good.

Behavior Shaping and More Nudging

The use of vast amounts of data from both traditional and novel sources to train AI-powered platforms and algorithms is becoming increasingly prevalent, enabling the sending of personalized messages to nudge behavior. Algorithmic nudging, which draws on behavioral economics and psychological science, is a form of behavior shaping that is being applied more and more in the workplace. Positive reinforcement, such as gamification and incentives, is used to gradually alter behavior until the desired outcome is achieved, whether it be adopting a healthier lifestyle or investing for retirement. Humu, a behavioral change technology company cofounded by Laszlo Bock, the former CHRO at Google and author of *Work Rules*, has developed an algorithmic "nudge engine" that can trigger push notifications to coax people into engaging in target behaviors they would not otherwise do on their own.[16]

Despite the value placed on data governance, privacy, and adherence to GDPR principles, critics argue that algorithmic nudging is not without bias, lacks transparency, and is a form of manipulation and control. Todd Haugh, a professor of business law and ethics at Indiana University, warns that nudges could push workers into behaving in ways that benefit their employers' interests over their own, such as redirecting attention to work-related tasks, increasing performance and productivity, and cost savings.[17]

Although algorithmic nudging holds promise and potential, ethical questions persist with respect to its manipulative nature and its ability to manage and control people. Even well-intentioned scholars inadvertently describe algorithmic nudging in terms of control. For example, Mareike Möhlmann, in her *Harvard Business Review* article "Algorithmic Nudges Don't Have to Be Unethical," asserts that "companies should not give up on algorithmic management to control workers through nudging."[18] However, Möhlmann does strongly advocate for an ethical approach to algorithmic nudging by creating a win-win situation for workers and employers alike, ensuring data transparency, and explaining the algorithm's underlying logic.[19]

Monitoring Nonexecutive Employees for Stock Dumping

The selling of company stock by executives is subject to strict laws and regulations regarding timing and duration. The Securities and Exchange Commission (SEC) is responsible for investigating potential insider trading and aggressively prosecuting executives who engage in "pump and dump" schemes. These schemes involve spreading false or misleading information to drive up the stock price and then selling shares at the inflated price.[20] Because senior executives have access to insider information, publicly traded companies self-monitor all stock trading activities among their C-suite personnel. However, this monitoring practice has recently expanded to rank-and-file employees as an HR analytics tool. At an employee survey consortium meeting, an industrial and organizational psychologist at a Fortune 100 firm proudly shared that his company routinely tracks "nonexecutive employees" who sell their stock as a sign of disloyalty and imminent attrition. In some cases, "these employees have been terminated,"[21] he said. A skilled attorney could make the case for wrongful termination if they were based on a systematic bias (i.e., termination for stock selling was a pretext for discrimination).

On a more fundamental level, it is worth considering the extent to which organizations should monitor nonexecutive employee stock transactions for HR analytics purposes. Personal financial decisions, including stock sales, are generally considered private and personal. Unless an employee has insider information, selling their company stock should be no different from any other personal financial decision, such as actively managing a stock portfolio, 401(k), or individual retirement plan (IRA).

Private Data Obtained from Social Media Websites

Over 10 years ago, the Associated Press reported on a job applicant who interviewed for a position only to be asked by the employer for his Facebook username and password so that they could view his private content and information. This request made the applicant uncomfortable, leading him to withdraw his application.[22] Similar incidents have occurred throughout the United States, leading several states to prohibit the practice due to its invasive nature and potential for discrimination based on factors such as race, religion, gender, marital status, or sexual orientation. Employers who pry into the personal lives of job seekers through social media may inadvertently obtain protected class information, creating legal and ethical implications. As a result, organizations should abandon these practices to avoid potential legal repercussions and uphold ethical standards.

Credit Checks as an Indicator of Responsibility

Organizations commonly conduct background checks on job candidates, including credit checks for roles involving financial responsibilities. The rationale behind this is to assess personal and financial responsibility, especially in positions within the accounting and finance department. However, some advocacy groups and lawmakers argue that credit history is not relevant to employment and can create barriers to upward mobility and exacerbate racial discrimination. Moreover, credit reports could potentially reveal deeply personal information, such as medical history, divorce, and domestic abuse.[23]

Several states have passed laws limiting the use of credit checks, but existing laws such as the Fair Credit Reporting Act have flaws and numerous exceptions for employers. It remains unclear whether algorithmic proxy measures like "credit scores" fall under these laws. In her book *Weapons of Math Destruction*, Cathy O'Neil warns about the dangers of unsupervised mathematical models and algorithms that can perpetuate biases and inaccuracies, leading organizations to exclude job applicants based on crude proxies like credit scores.[24] Considering the ethical implications and potential legal consequences, organizations should carefully reconsider the use of credit checks for employment purposes.

Scraping Data from Public Social Media Profiles

There are various platforms that scrape and analyze public social media data, such as changes made to LinkedIn profiles, summaries, and taglines, to indicate job seeking behavior and attrition. One example of such a platform is HiQ, which is an HCM technology company that uses data scraped from public LinkedIn profiles to create reports for clients. These reports identify which employees are most likely to leave the company and which are most likely to be targeted by recruiters.[25] Assuming that the reports include a probability score that is fairly accurate, how might employees react if they learned that their employer is monitoring their LinkedIn activities through this service?

Some employees might find this practice annoying at best and a little creepy, assuming they are aware of it. Consequently, clever employees are likely to frequently change their LinkedIn profile and tagline just to annoy their employer or, perhaps, as leverage to initiate a "stay conversation" with their manager in order to secure an advancement and promotion opportunity, higher pay, and/or a remote work arrangement.

Voice Analysis and Profiling

Voice analysis and profiling employ AI-powered platforms and algorithms to predict various business outcomes based on an analysis of a candidate's voice. For instance, voice analysis has been used to determine the truthfulness and honesty of a candidate and to predict job success based on the sound of a candidate's voice.[26] Companies such as Jobaline have developed AI-powered platforms that analyze vocal characteristics to classify job applicants based on how their voice is likely to impact others.

In their *Harvard Business Review* article "Should Your Voice Determine Whether You Get Hired?," Tomas Chamorro-Premuzic and Seymour Adler playfully construe the algorithm as a mechanical judge in a voice-based beauty contest in which "desirable voices are invited to the next round, where they are judged by humans, while undesirable voices are eliminated from the contest."[27] Voice profiling technology firms argue that their AI-powered platforms minimize human bias because AI and algorithms are blind. However, is the AI-powered platform truly blind and accurate when it comes to gender, race, or ethnicity?

A recent study showed that people perceive men with lower-pitched voices as more trustworthy and competent in terms of dominant leadership, whereas women tend to have a higher-pitched voice, which is an auditory cue for communal leadership. Interestingly, when women attempt to mimic a lower pitch voice, like Elizabeth Holmes, the former CEO of Theranos, it will likely have the opposite effect and come across as inauthentic and untrustworthy.[28] These are highly nuanced and hardwired evolutionary psychological processes that are beyond the capability of any

AI-powered platform. Similarly, how would a job candidate perform on a voice analysis if English were their second language or if they had a strong accent? Therefore, is it truly unbiased and fair to make a critical workforce decision based on a characteristic over which people have no control?

Video Interviewing Technology

Many organizations are seeking innovative ways to streamline and speed up their recruitment, screening, and hiring processes while minimizing human bias. In recent years, AI-powered video interviewing technology has been invaluable for scanning and extracting résumé keywords and candidate skills, as well as conducting video interviews. Today, organizations are increasingly automating much of their initial interview processes with these technologies. One such company is HireVue—a leading enterprise video interview software that compares and grades a candidate's word choice, tone, and facial movements with the vocabulary and nonverbal behaviors of an organization's exemplary employees. Using a proprietary deep learning algorithm, HireVue analyzes thousands of features and their relationships with the client organization's top performers, generating a ranking list and insight score for candidates. The final recruiting decision is made by a recruiter, and ultimately the hiring manager.

According to a 2020 SHRM Executive Network *In Focus* report, HireVue has drawn attention due to a complaint filed by the Electronic Privacy Information Center with the Federal Trade Commission (FTC).[29] More recently, CVS Health is facing a class action lawsuit when a job candidate, who had undergone a HireVue video interview, alleged that the technology was used as a lie detector and resulted in their job application being rejected.[30] These cases highlight the growing concerns surrounding advanced AI image processing, facial recognition technologies, and video interviewing. The validity, legality, and ethics of these technologies have faced scrutiny in recent times. Advanced AI image processing and facial recognition have been subject to critiques regarding their accuracy and potential biases.[31] Similarly, video interviewing technologies utilizing voice analysis to extract and assess various traits such as word choice, voice intonation, emotions, and honesty have not been immune to controversy. These advancements raise important questions about their fairness and potential adverse effects.

Several issues are associated with video interview technologies. First, candidates may face difficulties in adapting to unfamiliar video interviewing platforms, which can affect their performance during the interview process. Moreover, concerns arise from the imprecision of the technology and the limited datasets used to train the proprietary algorithms and platforms. Biases related to physical attractiveness, gender, sexual orientation, age, race, nationality, and language can manifest due to these limitations. The comparison of job candidates to an organization's current employees, with the aim of hiring individuals with similar characteristics, can lead to biased hiring practices and a lack of diversity—a phenomenon known as "unfair tribal hiring."[32] The rise of video interviewing technologies has brought about both praise and criticism. While these technologies offer potential benefits in the hiring process, concerns regarding their accuracy, fairness, and biases cannot be ignored.

The FTC and privacy advocacy groups are not the only ones looking into the misuse of AI for selection and hiring purposes. For example, the Equal Employment and Opportunity Commission (EEOC) recently launched an initiative to ensure AI-powered platforms, specifically "automated decision systems" (ADS) used in employment decisions comply with federal laws.[33] California is also drafting legislation around the use of ADS when it comes to making hiring decisions. The proposed legislation would make it unlawful to use ADS and other related AI technologies to "limit or screen out" job applicants unless they are shown to be related to the job.[34]

Micro-Expression Analysis

Micro-expressions are fleeting and involuntary facial expressions that occur in high-stakes situations, such as interviews and sales negotiations, when people try to conceal their true feelings.[35] They last only a fraction of a second and can include a broad range of emotions, such as happiness, sadness, disgust, surprise, contempt, anger, and fear. For decades, law enforcement professionals have relied on the science of micro-expressions for interrogating suspects, interviewing witnesses, and detecting deception. In the context of work, micro-expression analysis is a subskill of emotional intelligence that can be useful for effectively reading people during sales negotiations. More recently, micro-expression analysis capabilities have become a key feature in video interviewing technology, as alluded to earlier, to detect a wide variety of emotions and other dispositions and traits. However, it is virtually impossible to suppress or fake micro-expressions, making them a useful tool for detecting deception. It is important to note that the use of lie detectors and other mechanisms or devices to assess honesty is illegal in the United States under the Employee Polygraph Protection Act and in most states. Furthermore, the scientific evidence regarding AI-powered micro-expression analysis is inconclusive at best, with many open challenges and issues remaining.[36] Nonetheless, technology entrepreneurs continue to push the boundaries with AI-powered platforms, and organizations are willing to embrace them.

Giorgio's Story

In a recent interview for the head of people analytics position for a Fortune 100 firm, a job candidate named "Giorgio" went through a video-based interview involving an AI-powered platform. During the video-based interview, Giorgio intentionally used some exaggerated facial expressions, nervous laughter, cynical remarks, and sarcasm to "tease the tool" and test its effectiveness. Giorgio felt frustrated that the hiring company chose to use this tool to interview their future HR analytics leader. "They had to have known that I was aware of the underlying mechanisms and measures within the platform. The entire process was demeaning and disrespectful. . . . Considering the nature and level of the role, I expected an interview with a live person,"[37] he expressed. Giorgio's story illustrates the pervasiveness and perceived value of automated decision systems, video interviewing technology, voice analysis, and micro-expression analysis in candidate screening, employment decisions, and HR analytics. Despite their perceived usefulness, such tools should not be used as sole basis for making hiring decisions, as they can be subject to bias and misinterpretation. Giorgio's story also serves as a reminder that even senior level and highly experienced HR analytics leaders are not exempt nor spared from the practice.

Biometric Technology and Data

According to the Department of Homeland Security, biometrics refer to "measurable biological (anatomical and physiological) and behavioral characteristics that can be used for automated recognition."[38] Biometric technology is no longer limited to security and law enforcement purposes. It is now increasingly used in organizations for nonsecurity purposes as well. Biometrics technology uses people's physical and behavioral features to collect data such as fingerprints, palm prints, hand vein patterns, finger knuckle prints, facial features, ear shape, tongue prints, iris, retina, sclera, voice, keystroke dynamics, gait, signature, pulse, and DNA.[39] Similar to other areas discussed earlier, biometrics is subject to a variety of controversies and concerns, including privacy and ethical concerns. The importance of privacy issues related to biometrics, though mainly a legal matter, should not be underestimated, as biometric data is more sensitive than other forms of data.

Since biometrics is a vast area of study and practice, it is essential to address ethical issues related to technology in the workplace. According to Andrea North-Samardzic, some of the ethical issues that arise with biometrics and biometric technology include privacy rights, informed consent, regulatory guidelines, and discrimination.[40]

Technological advancements have made it possible to collect more biometric data, including physical and behavioral data, than ever before, but legislation has not kept pace with these advancements in terms of privacy rights. Some privacy and ethical concerns involve classifying and profiling people based on age, ethnicity, race, gender, and sexual orientation, which can lead to employee discrimination. Therefore, biometric technologies in the workplace should be used sparingly and for legitimate security purposes.

Workforce Surveillance Tools

Workforce surveillance and employee monitoring have been prevalent for decades, with call center workers, bank tellers, and financial representatives routinely monitored on the job. However, since the Covid-19 pandemic and the rise of remote work, workforce surveillance has become more pervasive and personal than ever before. Some of the tools used for monitoring employees include stealth monitoring, live video feeds, keyboard recording, random screen capturing, and location tracking, among others. For example, Sneek is a company that uses an always-on videoconference tool to take photos of employees at their desks every five minutes to manage productivity and monitor office presence. The leadership at

Sneek insists that the purpose of their platform is to cultivate "office culture" rather than workplace surveillance.[41]

Despite the proponents' arguments emphasizing the advantages of workforce surveillance, such as improved compliance, productivity, quality, and security, recent EU-sponsored research suggests that these practices actually undermine trust between workers and management, leading to reduced job satisfaction and increased stress, along with other psychosocial risks.[42] As mentioned earlier, SIOP conducted a survey exploring participants' perceptions of various passive data science scenarios, aiming to determine the "creepy or cool" factor associated with each practice. For instance, when it came to employers monitoring keystrokes as a measure of employee productivity, a significant 82.9 percent of respondents found the practice to be "totally creepy/no way," while 14.3 percent expressed "some nervousness" about it, and a mere 2.8 percent considered it "totally cool/no concerns."[43] These findings should give organizations pause and prompt them to reconsider their use of employee monitoring.

However, despite the concerns raised, workplace surveillance practices have seen a notable increase. A recent survey conducted by Express VPN revealed that 78 percent of organizations monitor their workforce, particularly their remote employees. Interestingly, 83 percent of these organizations admitted that employee monitoring raises ethical questions, yet they continue to spy on their employees to inform decisions regarding performance reviews, potential formation of workers' unions, employee terminations, and more.[44] This highlights the need for organizations to critically evaluate the impact and ethical implications of their surveillance practices.

This has recently prompted the US Congress to propose the Stop Spying Bosses Act. "The bill establishes requirements with respect to the collection and disclosure of certain worker data. For example, employers must disclose to their workers (including job applicants) any workplace surveillance by the employer, including (1) what data is collected, (2) how the data is used, and (3) how such surveillance affects workers' performance assessments. Further, employers may not use workplace surveillance for certain purposes, such as to (1) monitor a worker's activities related to a labor organization, (2) collect a worker's health information that is unrelated to the worker's job duties, (3) monitor a worker who is off duty or in a sensitive area, or (4) use an automated decision system (e.g., machine learning or artificial intelligence techniques) to predict the behavior of a worker that is unrelated to the worker's job. Further, employers must disclose to a worker any work-related decision that relies on workplace surveillance data and allow the worker to review the data. Employers also must meet certain requirements before transferring surveillance data to a third party."[45]

Gamification for Recruitment and Selection

Over the past decade, gamification has become increasingly popular in HR. Essentially, gamification involves using game technology and methods in nongame contexts. In the context of HR analytics, organizations are turning to video games as an alternative means of assessing and identifying talent. For instance, KnackApp has developed a series of games designed by a team of neuroscientists, psychologists, and data scientists to assess human potential. According to the website, the games generate an enormous amount of data and insights that can be used to assess leadership and entrepreneurial potential, creativity, persistence, resourcefulness, reasoning, risk-taking, and other characteristics.[46]

KnackApp has received significant praise and recognition as a breakthrough innovation that will minimize implicit bias and foster diversity and inclusion. The platform is supposedly grounded in science (game theory, behavioral and cognitive science, and AI) and relies on the use of microsensors and algorithms to measure various aspects of human potential.[47] However, the science, algorithmic, and game-based assessment of workers' potential is still emerging and evolving. Indeed, the adoption of novel talent identification tools, such as video games and game-based assessments, is still in its infancy. Moreover, the validity and reliability of these new tools are questionable when compared to traditional methods.[48]

Meanwhile, should job candidates be rejected based on how well they played a game? Should we rely on AI-powered gamification and stealth assessments to assess and select talent, abdicating our responsibility? These analytics may not be creepy, but they are at best dubious and are likely to leave employers and employees both confused and curious.

Sociometric Badges

Sociometric sensors that measure individual collaboration and team dynamics, as well as monitor whereabouts, have become popular in recent years. Sandy Pentland, professor and director of the MIT Media Lab, has pioneered the use of sociometric badges that collect data on employees' interactions throughout the workday. The badges capture information on communication and conversations, such as how much people talk, listen, and interrupt, among other things. In 2010, Pentland and his colleagues at MIT, including Ben Waber, created Sociometric Solutions, better known as Humanyze, to commercialize this badge technology.[49]

Currently, organizations tend to use sociometric technologies on a temporary, project basis. However, longer-term use of sociometric badges and sensors is on the horizon, particularly as the technology becomes more ubiquitous and cost-effective. As an example, in 2015, I was working on a consulting project with Facebook (now Meta). When I entered the lobby of the main building at their Menlo Park, California, location, the front desk representative used a large screen mounted on the wall, resembling a giant iPad, to identify the building and room number where my client was located and provide me with general directions. All employees on campus wear a badge equipped with a radio frequency identification (RFID) chip that enables this technology. I jokingly asked the representative whether the badges could determine when and where someone was using the bathroom, how long they were there, and which stall they were in. The representative nervously chuckled, but it was apparent that she did not share my sense of humor.

Humor aside, technologies that can track and monitor people's whereabouts in the workplace should give us pause. Although RFID badges are relatively simple, when equipped with sophisticated motion sensors and microphones, a brave new world emerges in terms of privacy and ethics. In his intriguing book *People Analytics: How Social Sensing Technology Will Transform Business and What It Tells Us About the Future of Work*, Ben Waber acknowledges that the trove of sensitive information derived from sociometric badges "could lead to egregious abuses." He argues that "this data could allow companies to determine when you're in the bathroom, how much time you wasted talking to your friend in another department, and so on."[50]

Both Waber and Pentland champion and adhere to what they refer to as the "new deal on data," which involves three core concepts pertaining to privacy and ethics:

- Data collection is opt-in and uses informed consent.
- Individuals control their own data.
- Any data sent to third parties must be aggregated.[51]

Toilet Timers

A Beijing-based technology company, Kuaishou, recently faced backlash on Chinese social media when videos of digital timers above employee toilet stalls went viral online. The photos revealed digital timers hanging over each stall and small sensors installed on the doors to activate the timers. Chinese social media users criticized the company for monitoring and timing its office workers' bathroom breaks to increase productivity and profits. Some called the practice a violation of human rights and privacy. However, others defended the company, stating that employees often misuse bathroom breaks, using them as an opportunity to waste time on their phones.[52]

Chip Parties
(Salsa and Bean Dip Optional)

Microchip implants are a recent development in the world of work. A few years ago, Three Square Market, a US-based company, hosted a "chip party" where employees were invited to have a microchip implant injected into their hands voluntarily. Developed by a Swedish company called Biohax, the technology is a RFID chip the size of a grain of rice.[53] Currently, microchip implants provide convenience when paying for food, public transit, or gaining access to buildings, among other uses.

However, as microchip technology becomes more advanced, privacy and ethical concerns are likely to arise. For example, in the near future, microchip implants could be used to track workers' geographic positions, which would be a significant invasion of privacy, especially outside the context of work or the workplace. Fears over privacy have led several states in the United States to pass laws banning mandatory microchipping of humans against their will.[54] In short, for many, microchipping humans represents the highest form of creepy analytics, likely to get under our skin figuratively and literally.

Are Genes Our Career Destiny?

Employment testing has long been a source of controversy, with various measures used by employers to screen and select workers being challenged by civil rights groups and courts. Genetic testing, however, is likely to spark even more debate. According to the EEOC, genetic information includes an individual's genetic tests and those of their family members, as well as information about the manifestation of a disease or disorder in an individual's family members, which is often used to determine whether someone has an increased risk of developing a future condition.[55]

In 2008, the Genetic Information Nondiscrimination Act (GINA) was signed into law, which prohibits discrimination against employees or applicants because of their genetic information. In other words, an employer may not use genetic information to make an employment decision, as genetic information is not relevant to an individual's current ability to work. However, there are some exceptions, such as the inadvertent acquisition of genetic information by an employer, family medical history obtained as part of a voluntary wellness program offered by the employer, and information acquired through commercially and publicly available sources, as long as the employer is not searching those sources with the intent of finding genetic information.[56]

Despite GINA's protections, there are concerns about the potential for genetic information to be used in the workplace. Scientists have linked hundreds of genes to intelligence and academic performance, and there are now online services that offer to quantify anyone's genetic IQ from a spit sample.[57] This has raised concerns about the revival of eugenics, with sociologist Catherine Bliss, in her book *Social by Nature: The Promise and Peril of Sociogenomics*, warning that genetic IQ testing could be used to predict potential and follow us everywhere we go, including the workplace and throughout our careers.[58]

AR, VR, and the Metaverse

Amid the social media chatter and hype, the metaverse reigns supreme as the next big thing. There has been a lot of talk about virtual reality (VR) and augmented reality (AR) in recent years, and both play a prominent role when it comes to the metaverse. The term itself was coined by author Neal Stephenson in his 1992 science fiction novel *Snow Crash*, which depicts a dystopian future where wealthy people escape into an immersive virtual world, a computer-generated universe that exists parallel to the real world.[59] Broadly speaking, VR and AR open up a world beyond reality that can be characterized by "persistent virtual worlds that continue to exist even when you're not playing as well as augmented reality that combines aspects of the digital and physical worlds."[60]

Companies, including Meta, are making substantial investments to leverage the potential of the metaverse concept. Similarly, industry giants like Apple, Google, and Microsoft, as well as various gaming companies like Epic Games, are also joining the metaverse trend. However, the metaverse is still a long way off and is largely a combination of wishful thinking and marketing hype.[61]

Even so, the notion of the metaverse is not without controversies and concerns. For example, questions about the metaverse's safety in terms of potential harassment, assaults, bullying, and hate speech have surfaced, according to a *New York Times* article. It is not hard to imagine a virtual reality that "plunges people into an all-encompassing digital environment where unwanted touches in the digital world can be made to feel real and the sensory experience is heightened."[62] Other concerns include data privacy as it pertains to the metaverse and virtual spaces. In a 2022 article in the *Washington Post*, the author, Tatum Hunter, contends that the metaverse and virtual reality will "give companies more opportunities to take and share data for profiling and advertising." It could also provide "employers with more ways to monitor our behavior and even our minds" in terms of workplace surveillance, control, and manipulation.[63]

Even Microsoft's cofounder, Bill Gates, expects the metaverse to be part of our workplaces "within the next two to three years," whereby we interact with colleagues and customers as digital avatars in a virtual world. According to Gates, "the idea is that you will eventually use your avatar to meet with people in a virtual space that replicates the feeling of being in an actual room with them."[64] However, when considering that we are still grappling with data privacy issues in the real world, the unfettered access to an unfathomable trove of personal data in a virtual world seems intrusive and beyond creepy.

Ready for Brain Transparency?

According to Nita Farahany, a futurist and law and philosophy professor at Duke University, the technology to read brainwaves already exists, which may sound like something out of science fiction. Farahany recently spoke about the topic at the 2023 World Economic Forum in Davos, Switzerland. With the help of AI, brain activity can be decoded in ways previously thought impossible. Farahany believes that "what you think, what you feel—it's all just data—data that in large patterns can be decoded using artificial intelligence."[65]

Wearable devices such as Apple Watches, Fitbits, hats, headbands, and tattoos, equipped with tiny sensors, can pick up brainwave activity and decode our thoughts and emotions using EEG and AI-powered technology. The potential of such technology is both incredible and dangerous, and its future is uncertain. Farahany sums it up well: "It is an exciting and promising future, but also a scary future. . . . Surveillance of the human brain can be powerful, helpful, useful, transform the workplace, and make our lives better. It also has a dystopian possibility of being used to exploit and bring to the surface our most secret self."[66]

For now, wearable technology cannot pick up and decode complex thoughts. However, in five to ten years, tracking our thoughts and emotions could become commonplace and acceptable. Outdated wearable devices will be replaced by sophisticated microchip implants, which will create vast datasets to train the AI and improve its overall predictive power and accuracy. As a result, brain transparency will no longer be confined to the realm of science fiction. It will challenge our fundamental right to self-determination and cognitive liberty and rise to the level of the creepiest analytics of all.

Fictional Creepy Analytics

Fictional stories about creepy analytics have existed for decades in popular books, articles, and movies in the dystopian genre. Examples include *Gattaca*, *The Minority Report*, and *The Matrix* series. Marvel's *Captain America: The Winter Soldier* is one of my all-time favorite movies involving creepy analytics and algorithms. The plot revolves around S.H.I.E.L.D. director Nick Fury telling Steve Rogers (aka Captain America) about a secret program called Project Insight, which connects the Helicarriers to spy satellites used to eliminate threats to national security before they even happen. According to Fury, Project Insight's technology and algorithm can read an individual's background to predict future threats and eliminate them. Morally perplexed, Captain America points out that punishment usually comes after the crime, and that "This isn't freedom. This is fear."[67] Later we learn that a supervillain and Nazi scientist, Dr. Arnim Zola, developed the sophisticated algorithm for Project Insight that can assess people's past to predict their future. Zola is dead, but his brilliant mind and memories were captured digitally and now represent part of an elaborate computer system. In his robotic form, Zola tells Captain America and Natasha Romanoff (aka Black Widow) that Hydra has been "secretly feeding crisis, reaping war," and that "it created a world so chaotic" that "humanity is finally ready to sacrifice its freedom to gain security."[68] Movies like this serve as a reminder of how out of control our surveillance society has become and how our personal and work lives have become an open digital book. The same can be said about HR analytics if we choose a dark, dystopian path. Time will tell if the HR analytics community is a hero, villain, or something in between.

Creepy Analytics According to ChatGPT

Recently, there has been much online chatter about ChatGPT, a chatbot launched by OpenAI in November 2022. ChatGPT is a generative AI-powered natural language processing tool that allows human-like conversations. Since its launch, alarm bells have been ringing in schools, colleges, and universities, with administrators and faculty frantically drafting policies to prevent the so-called "death of the college essay." Even Google has issued a "code red" about ChatGPT and plans to launch its own AI products and tools.[69]

Before ChatGPT's release, I spent the past year researching the many shades of gray and creepy analytics practices related to HR. Despite this, I thought it would be interesting (and a little fun) to ask ChatGPT what it thought were some of the creepiest HR analytics practices out there. In less than 10 seconds, ChatGPT's response was remarkably similar to my curated list. What follows is the unedited response to the prompt.

What Are the Creepiest HR Analytics Practices?

The creepiest HR analytics practices are those that invade the privacy of employees, without their consent, and that can make employees feel uncomfortable or even violated. Some examples of these include:

1. **Monitoring employee's internet use:** Tracking the websites and online activities of employees without their consent

and using this information to make decisions about their performance or behavior.

2. **Tracking employee's location:** Using GPS or other tracking devices to monitor the location of employees, without their consent, and using this information to make decisions about their performance or behavior.

3. **Facial recognition and emotion detection:** Using facial recognition technology to monitor employees' emotions such as stress levels, and facial expressions, without their consent, and using this information to make decisions about their performance or behavior.

4. **Personal data collection:** Collecting data on employees' personal lives, such as their health, family, or financial information, without their consent, and using this information to make decisions about their performance or behavior.

5. **Predictive analysis:** Using data and predictive analytics to identify potential problems, such as high-risk employees or potential turnover, without employee's consent, and making decisions based on this information.

6. **Constant monitoring of employee's screens:** Using software to monitor an employee's computer screen, keystrokes, and mouse movements in order to track their productivity and behavior.

7. **Microphone and camera monitoring:** Installing microphones and cameras in the workplace to monitor employee conversations, movements, and even facial expressions.

8. **Biometric data collection:** Collecting data on employee's biometric information, such as fingerprints, facial recognition, and eye tracking, without their consent.

9. **Behavioral profiling:** Using data to create detailed profiles of employee's behavior, preferences, and personal lives, without their consent.

10. **Social media monitoring:** Monitoring employee's social media accounts, without their consent, and using this information to make decisions about their performance or behavior.

ChatGPT was able to identify all of the usual suspects within seconds, which was impressive and unsettling at the same time. However, for the sake of my dignity, I was able to pinpoint several additional shades of gray and creepy HR analytics practices that were more intricate and nuanced. These include gamification, tracking nonexecutive employee stock sales, implanting microchips, genetic testing, monitoring toilet usage, AR and VR technology, the metaverse, and brain transparency. Let us also not forget about my clever inclusion of Project Insight from Marvel's *Captain America: The Winter Soldier.* Like any AI model, ChatGPT is not infallible and can produce information that is not entirely precise or evidence based.

In his book *I, Human: AI, Automation and the Quest to Reclaim What Makes Us Unique* Tomas Chamorro-Premuzic argues that our use of AI (in this case, ChatGPT) has been "reducing the value (and meaning) of our own experience and existence by eliminating much of the intellectual complexity and creative depth that has historically characterized us."[70] Hence, it would not have been very fulfilling to absolve myself from the mental anguish and imaginative gratification of the research conducted over the past year. But ChatGPT did validate my preconceptions and research, and now I can bask in the warm, cozy glow of my own confirmation bias.

CHAPTER 4

Evidence-Based and Ethical HR Analytics

Of course, 90% of everything is crap. That goes for academic research too. But hard facts help you decide who to believe. Are they claiming that the same old ideas are brand new? Are they claiming to be lone geniuses? Do they claim to have breakthrough ideas? All of us—I plead guilty too—are full of it at times.

—Robert Sutton

HR analytics is an inherently data-driven and evidence-based approach aimed at making smarter decisions for the workforce. However, the relationship between evidence-based management and HR analytics is often overlooked in the HR analytics community. Evidence-based management involves making decisions that are "based on a combination of critical thinking and the best available evidence."[1] Likewise, HR analytics follows a similar process of gathering and analyzing data for informed decision-making.

Despite being data-driven approaches, both are susceptible to bad actors, misuse, and ethical issues. Scholars and practitioners have been known to manipulate data and evidence to support their arguments, and ethical concerns continue to undermine the potential benefits of HR analytics. Therefore, in this chapter, the concept of evidence-based management in the context of HR and its relationship to HR analytics as well as common barriers to evidence-based practice are described. Additionally, the meaning of ethics and ethical decision-making in organizations is explored, while calling for an ethical ecosystem (i.e., cultivating an ethical mindset and perspective) throughout your HR analytics journey. Lastly, a basic framework is introduced that outlines specific ethical outcomes for each step in the HR analytics cycle to guide HR leaders in harnessing the power of HR analytics ethically and responsibility.

Evidence-Based HR

The proliferation of fads, trends, and dangerous half-truths has led to the emergence of the concept of evidence-based management.[2] In the context of HR, evidence-based management or evidence-based HR involves making critical workforce decisions based on scientific evidence rather than relying solely on individual intuition, experience, or preferences. This approach enhances the judgment of leaders and practitioners in the workplace by incorporating multiple sources of information.

Over the past two decades, several prominent HR scholars have advocated for an evidence-based approach to decision-making regarding HR programs, practices, and interventions.[3] More recently, Eric Barends and Denise Rousseau have authored a comprehensive book titled *Evidence-Based Management: How to Use Evidence to Make Better Organizational Decisions*, which offers an authoritative definition of evidence-based practice widely used across multiple applied disciplines, including HR.[4]

Evidence-based practice in management is about making decisions through the conscientious, explicit, and judicious use of the best available evidence from multiple sources by:

1. **Asking:** Translating a practical issue or problem into an answerable question.
2. **Acquiring:** Systematically searching for and retrieving the evidence.

3. **Appraising:** Critically judging the trustworthiness and relevance of the evidence.
4. **Aggregating:** Weighing and pulling together the evidence.
5. **Applying:** Incorporating the evidence into the decision-making process.
6. **Assessing:** Evaluating the outcome of the decision taken to increase the likelihood of a favorable outcome.

Several elements of this definition have practical relevance for HR leaders and other decision makers. The definition emphasizes the importance of conscientiously, explicitly, and judiciously using evidence, which involves a systematic approach to appraising the reliability and trustworthiness of evidence. It also highlights the importance of using "the best available evidence from multiple sources" to increase the probability of achieving desired business outcomes. It is important to note that this doesn't mean exhaustively collecting and codifying all the evidence but rather enough good evidence from the multiple sources.[5] The four sources of evidence are scientific literature such as empirical and conceptual studies, practitioners' professional expertise, organizations' internal data, and stakeholders' values and concerns (Figure 4.1).

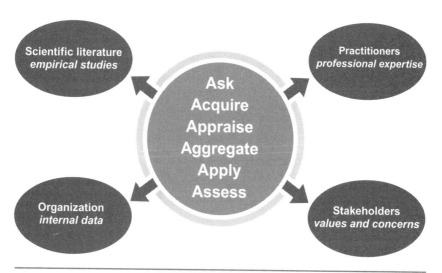

Figure 4.1 Sources of Evidence

Source: Re-created from Rob B. Briner and Eric Barends, "The Role of Scientific Findings in Evidence-Based HR," *People and Strategy* 39, no. 2 (2016): 18.

Scientific literature and empirical studies published in academic literature are not the only sources of evidence, and they are the least used in the context of HR analytics. Internal data derived from an organization's business intelligence and HR analytics efforts are a vital source of evidence. Another form of evidence comes from the experience and judgment of HR leaders and HR analytics practitioners. For instance, data-driven HR leaders should not abandon their intuition and well-seasoned expertise, but rather, recognize their biases and preconceptions about what works and what doesn't work, as well as their personal and professional agendas regarding the adoption of HR programs, practices, and interventions.

Lastly, stakeholder values and concerns are another vital source of evidence for appraising the value, worth, or trustworthiness of proposed programs, practices, interventions, and other significant workforce decisions, but at the same time they shouldn't be the only source irrespective of the power and prerogative they may hold. Therefore, it is critical for HR leaders and HR analytics practitioners to consider multiple sources of evidence.

HR leaders and HR analytics practitioners routinely use various forms of data and information to guide their decisions and work. However, they may not be effectively using all the available evidence. For example, the HR analytics community tends to focus narrowly on analyzing internal organizational data or mining and modeling unstructured and novel data sources that reside inside and outside the organization. This limited approach diminishes the potential value and impact of HR analytics on organizational outcomes. Recent research has demonstrated a linkage between HR technology, HR analytics, evidence-based management, and organizational performance. Specifically, evidence-based management was found to mediate the relationship between HR analytics and improved organizational performance.[6] Therefore, organizations must adopt an evidence-based management approach and fully leverage multiple sources of evidence to maximize the impact of HR analytics on organizational performance and other significant outcomes.

Barriers to Evidence-Based Practice

HR leaders are often too busy chasing after the latest trends and fads or succumbing to pressure to remove long-standing, evidence-based practices that are disliked by senior executives or employees.[7] This is due to the overwhelming noise generated by a multibillion-dollar management consulting industry made up of sales executives, consultants, human capital technologists, marketers, bloggers, industry analysts, and LinkedIn influencers who strive to grab the attention of potential customers and decision makers. Additionally, human capital management (HCM) technology companies and consulting firms of all sizes sponsor and present at national and international conferences to showcase their products and services and mingle with prospective clients, further contributing to the marketing madness. Consequently, the consulting and HCM technology industry has a near monopoly on the marketplace of ideas and innovations, profoundly shaping the collective mindshare of HR leaders and the HR analytics community and influencing strategic choices.

HR leaders and HR analytics practitioners are also bombarded with bestselling business books in the pop psychology genre, which they perceive as authoritative sources of information.[8] Furthermore, academic research published in journals is often unrelated to the real-world experience and interests of HR leaders and too difficult to interpret and apply, representing the proverbial research-to-practice gap.[9] Therefore, it's not surprising that HR leaders and HR analytics practitioners rely heavily on consultants and vendors, popular books, professional associations, and other practitioners for knowledge and information.

HR leaders and HR analytics practitioners are often fixated on the best practices of other organizations. Benchmarking involves sharing and comparing data and success stories about practices and interventions with other best-in-class firms within and across industries. In large and complex organizations with well-established cultures, it may be easier to emulate what other companies are doing rather than pursue an evidence-based, innovative strategy for achieving breakthrough performance (as presented in Chapter 11). According to Jeffrey Pfeffer and Robert Sutton's book *Hard Facts, Dangerous Half-Truths, and Total Nonsense: Profiting from Evidence-Based Management*, simply copying what other organizations do through "casual benchmarking" is a flawed and frequently misused practice. They argue that if an organization's strategy is to mimic others, then the best outcome they can expect is perfect imitation.[10]

Aside from the problem of blindly copying others, research suggests that senior leaders rely heavily on intuition and affective reasoning when making decisions about HR and other management practices.[11]

For instance, a senior executive might consider themselves a visionary or maverick leader who prefers to trust their instincts and may adopt unconventional or untested practices. Similarly, an executive may want to maintain the mystique of leadership, which can limit the executive's willingness to consider an evidence-based approach. A leader who relies solely on hard facts, data, and scientific evidence for decision-making may even be perceived as indecisive and lacking strong leadership.[12]

However, when leaders make impulsive workforce decisions or adopt questionable practices based on dubious knowledge or half-truths, they put their organizations at risk.[13] Moreover, using data to make decisions can alter the power dynamics within organizations, which may be unsettling for those in the C-suite.[14] For instance, a powerful or influential leader might prefer to rely on their own opinions, intuition, preconceived notions, and strategic agenda rather than data, facts, figures, and evidence. Lastly, HR analytics practitioners may resist evidence-based knowledge because scientific findings could challenge executive prerogative and the value placed on managerial experience and judgment.[15]

The core principle of evidence-based practice involves making decisions based on the best available evidence from multiple sources, as previously mentioned. Leaders have an ethical responsibility to adopt programs, practices, and interventions that are grounded in science to ensure the best possible outcomes for the people, teams, and organizations they serve. Additionally, leaders should consider potential ethical issues, including the short- and long-term impact of their workforce decisions. This same principle applies to HR analytics, which is inherently an evidence-based and data-driven approach for making smarter workforce decisions. It is therefore essential to use HR analytics ethically and responsibly, considering the welfare, respect, and dignity, as well as the fairness and equity, of all stakeholders involved.

What Is the Meaning of Ethics?

Ethics is the branch of philosophy that deals with moral principles and values, as previously mentioned. It pertains to questions of right and wrong, good and bad, as well as moral obligations and responsibilities in various personal, professional, and societal contexts. According to Denise Rousseau, "Ethics is not a science per se; they are moral standards that promote goodness, justice, and fairness."[16]

In terms of HR analytics and digital technologies, such as AI and automation in the workplace, ethics can vary depending on the context and stakeholders involved. Business leaders, who are bound by legal and regulatory obligations and fiduciary responsibilities, tend to prioritize profit and shareholder value as a business and an ethical imperative. Conversely, academics tend to view ethics through the lens of moral philosophy and theorize about what people should do without practical constraints. Therefore, while academics may argue against the adoption of questionable AI-powered technology or specific HR analytics practices, business leaders may have already decided to adopt such technologies and are primarily concerned with mitigating potential risks. As such, ethics can have different meanings for different people.

Ethical Concerns and Challenges

Leaders are constantly seeking new and emerging HCM technologies to streamline and accelerate their HR analytical insights process for critical workforce decisions. However, the extent to which such HR analytics practices are "automated or applied with little human intervention, oversight, or transparency" is becoming a growing concern and represents "simmering ethical challenges" for the HR analytics discipline.[17]

Over a decade ago, ethical questions began to arise about the potential abuses of HR analytics concerning the datafication of everything, including personal and often trivial characteristics, preferences, and behaviors with little relevance to job performance, as well as technological advancements.[18] More recently, research conducted by Insight222 found that privacy and ethical concerns are jeopardizing 81 percent of HR analytics projects.[19] Yet few organizations are meaningfully engaging with the important ethical challenges and risks when it comes to HR analytics. For example, few organizations have a formal HR analytics ethics policy or "ethics charter" in place to help mitigate the risks associated with HR analytics.[20] Even more concerning is that some organizations may be unaware of the potential paradoxes and pitfalls of HR analytics. However, it is essential that the HR profession and the HR analytics community proactively address the ethical challenges and risks that lie ahead. The ethical challenges and risks will not disappear on their own, no matter how much we try to ignore them. Hence, it is incumbent on the HR profession and HR analytics community to proactively take a stand.

Ethical Codes and Considerations

HR, like most professions, is built on norms, values, and ethical principles. As part of the Code of Ethics of the Society for Human Resource Management, HR professionals have an ethical responsibility to promote and foster fairness and justice for all employees and their organizations. HR professionals must demonstrate ethical leadership by maintaining the highest standard of ethical conduct. They must also consider and protect people's rights, particularly when it comes to gathering, analyzing, and appropriately using data and information for workforce decision-making. Similarly, the American Psychological Association's (APA) ethical principles and code of conduct require psychologists to abide by the general principle of "first, do no harm"

Recently, in response to growing concerns about the use of AI in employment decision-making, Division 14 of the APA, the Society for Industrial and Organizational Psychology (SIOP), released their task force recommendation for AI-based assessments, namely "Considerations and Recommendations for the Validation and Use of AI-Based Assessment for Employee Selection." The SIOP task force's recommendations are outlined in five sections:[21]

1. AI-based assessments should produce scores that predict future job performance or other relevant outcomes accurately.
2. AI-based assessments should produce consistent scores that reflect job-related characteristics (e.g., upon reassessment).
3. AI-based assessments should produce scores that are considered fair and unbiased.
4. Operational considerations and appropriate use of AI-based assessments for hiring.
5. All steps and decisions relating to the development and scoring of AI-based assessments should be documented for verification and auditing.

The recommendations essentially require that AI-based assessments meet the same level of scrutiny and standards as traditional employment tests with regard to validity, reliability, transparency, fairness, and appropriate use.

In addition to professional associations, governmental agencies are beginning to take notice and take action. For instance, on January 23, 2023, the EEOC organized a public hearing to examine this issue.[22] During the hearing, the EEOC received testimony from leading experts, including lawyers, advocacy group representatives, industrial and organizational psychologists, and computer scientists. The hearing's key takeaways indicate that employers have a responsibility to explore alternative selection procedures that are less discriminatory than AI and require transparency and explainability regarding black box AI they procure. Other key takeaways include the potential impact of AI on protected groups, especially through the inadvertent use of discriminatory proxies like zip codes or sport preferences. Another important takeaway is that statistical relationships and/or predictive utility alone are insufficient to justify the use of AI-powered assessment tools. Vendors and employers must also demonstrate how these tools relate to actual job-related skills and performance outcomes.

Even Mira Murati, the creator of ChatGPT, thinks AI should be regulated. In a *Time* magazine interview, Murati contemplated the risks of AI and concedes that "[AI] can be misused or used by bad actors. So, there are questions about how to govern the use of this technology globally. How do you govern the use of AI in a way that aligns with human values?"[23] Indeed, such questions are likely to continue to arise until country-specific legislation is in place. In the meantime, it is up to the HR analytics community to act ethically and responsibly.

Ethical Charters and Frameworks

Several credible consulting firms and educational advisory organizations have proactively put forth ethical guidelines and recommendations for the HR analytics community to consider. For instance, Jonathan Ferrar and David Green at Insight222 emphasize the significance of forming an "ethics and privacy council" and developing an organizational "ethics charter" regarding HR analytics practices.[24] To establish a data ethics charter, Insight222 proposes the following six-step process:[5]

1. Define what's important to you.
2. Align key stakeholders.
3. Demonstrate/communicate the specific individual benefit.
4. Create a process to get to your goal.
5. Develop an implementation plan.
6. Translate your (ethics) charter in action questions.

Some of the larger consulting firms have responded to the call for ethics, such as Deloitte, which recently introduced its "Technology Trust Ethics" framework for emerging technologies. The framework considers several dimensions, including privacy, transparency and explainability, fairness and impartiality, responsibility, accountability, robustness and reliability, and safety and security.[26] Deloitte also released its "Trustworthy AI" framework that depicts six key dimensions—specifically, AI should be transparent and explainable, fair and impartial, robust and reliable, respectful of privacy, safe and secure, and responsible and accountable. At its core, this framework includes governance, regulatory compliance, and trust.[27] Both of these frameworks have significant implications for ethical HR analytics.

In terms of educational advisory organizations, Al Adamsen, founder and CEO of People Analytics and Future of Work (PAFOW) has been a steadfast advocate of ethical HR analytics. PAFOW is "a global network committed to promoting People Data for Good: the responsible and ethical use of people data, analytics, and AI for the benefit of individuals, teams, groups, organizations, and society at large."[28] Adamsen hosts a popular *People Data for Good* podcast featuring candid interviews with HR leaders, HR analytics practitioners, consultants, academics, entrepreneurs, and technologists. Ethics and privacy concerns are some of the most frequently discussed topics on the podcast. In several of his podcasts, Adamsen emphasizes the importance of partnering with the organization's chief privacy and/or ethics officer, establishing a governance council, publishing a code of practice for ethics and privacy, and clearly articulating the benefits of HR analytics for people in the workplace.[29]

Data Governance and Transparency Is Not Enough

Each of the discussed ethical frameworks, guidelines, and recommendations calls for a mandate regarding data governance, transparency, and privacy, which is an essential first step. However, a generic data governance, transparency, and privacy policy is not enough. Organizations need to critically examine their underlying values, assumptions, and motivations in establishing evidence-based and ethical HR analytics capabilities. Specifically, organizations must consider how they derive, communicate, and, more importantly, use their HR analytical insights. A more progressive approach may require the need for a "Workforce Bill of Rights" that explicitly outlines not only how HR analytical insights will be used but also the situations and circumstances in which certain technologies, practices, data, and insights will never be used.[30] However, such an approach comes with an element of risk. Specifically, organizations may be reluctant to specify what they will and will not do when it comes to HR analytics for various reasons, such as potential legal liability or preemptively limiting options by boxing themselves in. Typically, organizational policies, ethics charters, and the like are not like contracts and, therefore, not legally binding. Nonetheless, until country-specific legislation catches up, organizations and the broader HR analytics community need to do more given the technological transformations that are underway.

HR Analytics at an Ethical Crossroad

The HR analytics community is currently at an ethical crossroad, and the choices made now will determine whether a quantified employee agenda truly exists. The question is, will HR analytics become something unrecognizable, dark, and dystopian or continue to be a positive force for good? (See Figure 4.2.)

Figure 4.2 Avoid Crossing the Line

As previously mentioned, ethics is often not black and white but rather gray. Figure 4.2 illustrates the potential paths HR analytics can take. The first path represents a principled approach to evidence-based and ethical

HR analytics as a force for good. This approach involves a proactive and systematic process for ethically gathering, analyzing, communicating, and using evidence-based HR research and analytical insights to make smarter workforce decisions and help organizations achieve their strategic objectives. It requires gathering and analyzing structured and unstructured data from both traditional and novel data sources in an ethical and responsible manner.

Evidence-based and ethical HR analytics also call for active and transparent data-gathering approaches that are communicated to the workforce. While this approach generally prefers theory-driven (top-down and deductive) methods, it is open to theory-free (bottom-up and inductive) approaches to HR analytical insights, provided it is conducted ethically and responsibly. Furthermore, evidence-based and ethical HR analytics prefers to measure various workforce characteristics, attitudes, aptitudes, preferences, behavioral intentions, and the like through direct measures such as valid and reliable scales, instruments, and tests. It also values and relies on insights derived from broader HR research and experimentation, as well as multiple sources of evidence, such as scientific research findings—which is a core tenet of evidence-based HR.

The quantified employee agenda is an alternative and arguably a dark and dystopian path for HR analytics. It is characterized as the ubiquitous datafication, surveillance, and analysis of the workforce, to shape and nudge desired behavioral changes, and manipulate, control, and optimize performance and productivity while undermining worker freedom and autonomy. While the goal of improving performance and productivity is typically seen as positive, the means by which the quantified employee agenda achieves it are dubious at best, and potentially unethical.

For instance, proponents of the quantified employee agenda rely heavily on mining and modeling unstructured data. This often entails covertly profiling the "digital exhaust" of potential talent, job applicants, and employees from novel data sources. Passive data gathering methods are typically employed, which involve the acquisition and analysis of data points that are largely invisible to the workforce. While passive data gathering has its advantages, such as reducing the burden on people to participate or respond, it is also likely to be viewed as intrusive once revealed, making the workforce unwilling participants.

As discussed earlier, proxy measures are another duplicitous approach used by proponents of the quantified employee agenda. A proxy measure is an indirect and often disingenuous measurement of something seemingly innocuous (e.g., pet preferences, hometown or zip code, magazine subscriptions) that is highly correlated with a desired outcome (e.g., preferred personality, culture fit, likelihood of attrition/turnover) that is unknown to a job applicant or employee.

The quantified employee agenda shares eerie similarities with the principles of surveillance capitalism previously discussed and has taken hold within the context of work, workforce, and workplace. Some researchers and industry observers suggest that the quantified employee agenda was always the underlying goal, though never explicitly stated. Sam Adler-Bell and Michelle Miller argue in their report, "The Datafication of Employment: How Surveillance and Capitalism Are Shaping Workers' Futures Without Their Knowledge," that datafication and surveillance practices "enable a pernicious form of rent-seeking—in which companies generate huge profits by packaging and selling worker data in marketplace hidden from workers' eyes—but also, it opens the door to an extreme informational asymmetry in the workplace that threatens to give employers nearly total control over every aspect of employment."[31]

It remains to be seen whether the HR analytics community will cross the creepy line consciously or unconsciously. Organizations may choose to tread a precarious path between the two perspectives, representing the creepy line and many shades of gray described in Chapter 3 (see Figure 4.2). HR analytics is still an evolving discipline, and navigating the ethical shades of gray, creepy analytics, and ever-shifting norms will define our professional values and ethics for years to come. Our success will depend on the collective ability of the HR analytics community to harness the power of advanced HR analytics ethically and responsibly, while raising the bar to be more evidence-based. Ferrar and Green wisely assert that "HR analytics is nothing without embedded ethical practices!"[32]

Cultivating an Ethical Mindset and Establishing an Ethical Ecosystem

To ensure that HR analytics remains a force for good, organizations and the HR analytics community as a whole must prioritize cultivating an ethical mindset and establishing an ethical ecosystem. This can be achieved through a series of essential steps. First, organizations need to foster a strong commitment to ethics, starting from top-level leadership. Leaders should actively demonstrate and communicate the importance of ethical practices in HR analytics, including ethical use and decision-making. As mentioned earlier, it is crucial to develop an ethics charter that outlines the organization's values, principles, and guidelines for ethical behavior in HR analytics.

Further, regular training and education programs should be provided to employees involved in HR analytics, focusing on ethical considerations, privacy, data security, and responsible use of AI-powered technologies and analytics tools. It is equally important to establish robust data privacy and security protocols to safeguard employee data and comply with relevant laws and regulations, such as GDPR. Transparency plays a key role in HR analytics initiatives, ensuring that employees understand the purpose, methods, and potential outcomes of data collection and analysis, while also obtaining informed consent.

Moreover, organizations should prioritize the use of anonymized and aggregated data to protect individual privacy and maintain confidentiality. A culture of continuous evaluation and improvement must be nurtured, regularly assessing the ethical impact of HR analytics initiatives and making necessary adjustments. Collaborating with external experts, professional associations (e.g., SIOP, SHRM), and ethical organizations helps organizations stay informed about emerging ethical practices and frameworks in HR analytics. Lastly, it is essential for organizations to embed ethical practices throughout their entire HR journey. By doing so, we can begin cultivating an ethical mindset and establishing an ethical ecosystem that encompasses the entire HR analytics cycle, as indicated in Figure 4.3.

Figure 4.3 Ethical Outcomes for Each Step in the HR Analytics Cycle

In Part II of the book, a comprehensive explanation of the seven-step HR analytics cycle is presented. At the end of each chapter, ethical practice tips are embedded into each step to encourage the ethical outcomes outlined earlier and avoid crossing the line while building your HR analytics capabilities.

PART II

The HR Analytics Cycle

CHAPTER 5

Step 1

Determine Stakeholder Requirements

---

*Always make those above you feel comfortably
superior. In your desire to please or impress them, do
not go too far in displaying your talents or you might
accomplish the opposite—inspire fear and insecurity.*

—Robert Greene

Determining stakeholder requirements is vital to the success of any HR analytics endeavor and represents the first crucial step in the HR analytics cycle. It is more than simply meeting with a few influential or vocal stakeholders to compile a list of data requests and reporting requirements. Instead, it involves establishing and nurturing key stakeholder relationships and adding value to the business through HR analytics. Specifically, partnering with stakeholders is a proactive and continuous process of building rapport, credibility, and trust in order to:

- Understand the business strategy and most pressing organizational issues.

- Conduct a strategic analysis to identify the organization's capabilities for success.
- Assess the organizational system.
- Establish an overall governance model and structure.
- Identify high-level needs, priorities, and expectations.
- Determine HR research and analytics requirements.
- Secure involvement, commitment, and support for key projects and practices.
- Foster ownership of the resulting HR analytical insights, both positive and negative.
- Ensure the ethical use of data and insights for workforce decision-making.
- Promote the adoption of evidence-based programs and practices.

In many ways, this first step is not a discrete step, but rather an ongoing process that pervades your entire HR analytics journey.

Stakeholders

Who are the stakeholders? A stakeholder in the broadest sense is anyone who is directly or indirectly involved in or affected by HR analytics. Internal stakeholders typically include:

- Senior executives (C-suite executives responsible for product development, manufacturing, sales, and other revenue-generating lines of business)
- Functional leaders (staff functions—such as finance, IT, legal, and marketing)
- Line managers
- HR leaders including the chief HR officer (CHRO)
- HR analytics practitioners including the HR analytics leader
- Employees and the broader workforce (potential talent, job applicants, contractors, gig workers)
- Labor unions and employee resource groups (ERGs)
- Data owners

External stakeholders may include:

- HCM technology vendors
- External consultants

- Privacy rights groups
- Universities
- Membership-based partnership research organizations
- Professional associations
- Federal, state, regional, provincial, and local governmental agencies
- Regulators and lawmakers
- Customers and clients

Each stakeholder has a unique perspective, set of expectations, and concerns regarding HR analytics. Line managers are typically most interested in visualizing data and reporting key metrics, while executives and senior HR leaders focus more on how HR analytical insights facilitate strategy, execution, workforce decisions, and other essential outcomes. Various employee resource groups (ERGs) are likely to voice potential ethics and privacy concerns, such as bias in hiring and promotion decisions. Functional leaders, including the chief information officer, IT staff members, and HCM technologists, are likely to weigh in on the HR digital stack and the types of technologies and tools used in HR analytics work. Naturally, the CHRO is likely to have strong perspectives and preconceived ideas about the HR strategy, the purpose, and the positioning of HR analytics. Ideally, these should be addressed before meeting with influential key stakeholders (covered in Chapter 11). Therefore, the HR analytics team must be aware of and remain vigilant to these competing interests and influences.

Stakeholder Interests and Influences

In his popular book *The Influence Agenda: A Systematic Approach to Aligning Stakeholders in Times of Change*, Mike Clayton provides a practical road map on how to influence, engage, and enlist the support of key stakeholders. He offers a simplified and broader definition of a stakeholder as "anyone who has any interest in what you are doing" or "anyone who can ruin your day."[1] Clayton argues that it's impossible to manage stakeholders, and any attempt to do so may be perceived as disrespectful and manipulative. Instead, he recommends an integrated and collaborative approach that considers stakeholder needs, priorities, and expectations as well as how various stakeholders interact and relate to one another. This is a proactive and ongoing process, and an act of effective leadership on the part of the HR analytics leader. Therefore, it's important to consider the wider context of interacting with and influencing stakeholders, including people and relationships, power and influence, and their hidden agendas and interests in HR analytics and the resultant insights.

There are several methods and tools available for stakeholder analysis, and one of the simplest is a stakeholder matrix, often referred to as a stakeholder map (Figure 5.1). A stakeholder matrix represents two dimensions, namely power and interest, on a continuum from low to high. Performing a basic stakeholder analysis can help the HR analytics team gain a shared understanding of people and relationship dynamics relative to their power and interests. For example, stakeholders with high power and interest are very relevant and require active management, while stakeholders with high power and low interest are somewhat relevant and should be kept informed.

Stakeholder power and influence in determining the direction and decisions of an organization depend on their positional authority or ability to persuade others in terms of an HR analytics project or workforce decision. In either case, stakeholders' power and interest carry significant ethical implications, particularly concerning the HR research and analytics agenda (covered in Chapter 6) and the potential harm and benefits of a workforce decision on the organization (covered in Chapter 11).[2]

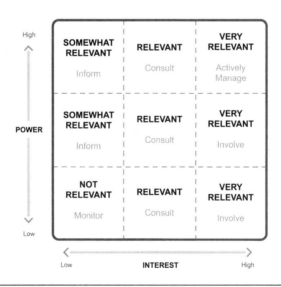

Figure 5.1 Stakeholder Matrix

Source: Adapted from Eric Barends and Denise M. Rousseau, *Evidence-Based Management: How to Use Evidence to Make Better Organizational Decisions* (London, Kogan Page, 2018).

Start with the Strategy

After identifying all of the key stakeholders, the HR analytics team should host and facilitate a series of stakeholder meetings. As mentioned, determining stakeholder requirements is not just about generating a "to-do" list of stakeholder data requests or reporting requirements. It's about engaging with stakeholders and having crucial conversations about the organization's capabilities for success with a focus on strategy alignment, execution, and adding value to the business. Therefore, it's vital that the HR analytics leader has an intimate understanding of the overall organization and its strategic goals and objectives. In his book *Strategic Analytics: Advancing Strategy Execution and Organizational Effectiveness*, Alec Levenson makes a strong case that focusing on business analytics or HR analytics alone will likely miss the mark. Instead, Levenson advocates for a complementary enterprise approach to analytics that aligns with the strategic objectives of the organization and considers the broader context of the organizational system.[3] Hence, the HR analytics leader should "start with the strategy" and work collaboratively with key stakeholders to conduct a systemwide strategic analysis to gain insight into the key capabilities for success.

Levenson recommends conducting a "strategic analytics diagnostic" that includes three fundamental steps of analysis as a road map, as shown in Figure 5.2.[4]

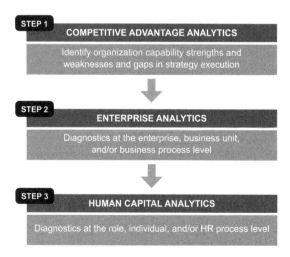

Figure 5.2   Strategic Analytics Road Map

Source: Re-created from Alec Levenson, *Strategic Analytics: Advancing Strategy Execution and Organizational Effectiveness* (Oakland: Berrett-Koehler Publishers, 2015). Used by permission of author.

According to Levenson, it's essential to "put the horse in front of the cart" and conduct each of the three steps in order. The first step, competitive advantage analytics, is considered crucial but is frequently skipped in the interest of time. It involves (a) identifying the organizational strengths and weaknesses in terms of strategic competitive advantage, (b) building a causal or linkage model that depicts the organization's capabilities to implement the strategy, which, in turn, leads to desired performance outcomes, and (c) ensuring alignment with key stakeholders in terms of HR analytics priorities.[5] The goal here is to keep stakeholders on track and focus on what really matters most—the organization's strategic objectives.

Assessing the Organizational System

To engage stakeholders effectively, it's vital to assess the overall organizational system, which aligns with Levenson's second step of enterprise analytics. This step should be an integral part of the stakeholder engagement process. Table 5.1 presents the key organizational factors to consider, along with strategies for assessing each. It's essential to evaluate factors such as organizational culture, communication channels, and decision-making processes to gain insight into how the organization operates and how it affects the success of HR analytics initiatives.

Table 5.1 Assessing the Organizational System

FACTOR	ASSESSMENT STRATEGY
Organizational mission, strategy, and values	Describe how the HR analytics function's mission and charter, if known, does or does not align with the organization's mission and strategy. Describe the organization's values.
Business goals and objectives	Describe the business goals and objectives. Anticipate the impact of HR analytics on current goals and objectives.

(continued)

Table 5.1   Assessing the Organizational System *(continued)*

FACTOR	ASSESSMENT STRATEGY
Organizational structure and decision rights	Describe how the organization is designed (levels, roles, responsibilities, and accountability).
	Does the organizational structure support the execution of the strategy?
	Are the right decisions being made by the right people?
Organizational capabilities	Describe the key capabilities and competencies for success.
	Describe how fiscal, human, and technological resources are allocated—are they aligned to support the execution of the strategy?
Culture	Describe the organizational culture.
	Assess the organization's readiness for change.
	Describe the behavior that is informally rewarded.
Ethics, corporate social responsibility, and sustainability	Identify the organization's corporate social responsibility mission, values, and goals in terms of the triple bottom line (people, planet, and profit).
	Describe the organization's commitment to sustainability.
	Describe the organization's policies and practices pertaining to ethics.
Governance model and structure	Describe the organization's governance model and structure—including its ethics, sustainability practices, and how it manages compliance and risks.

(continued)

Table 5.1 Assessing the Organizational System *(continued)*

FACTOR	ASSESSMENT STRATEGY
Evidence-based management	When it comes to adopting or implementing HR policies, programs, practices, or technologies, to what extent are they evidence-based (science-based)? What sources of information do decision makers rely on prior to adopting or implementing HR policies, programs, practices, or technologies (scientific literature, organization internal data, practitioners' professional expertise, stakeholder values and concerns, other)? To what extent are policies, programs, practices, or technology adoption decisions influenced by powerful stakeholders and/or fads and trends?
Political climate	Identify powerful stakeholders and key influencers who are directly and indirectly involved in the business strategy, HR strategy, workforce planning, workforce decision-making, and HR analytics. Identify data owners and any potential access issues.
Business policies, processes, and procedures	Describe current business policies, processes, and procedures that relate to HR analytics capabilities, practices, and projects. Anticipate the impact of HR analytics work on existing policies, processes, and procedures.
Communication channels	Describe how communication typically flows through the organization both formally and informally. Identify the most commonly used communication vehicles.

(continued)

Table 5.1   Assessing the Organizational System *(continued)*

FACTOR	ASSESSMENT STRATEGY
Fiscal and human resources	Identify trends in fiscal and human resources (cyclical patterns, budgetary constraints, employee turnover trends). Identify the human and financial resources required to support the HR analytics function, practices, and projects.
Problem history	Describe previous business problems and change efforts within the organization and business units/functions—including successes, failures, lessons learned.

In this step of the HR analytics cycle, there is no need to conduct a formal quantitative analysis across each of these factors. Instead, these factors can be informally and qualitatively assessed in relation to the strategy, stakeholder requirements, and the establishment and leveraging of HR analytics capabilities across the organization. Ideally, the HR analytics team should perform this assessment in collaboration with stakeholders to build credibility and trust. Furthermore, it is important to analyze the organizational system early in the HR analytics cycle before formalizing a governance structure for HR analytics.

Governance Model and Structure

Much has been written about the importance of corporate governance in the context of business and human resources. In terms of HR analytics, Jonathan Ferrar and David Green provide a superb definition of governance for the HR analytics community in their book *Excellence in People Analytics*. They define governance as "the mechanisms, processes, and procedures by which a company operates and manages risk for people (HR) analytics."[6] Ferrar and Green assert that good governance ensures alignment of HR analytics with the strategy, provides a mission and brand for the HR analytics function, and creates stewardship, accountability, and enablement.

To ensure alignment with the strategy, HR analytics leaders should engage with key stakeholders to discuss the organization's capabilities, strategy, and pressing business problems, as previously described. The HR analytics leader should have a solid understanding of the organization's strategic goals and objectives and proactively conduct a strategic analysis and assessment of the organizational system, as mentioned earlier, to pinpoint potential barriers up front. Lastly, the HR analytics leader should collaborate with stakeholders to identify strategic HR analytics priorities and expectations.

When creating a mission and brand for the HR analytics function, both philosophical and practical issues must be taken into account. Typically, a mission statement outlines the purpose, goals, and intended value of an organization or function. According to Ferrar and Green, a mission statement should reflect stakeholder views on what they deem essential.[7] However, the HR analytics leader must exercise caution in establishing leadership legitimacy, mission and charter ownership, and a strategic operating model that is neither too vague nor too restrictive.

An experienced HR analytics leader would not wish to limit their leadership legitimacy and influence by adopting a poorly conceived or narrow mission statement that restricts the nature and scope of HR analytics work. Instead, a broader and more influential role for the HR analytics leader and function is advocated for in this book, which requires a direct reporting relationship to the CHRO (covered in Chapter 12). A mission and charter with some teeth in driving strategies for change and influencing critical workforce decisions should accompany this (covered in Chapters 10 and 11).

While stakeholder involvement is crucial, stakeholders should not dictate or entirely take over the HR research and analytics agenda (covered in Chapter 6). Crucial conversations with the CHRO should occur beforehand, and the HR analytics leader should avoid relinquishing control to a small group of influential stakeholders or, worse, the so-called wisdom of the crowd.

When it comes to creating a governance model and structure, there are several key elements to consider. These include establishing an HR analytics oversight board, an ethics and privacy council, and an operating model for the HR analytics function (i.e., the structure and organization of the HR analytics function). Other important areas to consider include prioritizing HR analytics practices and projects, navigating potential data ownership and access issues, and demonstrating the value and return on investment (ROI).[8]

Furthermore, the HR analytics function should develop a distinct intake process for ad hoc data requirements and requests to avoid becoming bogged down in mundane minutiae during this stage of the HR analytics cycle. In short, governance is a highly collaborative process involving key stakeholders, all of whom bring good intentions, high expectations, and a multitude of questions to the table.

Stakeholder Intentions and Questions

As mentioned earlier, stakeholders' specific needs, priorities, and expectations will vary based on their influence, interest, and role in the organization. However, in general, stakeholders want what is best for the organizations they serve and usually have good intentions when it comes to HR analytics, workforce decisions, and achieving positive business outcomes.

When it comes to ethics, intent is crucial. Intent refers to "the desire to act ethically when facing a decision and to overcome the rationalization to not be ethical—this time."[9] This means that ethical decision-making is situational. Even if stakeholders want to do the right thing, there is a tendency to rationalize in order to justify potentially unethical behavior and business decisions. Therefore, it is essential to be mindful of stakeholders' intentions and to question them when they begin to rationalize their needs, priorities, or expectations. When this occurs, it is best to revisit the governance model and ethics charter to ensure that the organization is acting ethically and making decisions that align with its values and mission.

When meeting with stakeholders, it's likely that numerous questions will arise. Carl Sagan, in his book *The Demon-Haunted World: Science as a Candle in the Dark*, explains that "there are naive questions, tedious questions, ill-phrased questions, questions put after inadequate self-criticism. But every question is a cry to understand the world. There is no such thing as a dumb question."[10] While this statement is widely accepted and mostly true, HR analytics leaders may encounter unusual and potentially unethical questions from well-intentioned stakeholders.

Instead of posing questions for consideration, powerful stakeholders usually come to the table with an agenda and eagerly share their preconceived ideas and solutions. Max Blumberg, a highly respected people analytics advisor and business psychologist, argues that "we should expect stakeholders to come to the table with an agenda and their own ideas."[11] Indeed, as discussed in Chapter 4, stakeholders are inundated with the latest management fads, trends, and dangerous half-truths. For instance, consider the following scenario:

The HR analytics leader intends to conduct a series of meetings to introduce the HR analytics function, including its vision, mission, charter, and capabilities, to each major business unit and function within the organization. The goal is to discuss the business strategy, goals, and objectives, as well as to gather high-level stakeholder requirements and expectations regarding HR analytics practices and projects to address pressing workforce challenges. The first meeting is scheduled with the product development organization and includes the HR analytics leader, the CHRO, the executive VP of product development (PD), PD's chief of staff, and the HR business partner assigned to the group. The PD organization has recently experienced a higher-than-usual turnover rate, with many high-performing and high-potential employees leaving the company. However, instead of discussing the business strategy and the issue of unwanted turnover, the executive VP of PD opens the meeting with the following statement:

I read an article in [a popular business outlet], and it got me thinking about how we measure, manage, and reward performance. Personally, I am not a huge fan of traditional performance review and rating systems. They are too time consuming, and everyone hates them— including managers and employees. Don't you think? Progressive organizations are doing away with them altogether. I think we should abandon our performance review and rating system. Can you show me some data on this? How long are we going to continue using these antiquated methods for measuring the performance and achievement of our people?

As an HR analytics leader who has worked in various leadership roles in multiple organizations, she was aware that the dissatisfaction with performance management was at an all-time high. In recent years, senior leaders in various industries have been questioning the value of traditional performance review and rating systems, especially those involving forced ranking. Some well-known organizations have even adopted more frequent quarterly performance review processes or decided to abandon traditional performance review and rating systems altogether. However, the HR analytics leader was an evidence-based and ethical leader who knew that scientific evidence on performance management was essential. For instance, research has shown that performance appraisal and rating systems on various employee outcomes are more informative and impactful than some critics suggest.[12] In addition, a research report from a credible research institute reveals that "employee performance often drops at companies that nix their performance review and rating systems because managers lose a key reference tool and employees become less engaged."[13] Although there are inherent flaws in performance management systems, leading scholars have offered some practical, evidence-based strategies to "fix" performance management, such as training and encouraging managers and employees to engage in "consistent performance management behaviors" such as "communicating ongoing expectations, providing informal feedback in real time, and developing employees through experience," to name a few.[14]

Encounters with influential stakeholders who rely on non-evidence-based sources of information and have hidden agendas are commonplace. So, what is the best approach for an evidence-based and ethical HR analytics leader in such situations? The primary focus should be on reframing or redirecting the stakeholder's expectations and questions, rather than arguing the merits of their presenting problem or proposed solution. It is challenging to assist stakeholders in framing effective questions and redirecting their expectations, but it is essential. As a general guideline, it is important to ensure that stakeholder expectations and questions are:

- **Realistic:** Are the stakeholder's presenting problems and/ or questions practical, sensible, and achievable through HR analytics?

- **Value-added:** Are the stakeholder's presenting problems and/ or questions aligned with the business strategy and focused on specific business needs? Are they targeting the most pressing organizational problems and critical workforce issues?
- **Evidence-based:** Are the stakeholder's preconceived notions and/ or proposed solutions grounded in science?
- **Legal:** Are the stakeholder's requirements and expectations compliant with legal standards related to HR, including HR analytics?
- **Ethical:** Are the stakeholder's requirements and expectations ethical in terms of HR in general and HR analytics in particular?

Therefore, those who lead HR analytics play a crucial role and have a significant responsibility in assisting stakeholders to frame, reframe, and, in some cases, redirect questions and expectations. This is a collaborative and iterative process of refinement that continues as you define and prioritize the HR research and analytics agenda during Step 2 of the HR analytics cycle.

How to Avoid Crossing the Line

Ethical Outcome for Step 1: Ethical Expectations

In the initial step of the HR analytics cycle, it is essential to prioritize ethical outcomes by managing ethical expectations effectively. The following guidelines and tips can help in achieving this:

1. **Establish a governance model and ethics charter:** Set clear guidelines and principles that outline ethical expectations and behaviors within the organization. This governance model should serve as a reference point for stakeholders.

2. **Be aware of rationalization:** While stakeholders generally have good intentions, it's important to be vigilant if they start justifying potentially unethical behaviors or decisions. In such cases, revisit the governance model and ethics charter, and engage in open discussions to address any concerns.

3. **Help stakeholders frame their expectations and questions:** Assist stakeholders in formulating their HR research and analytics expectations to ensure that they are realistic, value-added, legally compliant, evidence-based, and ethical. Guide them toward asking meaningful and impactful questions that align with these criteria.

4. **Consider powerful stakeholders:** Recognize that influential stakeholders may assert their preconceived ideas and solutions. Instead of immediately challenging or dismissing their proposals, follow these steps:

   - Avoid immediate argumentation or critical appraisal.
   - Revisit your stakeholder matrix to identify key influencers in evidence-based and ethical decision-making within the organization.
   - Gather additional information to understand whether the stakeholder's idea accurately represents the perspectives of other influential decision makers.
   - Collaboratively and respectfully evaluate the stakeholder's evidence, considering practical and ethical implications. Assess the extent to which other influential stakeholders share the same perspective or proposed solutions.
   - Reflect on personal biases and assumptions regarding stakeholder expectations, comparing them with your own preconceived notions.

By adhering to these guidelines, HR analytics leaders can effectively manage ethical expectations throughout the HR analytics cycle, cultivating an ethical mindset and establishing an ethical ecosystem as described in Chapter 4.

CHAPTER 6

Step 2

Define HR Research and Analytics Agenda

Everyone has a hidden agenda. Except me!

—Michael Crichton

After identifying stakeholder expectations and priorities, the next step is to establish the HR research and analytics agenda. It is important to note that an HR research and analytics agenda in organizational settings differs from a scholar's research agenda in academic settings. In organizational settings, HR research and analytics practices and projects tend to focus on finding practical solutions to specific business and organizational challenges. In contrast, academic research tends to focus on a particular line of inquiry over time, aiming to generate new knowledge and theoretical frameworks.

The HR research and analytics agenda may be either long-term or short-term, depending on its goals and objectives, programs, practices, and projects. The constantly evolving nature of business and the "future of work" is reshaping what is considered long-term versus short-term. Today, with on-demand data aggregation and visualization, AI-powered platforms, and automation, long-term is no longer three to five years out. Instead, one year is now considered the long-term norm in most industries. On the other hand, short-term requirements typically coincide with the organization's quarterly or monthly results. It's worth noting that short-term doesn't necessarily mean tactical or reactive, nor is long-term equated with strategic. Short-term and long-term HR research and analytics requirements can be both strategic and tactical in nature. For instance, a short-term project could yield immediate results (e.g., market adjustments to employee salaries) that could have potential strategic and long-term implications.

Whether HR analytics work in and of itself is considered long-term or short-term depends on various factors, such as the nature of the business problem, level of urgency, goals and objectives, availability of data, time, and resources. An ongoing employee listening initiative, or the monthly operational reporting of HR metrics are generally considered long-term programs and practices. Conversely, an HR research initiative aimed at a specific business problem with defined start and end dates is typically seen as a project. In conclusion, HR analytics work may involve long-term, highly embedded programs and practices or short-term projects and interventions.

The Agenda Setting Process

In the political and policy spheres, the process of agenda setting can be a highly political and perilous endeavor. However, in the context of business and HR analytics, agenda setting is a collaborative and co-created process of defining the most important business challenges, opportunities, topics, and potential programs, practices, and projects. The primary goal of the agenda setting process is to define, prioritize, and share a balanced yet focused HR analytics portfolio with an eye toward ethics and privacy. When defining the HR research and analytics agenda, the following considerations should be considered:

- Organize the general stakeholder needs, priorities, and expectations using an organizational model, talent management framework, or employee life cycle.
- Formulate research questions for each need, requirement, and expectation, using stakeholders' language and terminology as much as possible.

- For each research question, generate specific hypotheses and consider potential rival hypotheses, as well as the ethical implications of the questions and hypotheses.
- Prioritize a balanced yet focused agenda that includes evidence-based and ethical long-term practices and short-term projects.
- Share the HR research and analytics agenda with key stakeholders and refine it through an iterative process.
- Allocate sufficient time and resources for covert operations and black projects.
- Lastly, avoid becoming a mere reporting function and create a distinct intake and prioritization process for ad hoc data requests and reporting.

By following these guidelines, HR analytics practitioners can create a well-organized, ethical, and effective HR research and analytics agenda that meets the needs of their stakeholders.

Organizing Stakeholder Expectations

After meeting with various stakeholders, the next step is to organize their needs, priorities, and expectations, including their preconceived notions, presenting problems, and proposed solutions. It's important to note that stakeholder needs, priorities, and expectations may vary as to whether they are realistic, value-added, evidence-based, legal, and ethical. However, at this point, prioritizing and considering the interests and influence of specific stakeholders should be avoided. Instead, the focus should be on organizing and codifying the information gathered from stakeholders. Several ways to organize stakeholder needs, priorities, and expectations were identified in Step 1, but a holistic approach is recommended. Organizational models, integrated talent management frameworks, or employee life cycles can serve as useful frameworks. Organizational models are diagnostic frameworks that include strategic factors and variables such as leadership, strategy, and culture, as well as key drivers of employee engagement, which in turn influence individual and organizational performance outcomes (see Case 1 and the Organizational Intelligence Model in Chapter 13). Integrated talent management frameworks and similar variants such as employee life cycles can also be used. Integrated talent management frameworks are comprehensive models that help organizations align their talent management programs and practices to the needs of the organization. Employee life cycles, on the other hand, typically depict the various stages that most employees will experience with their employer, such as attraction, recruitment, onboarding and engagement, development, rewards and recognition, progression and performance, retention, and exit (Figure 6.1).

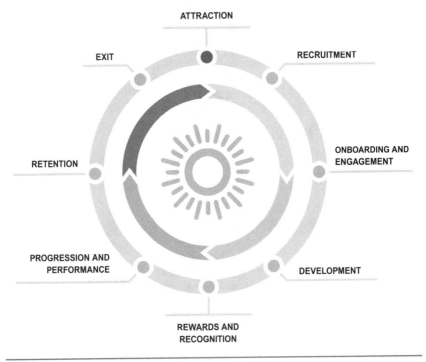

Figure 6.1 Employee Life Cycle

It is recommended that you select a model or framework that is comprehensive enough to cover all areas of focus, without overwhelming or confusing stakeholders. When establishing an HR research and analytics agenda, an employee life cycle is an acceptable and preferred approach, as it does not explicitly identify a specific HR function or center of expertise (CoE) in terms of ownership. It is important to note that stakeholder needs, priorities, and expectations may not always fit within a single stage of the employee life cycle. For instance, long-standing issues like employee engagement and retention often span across multiple stages in the employee life cycle. Nonetheless, using an employee life cycle approach is a practical framework and starting point for organizing the stakeholder needs, priorities, and expectations that were identified in Step 1 of the HR analytics cycle. Table 6.1 gives an example of how to apply this framework.

Table 6.1   Organizing Stakeholder Needs, Requirements, and Expectations

EMPLOYEE LIFE CYCLE STAGE	STAKEHOLDER NEEDS, PRIORITIES, AND EXPECTATIONS
Attraction	No employment brand outside the headquarters region.
	Unable to identify talent pools globally.
	Difficulty attracting diverse talent and job applicants.
	Highly skilled talent expects more remote work opportunities and/or flexible work arrangements.
Recruitment	Trouble anticipating staffing needs now and in the future.
	Struggling to hire the right people with the right skills at the right time.
	Slow and inefficient talent screening and selection process.
	Biases in our hiring practices and processes.
Onboarding and Engagement	Too slow at onboarding and integrating new employees—e.g., time to productivity/performance.
	Workforce seems disillusioned and disengaged—e.g., "quiet quitting."
Development	Little time to participate in formal learning and development events.
Rewards and Recognition	Rewards and incentives are working to attract top talent, but not working very well to retain the best and the brightest.
Progression and Performance	Limited advancement and promotion opportunities for high-potential talent and emerging leaders.
	No meaningful career paths.
	Well-known companies are abandoning their performance review and rating systems; "we should too."
Retention	Undesired turnover is high in certain business units, functions, and workforce segments (i.e., "my best people are leaving").
Exit	People are leaving the organization and unlikely to advocate for the organization as a "great place to work."

The stakeholder needs, priorities, and expectations that are presented in Table 6.1 convey a compelling story regarding the most pressing workforce-related challenges. All of them are expressed as presenting problems, which should not come as a surprise. However, these areas of focus, combined with the data gathered from the strategic analysis and organizational assessment in Step 1, offer a starting point for prioritizing what is most important to both the stakeholders and the organization.

As discussed in the previous chapter (Step 1), it is not practical or feasible to address all of the business problems and issues identified by stakeholders. Therefore, it is now time for the HR analytics team to carefully consider which business problems to include in the overall HR research and analytics agenda. Of all the problems and issues identified, the HR analytics team should prioritize and rank which ones can be effectively addressed through HR analytics. As previously mentioned, it is vital to evaluate the practicality, business value, and legal and ethical considerations of each potential HR analytics project. Other essential factors to consider include the availability of data, time, costs, and the analytical maturity and skill set of the HR analytics team. It is also vital to consider the nature of the HR analytics work that will be performed, such as whether it will focus on descriptive, diagnostic, predictive, and/or prescriptive HR analytics. Jean Paul Isson and Jesse Harriott, in their book *People Analytics in the Era of Big Data*, offer the following key questions for each:[1]

- **Descriptive:** What happened in the past?
- **Diagnostic:** What is happening now?
- **Predictive:** What will happen and why?
- **Prescriptive:** What should you do, knowing what will happen?

However, it is important not to rush into this decision. It is easier to determine whether a business problem and potential project requires a descriptive, diagnostic, predictive, and/or prescriptive approach once specific research questions and hypotheses are generated.

Framing Research Questions

The HR analytics leader has a responsibility to assist stakeholders in framing or reframing their expectations and questions. Framing questions is an effective way to clarify business problems and ensure that the HR analytics project is necessary and aligned with the strategy.[2] This is an iterative refinement process that should be carried out in collaboration with stakeholders. To refer back to our scenario in the previous chapter, it is essential to ensure that the questions are focused on a specific business need (problem or opportunity) to inform a critical workforce decision. The questions should be broad enough to capture the area of interest sufficiently and accurately, yet specific enough to inform action.[3] Therefore, in response to the executive VP of product development's observations and questions regarding the organization's performance review and rating system, for example, the HR analytics leader should assist in reframing stakeholders' expectations as questions. For instance:

- What is the purpose of the performance appraisal and rating system used in our organization?
- Is the current performance appraisal and rating system accurately and fairly measuring the performance contributions of the workforce?
- How are managers and employees experiencing the current performance appraisal and rating system?
- How can we reevaluate and redesign the performance appraisal and rating system?
- What are the possible consequences of adapting or abandoning the current performance appraisal and rating system?
- Are there any legal or ethical considerations that need to be considered?
- What internal data do we have on the quality and effectiveness of our performance appraisal and rating system?
- How are other organizations in our industry addressing the issue of performance appraisal and rating systems?
- What does the scientific literature and evidence say about the value and effectiveness of performance appraisal and rating systems, and how they can be improved?

While brainstorming and framing a list of research questions is a good start, the HR analytics team may not have the time and resources to address all of them. Therefore, it is advisable to collaborate with stakeholders to prioritize the most important questions before generating specific research hypotheses.

Generating Good Hypotheses

Once strategic priorities have been identified, it is time to translate stakeholder priorities and questions into specific hypotheses. Hypotheses are "formalized statements specifying key variables and their supposed relationships."[4] In other words, hypotheses propose a tentative explanation for a phenomenon of interest. Good hypotheses are both testable and falsifiable, and they provide answers to research questions. They should be simple statements that are understandable to stakeholders, as well as focused on solving business problems. For example, if an organization has difficulty attracting talent due to a lack of remote work opportunities or flexible work arrangements, research literature can be consulted to generate a research hypothesis. Upon examination of the research, it may be discovered that remote work opportunities improve employee satisfaction and engagement, which can lead to better job performance. Therefore, research hypotheses can be generated, such as:

- **Hypothesis 1:** Working from home positively affects employee engagement and performance.

Similarly, in the context of a performance appraisal and rating scenario, research may indicate a significant drop in employee performance at organizations that abandon their performance review and rating systems. It may also be found that by providing training and encouraging managers and employees to engage in consistent performance management behaviors, an organization can greatly improve the overall effectiveness of their performance review and rating system.[5] In this case, a research hypothesis can be generated, such as:

- **Hypothesis 2:** Training and encouraging managers and employees to engage in consistent performance management behaviors positively influences desired performance outcomes.

Theory-Driven Versus Data-Driven Hypotheses

It is important to note that the two examples presented are theory-driven hypotheses. In the context of big data and data science, data-driven approaches for generating hypotheses are popular. Theory-driven hypotheses employ a top-down and deductive approach based on existing theories and research, although often when limited evidence is available, a plausible supposition or explanation can be used to generate a working hypothesis and any potential rival hypotheses. On the other hand, data-driven hypotheses are generated using a bottom-up and inductive approach that is usually based on prior knowledge, personal experience, or observation. This involves exploring, extracting, and analyzing a large dataset to identify correlations and patterns. Subsequently, the insights gained from the data are used to generate or refine hypotheses. More information on theory-driven and data-driven approaches can be found in Chapter 9.

The field of HR analytics is constantly evolving, and new research questions and hypotheses are emerging all the time. According to Neil Schmitt and Richard Klimoski, in their classic and definitive textbook *Research Methods in Human Resource Management*, "a hypothesis is a tentative statement and usually takes the form 'If this . . . then . . .' "[6] Hence, the following is a list of common hypotheses statements that use an if-then approach:

- If organizations promote diversity and inclusion in their hiring practices, then they will experience higher levels of creativity and innovation.
- If employees have access to flexible work arrangements, then they will have higher levels of work-life balance and productivity.
- If organizations invest in employee training and development, then they will have higher levels of employee performance and retention.
- If leaders demonstrate high levels of emotional intelligence, then they will be more effective at managing and motivating their teams.
- If organizations provide opportunities for advancement and promotion to high-potential talent, then they will have higher levels of engagement and retention.
- If organizations prioritize employee well-being and mental health, then they will have lower levels of stress and absenteeism.
- If organizations use HR analytics to identify potential talent gaps, then they will be better equipped to attract and retain top talent.
- If employees have a strong sense of purpose and alignment with their organization's values, then they will have higher levels of engagement and performance.

- If organizations use HR analytics to identify and mitigate unconscious bias in their hiring and promotion processes, then they will have a more diverse and inclusive workforce.
- If organizations segment their talent and workforce, then they will be better able to offer a differentiated strategy when it comes to employee value propositions (EVPs) or drivers that matter most to employees.

Hypotheses are generated based on the variables of interest. To reiterate, a hypothesis is an educated prediction about the expected relationship or difference between the variables. The variables in any research project are the specific concepts or factors that HR analytics practitioners want to investigate. In other words, the variables of interest are the building blocks of research, and hypotheses are the glue that holds them together. Hypotheses guide HR analytics practitioners' decisions about how to measure the variables of interest, how to analyze the data, and what insights can be gleaned from the results. Hence, several types of variables must be considered in HR research and analytics, including independent, dependent, categorical, continuous, confounding, and other variables. Each type is discussed in Chapter 9.

Prioritizing and Communicating the Agenda

After framing the research questions and generating the research hypotheses, the HR research and analytics team initiates the process of prioritizing the agenda, which includes ongoing programs and practices, as well as new projects. With respect to new projects, it is vital to assess the extent to which they are realistic, value added, evidence-based, legal, and ethical as discussed previously. Additional criteria to consider includes:

- Stakeholder interest and influence
- Strategic alignment
- Importance
- Urgency
- Time
- Cost
- Availability of data
- HR analytics team's analytical maturity and skill set

Unless an organization is just starting its HR analytics journey, there are likely to be several HR analytics programs and practices already in progress. These may include an annual employee engagement survey, a 360-degree feedback system for development and performance reviews, HR reporting of metrics (such as head count and employee turnover), learning measurement and evaluation, and other data collection and reporting activities related to HR. These activities represent ongoing HR research and analytics programs and practices. Even if these ongoing programs and practices fall outside the mission and charter of the HR analytics function, it is essential to conduct a complete inventory and have unencumbered access to the data (Chapter 7 covers data sources).

As mentioned previously, the HR analytics cycle is a proactive process for establishing an evidence-based and ethical HR research and analytics agenda, which includes existing programs and practices as well as new projects. Generally, there are four major types of HR research and analytics activities:

- **Quick win projects:** These are "low-hanging fruit" projects aimed at establishing credibility, particularly during times of significant change or disruption.
- **Strategically aligned projects:** These are value-added projects focused on addressing a specific business need or solving an urgent organizational problem that aligns with the overall strategy.
- **Covert operations and black projects:** These are innovative and potentially disruptive projects that are sanctioned by the CHRO. However, they are conducted ethically and responsibly.
- **Existing programs and practices:** These are ongoing HR research and analytics programs and practices, such as an employee listening program or an annual employee engagement survey, or monthly reporting of HR metrics.

As evident from the preceding discussion, not all HR research and analytics is stakeholder driven. A study of HR analytics across the Fortune 1000 revealed that almost 40 percent of HR analytics priorities were determined by the HR research and analytics team, while the remaining 60 percent were driven by stakeholders.[7] While finalizing the HR analytics priorities, the HR analytics team should bring their own "HR intelligence" and business expertise to the table. Moreover, the team should think and act in terms of "change insurgents" and avoid relying on the status quo in the HR organization. This approach will inevitably influence the HR research and analytics agenda's content and focus. Therefore, the HR analytics team should allocate resources and time to covert operations and black projects with the CHRO's approval.

Besides covert operations and black projects, framing research questions, generating hypotheses, and establishing an HR research and analytics agenda form a collaborative process between the HR analytics team and key stakeholders in the organization. When meeting with stakeholders, the HR analytics leader should share the HR research and analytics agenda and help them understand how the research questions, hypotheses, and proposed projects will solve the identified business problems and issues. In short, stakeholders need to see the connection between the HR research and analytics agenda and their needs, priorities, and expectations.

Avoiding the Ad Hoc Data Fetching and Reporting Trap

Throughout my career as an HR analytics practitioner and consultant, organizations have often asked me how the HR analytics cycle accommodates ad hoc data requests and reporting. The short answer is that it doesn't. The HR analytics cycle is intended to be a proactive and systematic process for gathering, analyzing, communicating, and utilizing evidence-based HR research and analytical insights in order to facilitate smarter workforce decisions and help organizations achieve their strategic objectives. To effectively establish robust HR analytics capabilities that are both proactive and systematic, the HR analytics cycle must be positioned as a strategic capability that focuses on resolving the most pressing business problems. The HR analytics cycle was never intended to serve as an intake process or an order-taking system. Therefore, it is critical that the HR analytics team creates a distinct process for handling ad hoc data requests and reporting. This is why it is important to engage with key stakeholders to determine their requirements and establish an HR research and analytics agenda in advance. By doing so, you are more likely to avoid the ad hoc data fetching and reporting trap.

How to Avoid Crossing the Line

Ethical Outcome for Step 2:
Ethical Questions and Hypotheses

In Step 2 of the HR analytics cycle, it is crucial to assist stakeholders in framing ethical questions and hypotheses. The following guidelines and tips can facilitate this process:

1. **Understand stakeholder perspective:** Gain a clear understanding of the stakeholder's viewpoint and the specific business problem they are seeking to address. This will help you contextualize their questions and ideas.

2. **Consider potential harm:** Evaluate the potential negative consequences that may arise from certain questions, ideas, or solutions, particularly in relation to specific groups of people or participants. Prioritize the well-being and interests of all stakeholders involved.

3. **Provide guidance and ensure compliance:** Offer practical guidance to stakeholders, assisting them in framing their questions in a manner that aligns with applicable laws, regulations, and ethical principles outlined in the ethics charter. Help them shape their inquiries to ensure ethical compliance.

When generating ethical hypotheses, mutual understanding of the ethical principles outlined in the ethics charter is paramount. It is important to:

1. **Ensure testability and falsifiability:** Ensure that hypotheses are formulated in a way that allows them to be tested and potentially disproven. This fosters a scientific and rigorous approach to ethical HR research and analytics.

2. **Use understandable language:** Formulate hypotheses in a manner that is clear and comprehensible to stakeholders. This enhances transparency and facilitates meaningful discussions around the ethical implications of the hypotheses.

3. **Evaluate risks and benefits:** Assess the potential risks and benefits associated with each hypothesis, considering the impact on stakeholders and the organization as a whole.

4. **Generate rival or alternative hypotheses:** Encourage the exploration of multiple hypotheses that address the same business problem from different ethical perspectives. This promotes a comprehensive analysis of ethical considerations.

5. **Test for ethical implications:** Prioritize ethical analysis when testing hypotheses, ensuring that ethical standards are upheld throughout the HR research and analytics process.

6. **Revise and share hypotheses:** Continuously review and refine hypotheses as necessary, incorporating stakeholder feedback and insights. Share the finalized hypotheses with stakeholders to foster transparency and collaboration.

By following these guidelines, HR analytics practitioners can actively contribute to the framing of ethical questions and hypotheses, fostering an ethical mindset and ecosystem that respect the rights and well-being of all stakeholders involved.

CHAPTER 7

Step 3

Identify Data Sources

*Distinguishing the signal from the noise requires both
scientific knowledge and self-knowledge: the serenity to
accept the things we cannot predict, the courage to predict
the things we can, and the wisdom to know the difference.*

—Nate Silver

After establishing the HR research and analytics agenda, the next
step is to pinpoint the data sources that can aid in addressing the
research questions and hypotheses. Data sources can be categorized into traditional or novel, structured or unstructured, and public or
private. In this chapter, representing Step 3 of the HR analytics cycle, the
distinction between traditional and novel data sources is outlined, along
with a brief description of structured and unstructured data and public
and private information sources. The majority of the chapter comprises
a comprehensive list of data sources, encompassing both traditional and
novel sources. Lastly, a note of caution is provided against overreliance

on novel and potentially dubious data sources and practices, and some practical tips on how to avoid crossing the creepy line.

Types of Data Sources

In the context of HR analytics, traditional data sources typically refer to structured data that organizations have collected and stored over time. This includes employee data from HR information systems (HRIS), HR dashboards and scorecards, and employee survey results. These data sources have been used by organizations for decades to analyze trends, identify patterns, and make data-driven decisions.

On the other hand, novel data sources in HR analytics refer to the use of unstructured data or data derived from new sources that have not traditionally been used for HR analytics purposes. These data sources can include social media data, employee email and chat data, biometric data, sociometric sensors in the workplace, and other forms of digital exhaust generated by job candidates and employees. The key difference between traditional and novel data sources is that traditional data sources tend to be more structured and easier to analyze, while novel data sources tend to be unstructured and require more sophisticated data analysis techniques to extract meaningful information and insights (covered in Chapter 9). It's worth noting that not all traditional data sources are structured, and conversely, not all novel data sources are unstructured. For instance, new data can be collected from customized surveys or qualitative methods like semi-structured interviews. Nonetheless, the use of novel data sources in HR analytics, whether unstructured or structured, can provide organizations with valuable insights that traditional data sources cannot, such as real-time information on employee sentiment, communication patterns, and work behavior. By combining both traditional and novel data sources, organizations can gain a more comprehensive understanding of their workforce and make more informed decisions.

Structured and Unstructured Data

Structured data is data that has a clearly defined data model, such as a spreadsheet or database, and is organized in a highly structured and pre-defined format or schema. This means that the data is arranged consistently and predictably and can be easily searched, analyzed, and processed using traditional data management tools and methods. Conversely, unstructured data refers to data that is not organized in a predefined format or schema.[1] It can come in various forms such as text documents, images, audio and video files, social media posts, emails, and more. Unstructured data does not have a predefined structure and may contain information in varying formats, languages, and contexts. One key characteristic of unstructured data is that it often contains large volumes of useful information that can be difficult to extract using traditional data gathering and analysis tools.[2] For example, social media posts can contain insights about employee sentiment and behavior that can be valuable to an organization but may require more sophisticated techniques such as natural language processing and machine learning to extract and analyze as alluded to earlier.

Public and Private Data Sources

Apart from the different types of data sources, HR analytics data sources can be categorized as either public or private. Public data sources are those that are available to the general public and include university libraries, government databases such as the U.S. Department of Labor Statistics, and professional association websites such as SHRM, CIPD, and HRCI. Publicly available industry reports by Deloitte, Gallup, and McKinsey are also a form of public data sources. Additionally, public data on employers and organizations can also be accessed at Fortune.com and through the Great Place to Work Institute. Moreover, social media platforms such as LinkedIn, X (formerly known as Twitter), and Facebook and various job sites and communities such as CareerBliss, Fairygodboss, and Glassdoor can be great sources of public data.

Private data sources, on the other hand, are data collected and owned by the organization itself or a third-party entity. Private organizational data sources include HR information systems (HRIS), applicant tracking systems, and learning management systems, to name a few. Other forms of private data include external benchmarking data from "best-in-class" organizations and research reports and insights gathered by membership-based consortia such as The Conference Board, Gartner, the Institute for Corporate Productivity (i4CP), and academic think tanks such as the University of Southern California's Center for Effective Organizations.

Data Ownership

Whether data is public or private, structured or unstructured, traditional or novel, it is neither possible nor practical for the HR analytics function to own all the data. This is because data resides everywhere, both inside and outside of the organization. However, it is crucial that the HR analytics team has unencumbered access to all people-related data within the organization and has agreements in place to access data from other parts of the business and outside of the organization. During this step of the HR analytics cycle, data ownership issues are likely to arise. Data owners are key stakeholders in the HR analytics cycle, and potential data owners may have been identified earlier in Step 1. It is important to note that key stakeholders and data owners include employees and the broader workforce. Therefore, as you begin identifying potential data sources, both traditional and novel, it is important to identify the right data owners, clearly define your data needs, and establish data sharing agreements while ensuring transparency and data privacy and security as you build your HR analytics capabilities.

Traditional Data Sources

As previously noted, traditional data sources refer to those obtained from various well-established HR measurement and data collection activities. Following is a comprehensive list of traditional data sources, arranged alphabetically, that are widely considered mainstay HR research and analytics practices.

360-Degree or Multi-Rater Feedback
360-degree feedback, also known as multi-rater feedback, is a method that gathers feedback from multiple sources, including supervisors, peers, subordinates, and other stakeholders. The goal of 360-degree feedback is to provide a more comprehensive and well-rounded view of an individual's performance, skills, and behaviors and to identify areas for development and improvement.

Ad Hoc HRIS Data Mining and Analysis
Ad hoc HRIS data mining and analysis refers to exploring and analyzing data in a HRIS on an as-needed or one-time basis to answer specific

questions or solve particular business problems. Ad hoc analysis is typically conducted by HR professionals, analysts, or managers who require immediate or customized information from the HRIS. Examples of ad hoc HRIS data mining and analysis include analyzing employee turnover data to identify factors that contribute to turnover by various workforce segments, examining employee performance data to identify high-performing employees, or investigating employee compensation data for equity gaps by various demographics.

Employee Listening and Sensing

Employee listening and sensing represents an evolutionary leap from traditional employee and organizational surveys. Employee listening and sensing includes more frequently administered pulse surveys, micro-polling, and always-on continuous listening systems. Indeed, there has been a recent "push toward continuous listening" amid the many technological advancements in the marketplace.[3] There has been a proliferation of SaaS-based survey and sensing platforms that include advanced capabilities for capturing and analyzing employee sentiment and written comments.

Employee and Organizational Surveys

Employee and organizational surveys are one of the most long-standing and prevalent data collection methods used in organizations to understand the thoughts, feelings, and behaviors of employees. As such, a survey can be defined as "a systematic process of data collection designed to quantitatively measure specific aspects of organizational members' experience as they relate to work."[4] Employee and organizational surveys often serve as a primary data source for HR research and analytics, particularly when they are designed with a strategic intent and validity and reliability in mind.

Employee/Talent Profiling

Employee/talent profiling is a process used by organizations to create a profile or a comprehensive picture of their employees' skills, knowledge, experience, and characteristics. Such practices involve gathering and analyzing data about an employee's performance, behavior, competencies, credentials, personality, and other characteristics to make informed decisions about talent management such as identifying high-potential employees, those who are at risk of leaving the organization, or those who require additional support to enhance their performance. The data collected through employee profiling can be obtained through various methods, such as performance reviews, talent reviews, psychometric tests and profiling, and feedback from managers and coworkers.

HR Benchmarking

HR benchmarking is a common business practice of comparing an organization's HR practices and performance against industry standards or best practices. It typically involves collecting and analyzing data related to HR metrics such as employee turnover, compensation, recruitment, and training and development, and comparing the organization's performance to other organizations within or across the industry and sector. HR benchmarking is a frequently used tool for gaining competitive insight into best-in-class organizations to potentially adopt their HR practices and processes.

HR Metrics

HR metrics are key performance indicators (KPIs) that organizations use to assess the effectiveness and efficiency of the HR function and workforce. These metrics are used to track and analyze various aspects of HR, such as recruitment and hiring, employee engagement and retention, training and development, performance management, to name a few. Examples include turnover rate, time to hire, cost per hire, training completion rate, employee satisfaction or engagement scores, absenteeism rate, and performance review ratings. These metrics can provide valuable insights into the performance and impact of HR policies and practices, enabling organizations to identify areas for improvement and make data-driven decisions about how to manage their workforce more effectively.

HR Program Evaluation

HR program evaluation is a systematic and objective assessment of the quality, value, and effectiveness of HR policies, programs, and practices implemented within an organization. In their book *Evaluating Human Resources Programs: A 6-Phase Approach for Optimizing Performance*, Jack Edwards, John Scott, and Nambury Raju introduce an integrated process approach for evaluating HR program goals, processes, and outcomes.[5] Evaluation data in general is a rich data source from which to make critical HR decisions.

Labor Market Analysis

Labor market analysis is the process of examining the supply and demand of labor within a specific industry, region, or economy as a whole. It involves the collection and analysis of data on factors such as the number and types of jobs available, the skills and qualifications required for those jobs, the number of people seeking employment, and the wages and benefits offered to workers. A popular source of labor market data can be found at the Bureau of Labor Statistics. This data source is typically used in organizations for workforce planning purposes.

Learning and Performance Improvement Evaluation

Learning and performance improvement evaluation is similar to HR program evaluation. It is a process for evaluating the quality, value, and effectiveness of learning programs and other performance improvement interventions. Seung Youn (Yonnie) Chyung, in her book *10-Step Evaluation for Training and Performance Improvement*, provides a more recent definition of evaluation as the "systematic and systemic collection and analysis of information about the process and outcomes of a program in order to make improvements or judgements about the program's quality or value."[6] Learning and performance improvement evaluation typically involves collecting and analyzing data and other pertinent information before, during, and after the intervention to assess the extent to which it has achieved its intended objectives.[7]

Organizational Behavior Research and Modeling

Organizational behavior research and modeling involves the use of sophisticated research methods and theoretical models to study the behavior of individuals and groups in organizations. This type of research aims to understand the complex interactions between individuals, groups, and the organizational context in which they operate. The resultant insights of organizational behavior research and modeling can be used to pinpoint the factors and variables (e.g., antecedents, drivers, and employee value propositions) that matter most to employees and formulate strategies to improve employee engagement, organizational performance, and other outcomes (case studies are in Chapter 13).

Partnership or Outsourced Research

Partnership or outsourced research is applied research conducted in collaboration with universities, think tanks, research institutes, and membership-based research consortia. Examples of partnership research include joint research studies between an organization and university or professional association (e.g., CIPD, HRCI, SHRM, SIOP). Outsourced research typically includes HR industry analysis, benchmarking reports, insights, and toolkits obtained from membership-based consortia such as Gartner, McLean & Company, i4CP, and The Conference Board, as well as academic think tanks such as Cornell's Center for Advanced Human Resource Studies (CAHRS) and the University of Southern California's Center for Effective Organizations (CEO).

Psychometric Testing

Psychometric testing is a high-stakes assessment method for employee selection and development decision-making. Instruments used in psychometric testing are grounded in science and the psychological measurement of individual differences. There are psychometric tests that are designed to measure ability, aptitude, attainment, and achievement, while other tests measure personality, integrity, mood, interests, motivation, values, attitudes, and beliefs. The most acceptable personality instruments are those based on the Big Five personality traits or Five-Factor Model of personality—namely openness, conscientiousness, extraversion, agreeableness, and neuroticism. Credible organizations and institutes that administer valid and reliable psychometrics tests include Deeper Signals, Hogan Assessments, SHL, and The Psychometrics Centre of the Cambridge Judge Business School.

Although psychometric testing is widely used in the context of HR analytics and for hiring and promotion decisions, they are not without controversy. In her fascinating book *The Cult of Personality*, Annie Murphy Paul argues that these supposedly neutral tests are fraught with intrusive questions, biased assumptions, and limiting labels that are actually shaped by industry and government agendas. According to Paul, personality tests in particular generate narrow categorizations and characterizations of individuals that reflect a cult of personality that values and rewards superficial-level traits rather than substance, and static rather than dynamic qualities.[8] Instead of celebrating individuals' distinctive and unique qualities, these tests prioritize standard and average traits and attributes, which is deeply troubling and feeds into the quantitative employee agenda described earlier.

Return on Investment (ROI)

Return on investment (ROI) is a strategic HR metric that is considered the ultimate measure of success in terms of HR accountability. Organizations routinely engage in various ROI projects to measure the value and impact of their human capital investments. Jack Phillips and Patti Phillips at the ROI Institute have written numerous books on the topic of ROI in the context of HR, talent management, and training and performance improvement, among other areas, and have a proven methodology that measures the ROI and success of HR programs, practices, and interventions.[9] Both are considered HR measurement pioneers who played an influential role in launching the HR analytics movement that continues to this day.

Scientific Research Literature

Scientific research literature is a source of evidence published in academic journals. Scientific research literature includes the findings and results from empirical and conceptual studies published in peer-reviewed outlets. In the context of HR analytics and evidence-based decision-making, it is essential for practitioners to know how to search for research studies and to be able to evaluate and judge how trustworthy and relevant they are as a source of information and evidence.[10]

Selection Research

Selection research is a type of research conducted to determine the most effective methods for selecting and hiring employees. The main objective of selection research is to identify the selection tools (e.g., personality tests and other psychometric instruments) and procedures that are best suited for a particular organization, job, and role. Selection research considers factors such as the validity and reliability of selection methods, the legal defensibility of selection tools and processes, and their impact on various demographic groups.

Sentiment Analysis

Sentiment analysis is a technique used in natural language processing and machine learning to determine the emotional tone or sentiment expressed in a piece of text. It involves analyzing text data, such as employee survey written comments or social media posts, to identify the overall sentiment of the text as positive, negative, or neutral. AI-powered sentiment analysis is a significant advancement as compared to manual thematic analysis techniques.

Site or Location Identification Research

Site or location identification research is focused on identifying the best locations for business operations, such as manufacturing plants, office space, or retail outlets. This research helps organizations to determine the most suitable location for their business based on a number of factors such as accessibility, infrastructure, labor market, local regulations, taxes, and other business factors. Site or location identification research can involve gathering data through market analysis, online research, site visits, and interviews with local business, community, and political leaders.

Talent Pool Research

Talent pool research involves identifying potential candidates for specific job roles or future organizational needs. This research helps organizations to understand the available talent in the market and develop strategies to attract and retain the best candidates. Talent pool research typically involves gathering data on factors such as job market trends, candidate demographics, skill sets and experience, education and training, and compensation and benefits.

Talent Supply Chain Analytics

Talent supply chain analytics involves the analysis of data from various sources for optimizing talent demands in terms of changing business conditions. Talent supply chain analytics can help organizations anticipate and address talent shortages and gaps and optimize work schedules in real time.[11]

Workforce Forecasting

Workforce forecasting is a workforce planning technique for predicting future workforce needs based on an organization's business objectives, growth projections, and workforce data. It typically involves performing supply and demand analysis to forecast and subsequently develop strategies to ensure that the organization has the right number of people with the right skills at the right time. Workforce forecasting is a critical component of workforce planning and helps organizations to ensure that they have the right talent to achieve their business objectives.

Novel Data Sources

Over the past decade, there has been a surge in the abundance of data, resulting in the discovery of new data sources for HR analytics. Examples include the following.

Biometric Data

Biometric data such as fingerprints, retinal scans, and facial or voice recognition can be used to access restricted areas, monitor employee attendance and performance, and other workplace behaviors. Biometric data also can be used to create a more personalized employee experience, such as adjusting lighting or temperature settings based on an individual's preferences.

Calendar Analysis

Calendar analysis can be used to collect data (e.g., topic, accepting/declining meeting invites) and analyze trends on how employees spend their time to optimize work schedules, enhance resource allocation, improve work-life balance, and track team performance.

Credit Screening

Credit screening is generally used to screen job candidates and employees to assess their risk level, particularly those serving in financial roles. More recently, credit screening is being used by organizations for general hiring decisions as a general indicator of overall responsibility and reliability.

Custom Surveys

Highly custom surveys are being used to explore job applicants' or employees' attitudes, preferences, characteristics, and values, among other variables. In his book *Employee Surveys That Work*, Alec Levenson recommended that organizations generate new and novel data through highly customized or bespoke surveys that do not repeat the same questions year after year. In contrast, common practice today is for organizations to spend inordinate amounts of time annually collecting and analyzing the same questions, which are often drawn from a predetermined set of vendor-supplied survey options.[12]

Digital Exhaust Analysis

Digital exhaust analysis refers to the vast amount of data that is generated by an employee's online activity, often without their awareness or explicit consent. This data includes information such as browser history, and meta-data generated by various workplace apps and devices. Digital exhaust analysis can be used by organizations to track employee behavior and gain critical insights into employees' future behavior and performance.

Digital Footprint Analysis
Digital footprint analysis is related to digital exhaust, but is a distinct source of data. It can be used to analyze employees' online behavior, such as the websites they visit, the articles they read, and the videos they watch. Digital footprints can provide insights into employee interests, skill sets, and potential areas for development, among others.

Email Analysis
Email analysis can be used to collect data on employee communication patterns such as response times, message lengths, CC/BC behavior, and tone. Email analysis can be used to understand employee sentiment, engagement, collaboration, and productivity.

Employee Badges
Employee badges equipped with sensors can collect data on employee whereabouts, movements, and interactions within the workplace. This can be used to analyze team dynamics, collaboration, workspaces utilization, and productivity.

Health Profiling
Health profiling is a process in which organizations can use third-partner consulting firms to predict the health risks of employees.

Home and Hometown Analytics
Home and hometown analysis can be used to make hiring decisions based on where people live (e.g., the closer employees reside to the office, the less likely they are to leave than those who live farther away). It can also be used to identify a job applicant's hometown as a relatively accurate predictor of attrition.

Microchip Implants in the Workplace
Microchip implants in the workplace refer to the use of small radio frequency identification (RFID) devices that are implanted under an employee's skin, usually in the hand. These devices can be used to track

employee movements, monitor productivity, and control access to secure areas or equipment. The use of microchip implants is both rare and controversial and not universally legal.

Micro-Expression Analysis

Micro-expression analysis can be used to analyze people's facial expressions in order to gain insight into their emotions, attitudes, and behaviors. Micro-expressions are brief, involuntary facial expressions that occur in response to emotional stimuli and are often difficult to detect because they occur for only a fraction of a second. Additionally, and although generally illegal, micro-expression analysis can be used to detect deception during interviews and other interactions, which can help organizations make more informed hiring decisions.

Monitoring Personal Financial Choices

Monitoring personal financial choices can help organizations identify overall financial wellness, which has been linked to overall well-being and job performance. Analyzing financial choices can also help organizations evaluate the effectiveness of their total compensation packages and identify potential fraud and unethical behavior. As mentioned in Chapter 3, there have been some reports in which organizations are monitoring nonexecutive employees who "dump" their stock as an accurate indicator of imminent attrition.

Organizational Network Analysis (ONA)

ONA can be used to analyze the patterns of communication, information flow, and relationships among individuals or groups within an organization. It involves using data visualization and social network analysis techniques to gain insights into how work is performed, how decisions are made, and how knowledge is shared within an organization. By analyzing the social networks within an organization, ONA can help organizations improve communication and collaboration, enhance decision-making, and increase productivity.

Social Media

Social media is a treasure trove of novel data sources. Social media platforms such as LinkedIn, X, and Facebook can be used to analyze employee social connections, sentiment, engagement, interests, and behavior including job seeking behavior (e.g., third-party platforms are available that monitor changes made to LinkedIn profile, summary, or tagline as an indicator of job seeking or attrition).

Text and Speech Analytics

Text and speech analytics can be used to analyze the content of emails, chat logs, and voice recordings to gain insights into employee sentiment, communication patterns, and engagement.

Voice Analysis

Voice analysis technology can be used to analyze employee speech patterns and tone to detect signs of stress, fatigue, disengagement, and dishonesty. Voice analysis can be conducted through various channels, such as call center recordings, videoconferences, and chatbots.

Wearable Devices

Wearable devices such as fitness trackers and smartwatches (e.g., Fitbit and Apple Watch) can provide data on employees' physical activity, sleep patterns, and other health-related metrics, which can be used to inform wellness programs and other initiatives.

Wellness Program Data

Wellness program data can be used to track employee participation in exercise programs, nutrition counseling, or mental health assistance to provide insights into employee engagement, well-being, health, and productivity.

Workplace Surveillance Technologies

Workplace surveillance technologies are tools and systems used by employers to monitor their employees' activities and behaviors while on the job. The use of such technologies is controversial. For example, there are tools available that take photos of employees at their desks and/or their computer screen every five minutes to manage productivity and office presence. Other software solutions are available to track employees' internet and email usage, keystrokes, and other digital activities. GPS tracking devices that monitor employee locations and movements are also popular surveillance technologies.

Overall, the use of novel data sources is rapidly expanding, and organizations are finding new and innovative ways to gather and analyze such data for HR analytics purposes both actively and passively.

Words of Wisdom, Warning, and Whatnot

When it comes to using new data sources and implementing emerging HR analytics practices, organizations should conduct thorough research before venturing into unfamiliar territory or pursuing the latest human capital management (HCM) technology or artificial intelligence (AI) platform. It is worth noting that the HR analytics community tends to be both gullible and beguiled when it comes to HCM technologies and novel data sources. While these new technologies show potential, they typically rely on proprietary algorithms and inscrutable "black boxes" that seldom clarify the underlying mechanisms involved (i.e., which factors or reasons led to a workforce prediction or decision, and how). HR analytics must be founded on an understanding of the data to be employed and the context in which that data was gathered if any meaningful insights are to be gained.[13] From my perspective, if an HCM technology vendor refuses to disclose the inner workings of their black box, it is best not to work with them.

When it comes to using novel and untested data sources, it is crucial to consider both the potential rewards and risks, including legal and ethical implications. One important question to ask is how much competitive advantage a specific data source, technology, or practice can realistically offer. Many of these innovative data sources are controversial and dubious at best. However, whether these new data sources and accompanying HR analytics practices are ethical or questionable ultimately hinges on the values and ethics of the organization, as well as our own personal and professional ethical standards. Questions about ethics and privacy are likely to arise and should be addressed.

Nate Silver's bestselling book *The Signal and the Noise: Why So Many Predictions Fail—but Some Don't* famously stated, "distinguishing the signal from the noise requires both scientific knowledge and self-knowledge: the serenity to accept the things we cannot predict, the courage to predict the things we can, and the wisdom to know the difference."[14] It is also important to have the courage not to predict things just because we can. Additionally, we may need to question the relevance of traditional HR research and analytics practices and make difficult decisions about adapting or discontinuing outdated or symbolic practices while avoiding dubious data sources and practices.

How to Avoid Crossing the Line

Ethical Outcome for Step 3:
Ethical Sources

In Step 3 of the HR analytics cycle, it is essential to think critically about your data sources. The following guidelines and tips can facilitate this process:

1. **Consider potential rewards and risks:** Evaluate the potential benefits and risks, including legal, privacy, and ethical implications associated with novel data sources. Ensure that the use of such data aligns with ethical principles and regulations.

2. **Assess competitive advantage:** Reflect on the extent to which your organization will attain strategic competitive advantage through the use of specific data sources or the adoption of certain AI technologies or HR analytics practices. Consider the ethical implications of seeking competitive advantage, and prioritize responsible and ethical decision-making.

3. **Advocate for explainable AI:** Emphasize the importance of explainable AI in HR analytics. Avoid black box AI solutions that lack transparency and understanding. Instead, seek white box AI solutions that provide clear explanations of the algorithms used and allow for scrutiny of potential bias and discrimination. When engaging with HCM technology vendors or AI-powered platforms, inquire about the data used to train the algorithm and their commitment to addressing bias and discrimination.

4. **Technology procurement:** If an HCM technology vendor is unwilling or unable to provide transparency and open their black box to address concerns related to bias and discrimination, consider alternative options. Prioritize working with vendors who demonstrate a commitment to ethical practices and transparency.

By adhering to these guidelines, HR analytics practitioners can foster ethical decision-making, promote transparency, and ensure that the use of data and AI technologies in HR analytics aligns with ethical principles, legal requirements, and the well-being of employees and stakeholders.

CHAPTER 8

Step 4
Gather Data

Data is like garbage. You'd better know what you are going to do with it before you collect it.

—Mark Twain

This step of the HR analytics cycle involves the process of gathering data for HR research and analytics. It includes collecting data from various sources, as discussed in the previous step. Data gathering is a crucial step in the HR analytics cycle because the quality of the data collected can greatly impact the accuracy and reliability of the insights derived from HR analytics. The HR analytics practitioner must determine which means and methods are most appropriate and relevant to the research questions and specific hypotheses generated.

There are various types of data gathering tools, technologies, and techniques that can be used in the context of HR analytics work. Therefore, in this chapter, I first distinguish between several interrelated types of data gathering, specifically primary and secondary data gathering, and active and passive data gathering. I also discuss the most common quantitative and qualitative data collection tools used in HR analytics, such as surveys, interviews, focus groups, observations, psychometric tests, and key business and HR metrics. Although these technologies have been discussed previously throughout the book, I briefly highlight the most frequently used technologies when it comes to gathering, storing, and organizing data, such as HRIS, talent management software, AI/ML platforms, social networking systems, and collaboration and productivity tools. Moreover, I explain various data-gathering techniques used in HR analytics work, such as workforce segmentation, research design, sampling strategy, and tool quality in terms of validity and reliability, to produce credible evidence. Lastly, I offer some practical guidelines when it comes to gathering data ethically and responsibility.

Types of Data Gathering

In the context of HR analytics, data can be gathered in two ways, namely primary or secondary. Additionally, data can be collected actively or passively. The type of data gathering chosen will depend on various factors, including the research questions and hypotheses, the HR analytics team's skill set, and the availability of technological and analytical tools, as well as privacy and ethical considerations.

Primary and Secondary Data Gathering

Primary data gathering entails collecting original data from the source for a particular purpose and HR research and analytics project. The data is collected through a variety of methods and tools such as surveys, interviews, focus groups, observations, and psychometric tests, among others. Primary data represents original research and data that is collected for the first time, and the HR analytics practitioner has complete control over the data gathering process. The advantages of primary data are that it is fresh and relevant to the research questions and hypotheses generated and can be customized as needed. However, primary data gathering can be time-consuming and costly to perform in terms of resources and the skill sets needed to do it right.

On the other hand, secondary data gathering involves data and information that has already been collected for different purposes. Secondary data can be obtained from sources such as university libraries, government agencies, research institutions, and public databases as discussed in Chapter 7. Examples of secondary data include reports, articles, and statistics.

The advantages of secondary data are that it is usually less expensive and less time-consuming to obtain than primary data, and it can provide historical trends and contextual data. However, secondary data may not be as relevant to the specific research questions or hypotheses, and the HR analytics practitioner has less control over the quality and veracity of the data gathered. This is why it is critically important to gather existing data from credible sources (e.g., literature review of journal articles and reports from credible institutes, HR benchmarking, labor market databases).

Active and Passive Data Gathering

In addition to primary and secondary data gathering, it is important to consider the extent to which the data is actively or passively collected. In the context of HR analytics, active data gathering generally refers to methods that involve interacting with individual participants such as conducting surveys, facilitating interviews or focus groups, or administering psychometric tests.[1] There are two primary types of active data gathering in HR analytics that warrant mention: active self-reporting and active behavioral observation. Active self-reporting involves directly asking employees to provide information about their own experiences, attitudes, behaviors, or opinions (e.g., using surveys, interviews, and focus groups).[2] Conversely, active behavioral observation involves directly observing individuals in real-world or simulated settings to collect data about their actions, movements, behaviors, and social interactions (e.g., using observations, leadership simulations, and sociometric sensors).[3]

Passive data gathering, on the other hand, involves collecting data through indirect methods that do not require direct interaction with individual participants in the workplace. This approach typically involves collecting data through existing sources, such as an employee's regular workflow and day-to-day interactions, network data, website analytics, and biometric data.[4] Passive data gathering does not require the active participation of the individuals being studied or observed, and the data collected is often broader in scope and less specific than that collected through active data gathering. In HR analytics, passive data gathering can provide valuable insights into patterns and trends over time, while active data gathering can provide more detailed and specific information about individual experiences, behaviors, and attitudes that in turn compels action. Both approaches have their advantages and disadvantages, and the choice of which method to use will depend on a variety of factors including the research questions and hypotheses, privacy and ethical factors, and the level of sophistication of the HR analytics team, as well as the tools, technologies, and techniques used.

Data Gathering Tools

There are several tools available for data gathering in HR analytics. Some of these tools are designed for collecting quantitative data, while others are used for qualitative data collection. When thinking of HR analytics, quantitative data gathering approaches such as surveys, numerical data, and metrics are typically the first options that come to mind. However, the use of qualitative data gathering methods is gaining popularity. Qualitative data can be particularly useful in exploring complex or sensitive topics, such as strategy and execution, workplace culture, and diversity and inclusion. Many organizations now recognize the value of combining both quantitative and qualitative data gathering methods to obtain a more complete understanding of their workforce. By gathering and incorporating both types of data, HR analytics practitioners can triangulate the information to gain a more holistic understanding of the phenomenon under study or the topic of interest. Therefore, the following data gathering tools are described in detail.

Surveys
One of the widely used tools in HR analytics is the survey, which allows HR analytics practitioners to easily collect data and information from a large number of people. Surveys can be used for various purposes, such as:

- Capturing internal and external business and/or HR intelligence for strategy creation and innovation.
- Identifying the most pressing business challenges and opportunities for improvement.
- Aligning individuals, teams, and the organizational culture with the strategy and goals of the organization.
- Benchmarking functional and industry-specific metrics and analytics for effective strategy execution.
- Communicating and reinforcing the organizational vision, mission, and strategic objectives and initiatives.
- Gathering data and information from customers, employees, and other stakeholders.
- Assessing the organization's readiness for change and its ability to adapt to and sustain change.

- Diagnosing organizational culture and climate, M&A fit and cultural integration, and workgroup trust.
- Pinpointing leadership and management capabilities and learning and development gaps.
- Evaluating the quality, value, and impact of products, services, programs, and solutions.

Surveys can be designed in different technological formats, but the general steps for constructing a survey remain the same. To begin with, the first step is to create a list of items to be included in the survey. These items should be relevant to the research questions, hypotheses, and specifically, the variables of interest (such as employee engagement, culture, work-life balance, and flexible work arrangements) in the project. Brainstorming is an effective way to generate such items unless you are using an existing survey instrument. It is crucial to avoid creating or using double-barreled items. Double-barreled items are questions or statements that combine two separate ideas into one item, which may cause confusion or misunderstanding for respondents.[5]

After creating a pool of survey items, they should be categorized under specific headings, and any redundant or unnecessary items should be eliminated. Once the items have been constructed, appropriate response alternatives or choices for each item should be selected. It is important to note that not all survey items require the same response alternatives. There are several response alternatives commonly used on surveys, including rating scales, multiple choice, binary (yes/no or true/false questions), ranking, checklist, and open-ended questions. The two most frequently used response alternatives are closed-ended items (which can be unipolar or bipolar) with rating scales and open-ended items to obtain written comments.[6] Closed-ended items require individuals to choose from a list of specified response alternatives to answer the question, while open-ended items allow respondents to provide their answers in their own words.

Regarding closed-ended items, the response alternative labels provide meaning to the numbers on the scale. As alluded to, closed-ended items can be unipolar or bipolar. Unipolar scales ask respondents to rate the relative presence or absence of a single quality or attribute usually ranging from nothing to something (e.g., extent scales). Conversely, bipolar scales deal with two attributes and ask respondents to rate two opposite attributes (e.g., strongly disagree to strongly agree). Table 8.1 illustrates five-point rating scales that are unipolar or bipolar in nature, but longer scales can also be used. A longer scale, such as a seven- or nine-point scale,

Table 8.1 Five-Point Likert-Type Rating Scales

	1	2	3	4	5
Acceptability	Totally unacceptable	Unacceptable	Neutral	Acceptable	Totally acceptable
Accuracy	Never true	Rarely true	Sometimes true	Often true	Always true
Affect	No affect	Minor affect	Neutral	Moderate affect	Major affect
Agreement	Strongly disagree	Disagree	Neither disagree nor agree	Agree	Strongly agree
Appropriateness	Absolutely inappropriate	Inappropriate	Neither inappropriate nor appropriate	Appropriate	Absolutely appropriate
Beliefs	Untrue of what I believe	Somewhat untrue of what I believe	Neutral	Somewhat true of what I believe	True of what I believe
Concern	Not at all concerned	Slightly concerned	Somewhat concerned	Very concerned	Extremely concerned
Desirability	Very undesirable	Undesirable	Neither undesirable nor desirable	Desirable	Very desirable
Difficulty	Very difficult	Difficult	Neutral	Easy	Very easy
Effectiveness	Very ineffective	Ineffective	Neutral	Effective	Very effective
Expectancy	Much worse than expected	Worse than expected	As expected	Better than expected	Much better than expected
Extent	Not at all	To a small extent	To a moderate extent	To a great extent	To a very great extent
Familiarity	Not at all familiar	Slightly familiar	Somewhat familiar	Moderately familiar	Extremely familiar

	1	2	3	4	5
Frequency	Never	Rarely	Sometimes	Often	Always
Importance	Not at all	Somewhat important	Important	Very important	Extremely important
Intensity	None	Very mild	Mild	Moderate	Severe
Likelihood	Extremely unlikely	Unlikely	Neutral	Likely	Extremely likely
Priority	Not a priority	Low priority	Medium priority	High priority	Essential
Probability	Not probable	Somewhat improbable	Neutral	Somewhat probable	Very probable
Problem	No problem	Very small problem	Small problem	Moderate problem	Big problem
Quality	Very poor	Poor	Average	Good	Very good
Reflect Me	Very untrue of me	Somewhat untrue of me	Neutral	Somewhat true of me	Very true of me
Satisfaction	Very dissatisfied	Dissatisfied	Neither dissatisfied nor satisfied	Satisfied	Very satisfied
Support/Opposition	Strongly oppose	Somewhat oppose	Neither oppose nor favor	Somewhat favor	Strongly favor

Source: Adapted from Arlene Fink, *The Survey Handbook* (Thousand Oaks: Sage, 1995); Wendy L. Combs and Salvatore V. Falletta, *The Targeted Evaluation Process* (Alexandria: ASTD, 2000); Allan H. Church and Janine Waclawski, *Designing and Using Organizational Surveys* (San Francisco: Jossey-Bass, 2001); Wade M. Vagias, "Likert-Type Scale Response Anchors," Clemson International Institute for Tourism and Research Development, Department of Parks, Recreation and Tourism Management, Clemson University, http://media.clemscn.edu/cbshs/prtm/research/resources-for-research-page -2/Vagias-Likert-Type-Scale-Response-Anchors.pdf.

allows for more discrimination among responses. Moreover, using an even-numbered scale compels respondents to select one side of the scale over the other in a bipolar manner, rather than a middle point. However, odd-numbered scales, either five-point or seven-point, are recommended for most workforce-related surveys.[7]

Open-ended items allow individuals to provide their own response to the item in their own words. They are suitable to use when the HR analytics practitioner is uncertain about all possible responses that individuals may provide. However, open-ended items on surveys may result in some complications. For instance, people may provide information that is only indirectly related to the question. Moreover, analyzing written responses using traditional content analysis approaches may be challenging. Nonetheless, recent advancements in AI/ML text analytics, especially with regard to using deep learning techniques with natural language processing (NLP) are quite promising.[8]

Regardless of the type of response alternative used, it is important to specify how respondents should answer each item. For example, if an item pertains to position, all possible positions should be represented in the response alternatives as much as possible. A common best practice is to include an additional response alternative labeled "other" with a box for respondents to fill in if their position is not listed. Respondents should also be informed of the appropriate number of responses for each item (e.g., "check all that apply"). Lastly, response alternatives should match the respective item, meaning that they should be appropriate and relevant to the survey item.[9]

Clear instructions on how to complete the survey and the estimated time it will take should be prominently displayed. The purpose of the survey should be clearly stated, and the business owner or sponsor should be identified so that respondents understand the goals of the survey. To ensure that respondents have a shared understanding of the meaning of items, important terms or concepts should be defined. According to Arlene Fink in her book *How to Conduct Surveys: A Step-by-Step Guide*, sensitive questions or items should be placed well after the start of the survey but before its conclusion. Demographic questions should be the last items on the survey to increase the likelihood of completion.[10]

The final consideration is the layout of the survey. The font should be easy to read and an appropriate size and shape. Underlining, italics, or boldface type can be used to make distinctions between items and enhance the overall appearance of the survey. Layout decisions should be made based on the technology used, and online survey solutions such as QuestionPro and Qualtrics offer robust capabilities and features (e.g., survey templates, multiple response alternative types, branching/skip logic, and data analysis) to design, deploy, and analyze a survey in various layouts and formats. Before administration or deployment, stakeholders should review the survey to ensure it meets their data and informational needs. It is crucial to pilot test all surveys to identify errors and potential issues.

The survey is a useful HR analytics tool with both advantages and disadvantages. One significant advantage is the ability to gather a large amount of information quickly and easily. In-house design allows for customized items to be included, and technology like online survey solutions and SaaS-based platforms can streamline the process. However, a major disadvantage is the time it takes to design, administer, analyze, and derive insights from surveys, as well as the time-consuming action planning and change process that often follows. When it comes to employee engagement surveys, for example, real-time insights rarely lead to real-time decisions and actions, particularly in politically sensitive areas like salary increases, advancement and promotions opportunities, and flexible work arrangements. Nevertheless, surveys remain one of the most commonly used tools in HR analytics, with a wide range of uses in HR research and analytics. Examples of the multiple uses of surveys in the context of HR research and analytics include:

- Prehire/job applicant surveys
- Employee and organizational surveys
- Employee engagement surveys
- Employee experience surveys
- Employee value proposition (EVP) surveys
- Workplace culture surveys
- Onboarding/new hire surveys
- Organizational needs assessment surveys
- Organizational diagnostic surveys
- Organizational capability surveys
- Leadership and management capability surveys
- Strategy alignment and execution surveys
- Learning and performance improvement evaluation surveys
- Change readiness surveys
- M&A integration surveys

- Pulse surveys
- Employee exit surveys
- Highly specialized surveys for HR research and experimentation

Interviews

Conducting interviews is another method for collecting data and information for HR analytics purposes. Interviews can be done in person, over the telephone, or through video technology such as Zoom or Microsoft Teams. To ensure consistency in results, interviews should be conducted in a consistent manner. There are several steps for preparing for interviews. The first step is to determine whether the interview will be conducted in person, over the telephone, or through video technology. Telephone or video interviews are less costly since participants do not need to travel to their workplace. They are also more convenient for respondents and can be completed more quickly.

Once the interview method is decided, the questions to be asked should be generated, aligned with the research topic and questions, and written in a natural conversational tone. It is crucial that the question stems begin with "who, what, when, how, and why" and be simple enough for the interviewer to read to the respondent without any confusion.[11] All respondents should be asked the same questions in the same way to ensure comparable responses. A semi-structured approach is commonly used in organizational settings to maintain a consistent set of questions and allow flexibility for participants to discuss what they think is important.

After creating the interview protocol, a recording form is generated, which includes instructions to establish rapport, explain the purpose of the interview, and how the data will be used. If vague or incomplete answers are given, the interviewer may need to ask question extensions (probes or follow-up questions), and these extensions should be listed on the interview protocol.[12] Interviewers should also receive training on interviewing techniques to minimize unintentional biases. Obtaining consent in advance of the interview is essential, especially if it is recorded.

Interviews provide the opportunity to clarify answers and probe for more detail, making it an advantageous method for HR analytics practitioners. However, it is relatively time-consuming, and scheduling an interview may require several contacts. Therefore, providing advance notice, limiting interview length, and scheduling at a convenient time for the respondent increases the likelihood of participation.

Focus Groups

Focus groups are a valuable tool for gathering data in HR analytics and can be used to investigate a specific topic or issue in greater depth. The questions asked during focus groups require thoughtful reflection and interaction among participants, which is why it is recommended to limit the number of questions asked during a standard session. To ensure meaningful results, the session's strategy is planned in advance. As a qualitative data gathering tool, focus groups can be used to explore stakeholders' experiences or perspectives related to HR analytics projects or to investigate attitudes and opinions on important topics like workplace culture or flexible work arrangements.

The first step in the process of using focus groups as a data gathering tool is to define the session's purpose, which depends on the research questions, hypotheses, and topics of interest. Once the purpose is established, specific questions and discussion strategies are designed. The success of the focus group depends on the moderator's skills and the session's design.[13] Without proper preparation and facilitation skills, the data collected may not be meaningful or useful.

The moderator's role is to create a permissive and nonthreatening atmosphere where participants feel comfortable sharing their observations and experiences related to the topic. At the beginning of the session, the moderator should introduce the sponsor and purpose of the session, describe how the information will be used, and provide background information about the topic. Throughout the session, the moderator should ask for clarification and elaboration as necessary to facilitate group discussion.

The number and composition of participants depend on the purpose and nature of the topic or issue. Conducting several small groups may be necessary to appropriately group participants. A focus group can include 3 to 10 participants and last between 90 minutes to two hours to ensure thorough exploration of questions and issues.[14] Individuals should be grouped together based on similarities, such as managers in one session and employees in another.

The advantage of using focus groups as a data gathering tool is the opportunity to explore a topic or issue in greater depth than other methods. It allows the moderator "to get a sense of the voice of people in a group setting" according to Jen Katz-Buonincontro. Moreover, "focus group members can 'riff,' or build off of each other's ideas; discuss a topic or debate; and disagree with each other."[15] However, a disadvantage is the potential for the moderator to bias the discussion unintentionally, and participants may be influenced by others, resulting in an unrepresentative sample. Lastly, the information collected through focus groups may be descriptive and reveal negative information that stakeholders did not anticipate.

Observation

Observation is another valuable tool for HR analytics practitioners. It involves firsthand examination of an object, such as an activity, process, behavior, performance, work sample, or product, and the use of checklists or rating scales to describe or rate certain important features of the object.[16] However, observation is only appropriate when the object can be easily and directly observed and may require technological mechanisms and methods to capture subtle changes or complex activities (e.g., workplace surveillance technologies, sociometric sensors, wearable devices).

Checklists and rating scales can be used to aid in the observation process, with checklists used to document required elements and rating scales enabling discrimination among levels of quality or other criteria.[17] It is important for observers to receive explicit instructions on how to perform the observation and complete the rating form, and for inter-rater reliability to be calculated if multiple individuals rate an object. Those who will be observed should be informed in advance, and observers should not give directions or nonverbal cues that may influence behavior or performance. Passive data gathering approaches can also be used to observe employees, with or without their knowledge, using various technologies as mentioned previously.

Psychometric Tests

Psychometric tests are standardized measures used to assess an individual's mental abilities, aptitudes, academic achievement, personality traits, preferences, motivations, values, attitudes, and beliefs, among other factors. There exists a whole body of knowledge dedicated to the science of psychological assessments, particularly with respect to tests and measurement and individual differences.[18] In general, psychometric tests can be classified into two broad categories: knowledge-based and person-based. Examples of knowledge-based tests include the following:

- **Intelligence tests** measure an individual's general cognitive abilities, including reasoning, problem-solving, and abstract thinking (e.g., Wechsler Adult Intelligence Scale and the Stanford-Binet Intelligence Scale).

- **Aptitude tests** measure an individual's ability to perform specific tasks or learn new skills (e.g., Armed Services Vocational Aptitude Battery and the Differential Aptitude Tests).
- **Achievement tests** measure an individual's knowledge and proficiency in a particular subject area (e.g., SAT, ACT, GMAT, and GRE).

Common person-centered psychometric tests include:

- **Personality tests** measure an individual's personality traits and characteristics, such as introversion/extroversion, emotional stability, and openness to new experiences (e.g., the Big Five personality traits or Five-Factor Model—specifically Deeper Signals' Core Drivers, Hogan Personality Inventory, and NEO Personality Inventory), including dark traits (e.g., narcissism). Other trait-based personality instruments include the 16 Personality Factor Questionnaire.
- **Behavioral assessments** measure an individual's behavior and tendencies, such as leadership skills, communication skills, and decision-making abilities (e.g., situational judgment tests).
- **Popular personality tests** measure an individual's personality type, preferences, and strengths (e.g., Myers-Briggs Type Indicator, DiSC, Enneagram, and CliftonStrengths).

Psychometric tests are commonly utilized to make decisions about selection, development, talent management, and promotion. However, it is important to recognize that psychometric tests are not immune to controversy. Opponents argue that certain types of psychometric tests are biased toward specific cultures.[19] Furthermore, the EEOC has found that personality tests had an adverse effect on job applicants based on race and national origin.[20] Therefore, it is important to use these tests in combination with other assessment methods and to interpret the results with caution.

Organizations typically do not endeavor to create their own psychometric tests, even if they have a team of psychologists on staff. First, there are numerous psychometric tests available that have been tested for their validity and reliability over many years.[21] Second, constructing and validating psychometric tests are very challenging tasks, unlike customized surveys used for HR research and experimentation. However, organizations are increasingly abandoning traditional and well-established assessments in favor of customized and/or pseudoscientific psychometric tests to achieve strategic competitive advantage.[22] Nonetheless, it is recommended that organizations use established and widely recognized psychometric tests and scales instead of reinventing the wheel or chasing the next pseudoscientific fad or trend.

HR Metrics

Instead of creating tools specifically for data collection, organizations often monitor HR metrics. These metrics include head count, cost per hire, time to hire, quality of hire, time to productivity, HR-to-employee ratio, employee engagement scores, training and development expenditure per employee, productivity rate, performance review/appraisal ratings, diversity ratios, absenteeism rate, and employee turnover rate. It is important to note that there are many HR metrics to choose from, and the selection depends on the organization's strategic objectives and goals, industry, and size, among other factors. Leading research and consulting firms such as McLean & Company offer a library of HR metrics to help organizations get started, with 200 distinct HR metrics available.[23] Tracking HR metrics is a vital component of evidence-based HR and an effective tool for HR analytics practitioners to measure performance, identify areas for improvement, and make data-driven decisions.

When implementing the HR analytics cycle, the HR analytics practitioner must choose from various data-gathering tools. The selection of which tool or tools to use should be based on the research questions, hypotheses, and variables of interest. Additionally, the HR analytics practitioner must consider the stakeholders' perceptions of the credibility of the selected tool.

Data Gathering Technologies

New technological advancements have introduced innovative ways of gathering, organizing, analyzing, and reporting data. HCM technology vendors showcase these technologies every year at conferences and expositions, as previously mentioned. Undoubtedly, HR analytics has become increasingly reliant on technology to enable prompt data-driven insights and workforce decisions, as discussed in Chapters 2 and 3. The following are examples of technologies used for data gathering, storing, and organizing in HR analytics:

- HR information systems
- Applicant tracking systems
- Performance management systems
- Time and attendance systems
- Learning management systems
- Talent management solutions
- Online survey solutions
- SaaS-based employee engagement and feedback tools
- Collaboration and productivity tools
- Social networking systems
- Specialized AI/ML platforms
- Data aggregation tools
- Biometric devices
- Sociometric sensors and badges
- Wearable technologies

Data gathering technologies will continue to evolve as organizations continue to push the boundaries and explore new data sources and passive data-gathering approaches. These innovations have profound privacy and ethical implications to consider. Specific technologies used for data mining and analysis are discussed in Chapter 9, "Step 5: Analyze and Transform Data," in the HR analytics cycle.

Data Gathering Techniques

Before planning any data gathering related to an HR research or analytics project, HR analytics practitioners should consider four important techniques. Unfortunately, inexperienced HR analytics practitioners often overlook these techniques as they can be somewhat technical. The techniques are workforce segmentation, research design, sampling strategy, and tool quality—reliability and validity.

Workforce Segmentation

Workforce segmentation, often referred to as talent segmentation, is a crucial technique in HR analytics that should be considered up front, rather than after the data has been gathered and analyzed. This process involves identifying distinct groups or subgroups based on specific characteristics such as skills, experience, performance, potential, or other relevant factors. In their influential book *Workforce of One: Revolutionizing Talent Management Through Customization*, Susan Cantrell and David Smith argue that organizations serious about talent management must replace generic, one-size-fits-all approaches with personalized strategies tailored to each individual's unique strengths, motivations, career aspirations, and values.[24] This approach goes beyond providing targeted learning and development opportunities for employees. It involves the identification of employee value propositions and application of differentiated strategies to attract, develop, reward, recognize, engage, and retain employees by critical talent segments.

Common examples of workforce segments in the context of talent management include high-potential employees, high performers, emerging leaders, existing leaders, critical roles and skill sets, and diversity demographics (e.g., gender, race/ethnicity, LGBTQ, age, generation), among others. Various professional roles, such as sales, marketing, engineering, product development, manufacturing, administration, operations, IT, legal, and HR, represent other examples of workforce or talent segments. Unfortunately, HR is a talent segment that does not always receive the attention it deserves when it comes to talent management practices (see Case 3 in Chapter 13). Therefore, HR analytics practitioners must prioritize identifying their most critical talent segments from the outset.

Research Design

The research design refers to the plan used to answer the research questions and test relevant research hypotheses.[25] The purpose of using an appropriate research design is to increase the number of comparisons and interpretations that can be made from the resulting data and insights derived through HR analytics. A well-designed HR research and analytics project is essential to ensure that the collected data is reliable, valid, and generalizable to the population of interest. Although there are many research designs to choose from, the following are commonly used in HR analytics.

In general, there are three broad types of research designs: pre-experimental, quasi-experimental, and true experimental.[26] The simplest pre-experimental design is the one-group post-only design, sometimes referred to as the one-shot case study. This design involves a single group of participants, and at least one data-gathering tool is used after the intervention is implemented. Since no comparison data is available, the data is primarily descriptive.

Another commonly used pre-experimental design is the one-group pre/post design.[27] This design involves administering a data gathering tool, such as a survey, twice: once before the introduction of the HR program, practice, or intervention as a baseline measurement, and once after it has been implemented. This allows the HR analytics practitioner to determine whether there was a significant difference in or effect on the desired outcome as a result of the program, practice, or intervention.

Another commonly used design in HR research and analytics is the pre/post control group design, which can be classified as either quasi-experimental or true experimental, depending on whether participants were randomly selected and assigned to each group.[28] However, in practical settings, random selection and assignment are often challenging. Therefore, in applied HR research and analytics in organizational contexts, the pre/post control group design is generally considered quasi-experimental. In this design, a group of employees from another work group is selected to participate in the HR analytics project for comparison purposes (this is the control group). The data gathering tool or test is administered once before the intervention and again after the intervention has been implemented. The control group should not be impacted by the intervention, although data is gathered from this group. This approach allows for a comparison of the outcomes between the two groups, enabling HR analytics practitioners to determine whether there are any meaningful differences and/or a desired effect. From these findings, HR practitioners may infer that other work groups within the organization could also benefit from the same intervention.

One of the most commonly used research designs in HR analytics is the correlational design, which involves measuring two or more variables to determine whether there is a relationship between them. For instance, HR analytics practitioners frequently engage in research and experimentation to identify the factors and variables that are associated with employee engagement (as discussed in Chapter 13). In this design, the researcher measures the variables of interest, such as meaningful work and employee engagement, in a sample of participants and then analyzes the data to determine whether there is a statistically significant relationship between the variables. Correlational research is useful when the researcher wants to investigate the strength and direction of the relationship between variables but cannot manipulate or control them. Although correlation does not necessarily indicate causation, the HR analytics practitioner can use more advanced predictive analytics and research designs to establish cause-and-effect relationships. Put another way, the "benefit in finding a correlation that isn't causal in nature is that it is a potential step on the path of finding a cause."[29]

As mentioned previously, the research design is often disregarded in the interest of saving time. Inexperienced HR analytics practitioners may feel like they are asking too much of participants if they require them to complete multiple data collection tools. Nevertheless, the use of a research design is a fundamental principle for producing scientifically reliable insights. Furthermore, by employing a sampling strategy—which will be discussed next—not all members of the workforce are required to participate.

Sampling Strategy

The sampling strategy determines the number of individuals who will participate in an HR research and analytics project and the reasoning behind their participation. The sampling strategy is connected to the research design in terms of when the groups will participate. HR analytics practitioners have access to various sampling strategies, including simple random sampling, stratified random sampling, cluster sampling, convenience sampling, and quota sampling.[30] The most commonly used and discussed here is simple random sampling. In this method, the entire population list (all possible participants) is obtained, and individuals are randomly selected from the list. Every individual should have an equal chance of being selected, and the sample should represent the population of participants. Nowadays, a random sample can be easily generated through various technological methods and tools (e.g., Excel, various online tools, SPSS, R). The benefit of random sampling is the elimination of potential bias in the selection process.

There may be instances where it is necessary to include all individuals within the organization in the HR research and analytics project. This is especially applicable if the group being studied is small. In employee surveys and sensing, for example, census surveys are usually conducted to ensure that all employees are given the opportunity to provide their feedback and voice their opinions. This may provide a psychological benefit in terms of job satisfaction and employee engagement, regardless of the associated costs. Additionally, legal compliance, ethical considerations regarding fairness, and adherence to organizational practices and policies pertaining to diversity and inclusion are other reasons for including all employees in an HR analytics practice or project.

Moreover, it is important to note that the sampling plan used for one data collection tool may not be applicable for another. For instance, while a survey may be distributed to all employees impacted by an intervention, only a few individuals might be selected randomly for direct behavioral observation. Whether a sampling strategy is employed or not, the reasoning behind the selection of specific groups should be evident and intentional.

Tool Quality—Reliability and Validity

The final technique employed by HR analytics practitioners is arguably the most important one. It allows them to evaluate the reliability and validity of the selected data collection tools (e.g., tests, assessments, surveys, or scales) and/or technologies. Reliability refers to the extent to which a tool and/or technology "measures something consistently."[31] In other words, does the tool provide the same results when the measurement is repeated? Validity, on the other hand, refers to the extent to which a data gathering tool and/or technology "measures what it is supposed to and works well for its intended purpose."[32]

By assessing the reliability and validity of the data collection tools, HR analytics practitioners can ensure the quality of the tools before using them. There are various techniques for calculating reliability and increasing validity. Generally, reliability is easier to determine than validity. The techniques for calculating reliability include test-retest reliability, parallel forms reliability, split-half reliability, internal consistency reliability, and inter-rater reliability.[33]

To calculate test-retest reliability, an identical test is administered to a group of individuals twice, with a period of time elapsing between the administrations. A correlation coefficient is then calculated to determine the extent to which individuals' scores are related. Ideally, the scores on the first test should correlate highly with the scores on the second test.[34]

Alternatively, parallel forms reliability can be used in a similar manner. This technique involves designing two equivalent tests that cover similar content but have different items or questions. The level of difficulty of the items must be equal for both tests. When administering both tests, the correlation between the assessments should be high.[35]

An alternative method to parallel forms reliability is split-half reliability. This technique involves the administration of only one test or assessment. The items on the test are randomly split into two halves, each containing equivalent numbers of easy, moderate, and difficult items.

Individuals' scores on one half of the test are correlated with their scores on the other half. This technique is useful when parallel or equivalent forms of an assessment are not available or if there is no opportunity for a second administration of the test.[36]

To determine if the items on a test are measuring the same thing, internal consistency reliability can be calculated. This involves assessing whether there is consistency in scores across the items within a data collection tool such as a test or survey.[37] Coefficient alpha, also known as Cronbach's alpha, is the most commonly used method for surveys that use Likert-type scales. HR analytics practitioners and researchers in social, behavioral, and organizational sciences often use 0.7 as a cutoff for Cronbach's alpha. If the coefficient is at or above this level, it indicates that the items are sufficiently consistent, and the measure is reliable.

Another way to ensure reliability in data collection is by assessing the consistency of multiple observers, raters, or interviewers. This technique, known as inter-rater reliability, aims to eliminate the possibility of bias by any individual involved in the data collection process. By assigning a unique code to each rater, participants' responses can be associated with their respective raters. While participants' responses may differ, there should be no systematic differences associated with any particular rater. Alternatively, a percentage of agreement between raters can be calculated, but this method is not a true measure of reliability.[38]

The validity of a data gathering tool is more difficult to assess. If a tool is not reliable, then certainly it will not be valid. However, a reliable tool still may not be valid; in other words, the tool may consistently measure a characteristic, but it may not be the characteristic that you intend to measure. Hence, the validity of data gathering tools must also be considered.

The different types of validity related to data gathering tools in HR analytics are face validity, content validity, concurrent validity, predictive validity, and construct validity.[39] Face validity refers to the extent to which a tool, such as a test or assessment, appears to measure what it claims to measure. For example, a test for cable installers would have high face validity for the employee if the questions on the test clearly relate to the activities involved in cable installation. Face validity is not an important parameter to measure, but if irrelevant items are included on a data gathering tool, participants may question the nature of these items and believe that the test or assessment is a waste of time. As discussed earlier, proxy measures lack transparency and face validity by design (see Chapter 3).

Content validity refers to the extent to which a test has items that "fairly represent all of the items that could be on the test."[40] Content validity is similar to face validity, except that an HR analytics practitioner with the right background and subject matter expertise performs an item analysis to judge whether the items on the data collection tool are valid for the purpose of the test. Content validation is commonly performed by HR research and analytics practitioners, and it does not involve a statistical calculation.

Concurrent validity, predictive validity, and construct validity are the most technical types of validity. Concurrent validity is a form of criterion-related validity that measures the extent to which scores on one test correlate with scores on another measure. It assesses how well a new test compares to a well-established test or "gold standard" instrument that it aims to replace.[41] On the other hand, predictive validity refers to how accurately a test can predict future behavior or performance. It is considered the holy grail in HR analytics when it comes to making high-stakes talent decisions. Finally, construct validity is the degree to which a test's scores reflect the construct that the test is intended to measure. It evaluates the extent to which the items on a test, survey, or scale represent specific constructs of interest, such as leadership or employee engagement. This is necessary when developing psychometrically validated scales, personality tests, and employee survey instruments that measure a variety of factors and variables.

How to Avoid Crossing the Line

Ethical Outcome for Step 4:
Ethical Methods

In Step 4 of the HR analytics cycle, it is critical to consider the ethical aspects of your data gathering methods. The following guidelines and tips can facilitate this process:

1. **Collect necessary data:** Gather only the data that is essential for the specific purpose and avoid collecting irrelevant or unnecessary information. Avoid collecting data simply because you can or for the sake of having it.

2. **Include qualitative data:** While quantitative data gathering approaches are commonly used in HR analytics, consider incorporating qualitative data gathering methods as well.

Qualitative data can provide valuable insights into complex or sensitive topics, such as strategy and execution, workplace culture, and diversity and inclusion. By combining both quantitative and qualitative data, you can gain a more comprehensive understanding of your workforce.

3. **Provide opt-out options:** Respect employee autonomy by offering them the choice to opt out of HR analytics projects and certain data gathering activities. Allow employees to have control over their participation in data collection and ensure that their privacy and preferences are respected.

4. **Reflect on passive data gathering:** Consider the ethical implications of using passive data gathering methods compared to active approaches. Passive data collection, such as monitoring digital activities or using sensor technologies, may raise privacy concerns. Evaluate the necessity and ethical justifiability of such methods, ensuring that employee privacy is protected.

5. **Use psychometrically validated scales and measurement tools:** Instead of relying on proxy measures that lack transparency, use validated scales and measurement tools. These tools have undergone rigorous testing to ensure accuracy and fairness, providing more reliable data for analysis.

6. **Maintain data confidentiality:** Safeguard the confidentiality of employee data by limiting access to authorized personnel only. Implement appropriate security measures to prevent unauthorized access, theft, or misuse of data.

7. **Communicate transparently about data usage:** Foster transparency by clearly communicating to employees how their data will be used and the potential benefits it can bring. Ensure that employees have a clear understanding of the purpose and intended outcomes of data collection, building trust and promoting a positive perception of HR analytics initiatives.

By following these guidelines, HR analytics practitioners can uphold ethical standards in data gathering, prioritize employee privacy and autonomy, and foster a culture of trust and transparency within the organization.

CHAPTER 9

Step 5

Analyze and Transform Data

If you torture the data long enough,
it will confess to anything.

—Ronald Coase

A
nalyzing and transforming data into useful and meaningful insights is considered to be the most important, yet challenging, step in the HR analytics cycle. Leading software firms such as Oracle, Salesforce, SAP, and Workday have made significant advancements in incorporating HR analytical capabilities within their suite of products, such as predictive analytics, process analytics, text and sentiment analytics, and real-time analytics. Additionally, several data aggregation and visualization platforms have entered the market. However, these enterprise platforms and SaaS-based tools cannot magically codify, analyze, visualize, and interpret all the disparate data available. This is especially true for evidence-based findings and insights derived through scholarly research as well as applied HR research and experimentation projects performed in organizations. A significant portion of this work is still performed by

qualified HR researchers, analysts, statisticians, and data scientists who specify and run the analysis through various statistical software packages (e.g., SPSS, SAS, R), rather than using a vendor's "black box" solution where the model building and analysis is preset for the end user.

Step 5 in the HR analytics cycle involves analyzing and transforming data for HR analytical insights. Much of the groundwork for analyzing data for individual projects was presented in the previous chapter (Step 4), where data gathering tools, technology, and techniques are selected and designed to answer research questions and hypotheses. Data analysis activities are driven by those tools, technology, and techniques. This chapter explains how to clean, analyze, and interpret gathered data. Basic data cleaning steps are enumerated, followed by an outline of the most common statistical concepts and tests used in HR analytics. Data science concepts such as data mining and analysis, predictive modeling, and natural language processing (NPL) are also described. Moreover, the notion of meta-analysis and the process of data warehousing in terms of extracting, loading, and transforming data from disparate sources are briefly discussed. Further, interpreting the data is discussed in terms of making sense of the results and insights. Lastly, ethical issues associated with HR analytics data are presented in this chapter as something that must be considered throughout the analysis process and before communicating the results and insights.

Cleaning Data for Analysis

The process of cleaning and preparing data for analysis can be an onerous task whether it is performed manually for an individual HR research and analytics project or larger data science initiative involving data warehousing and multiple data sources. When using data for workforce decisions, most people agree that your HR analytical insights are only as good as the data you are using. Hence, the proverbial mantra "garbage in, garbage out," or GIGO.

Data cleaning is a vital step in the overall data management process to ensure data quality for analysis. In a nutshell, data cleaning is the process of fixing or removing incorrect, corrupted, incorrectly formatted, duplicate, or incomplete data within a dataset. There are numerous books, articles, and online resources available on data cleaning in the context of big data and data science. Many of these data cleaning processes and techniques involve using simple spreadsheets such as Excel, standard statistical analysis software (SPSS, SAS), or more sophisticated data analysis tools such as R and Python.

Regardless of the specific analytical tools used and assuming the data gathered is valid and reliable (explained in Chapter 8), the Academy to Innovate HR recommends the following practice steps:[1]

1. **Check if the data is up to date.** Data should be up to date in order to obtain maximum value from the data analysis.
2. **Check for reoccurring unique identifiers.** Duplicate IDs indicate multiple records for one individual.
3. **Check data labels across multiple fields and merged datasets and see if all the data matches.** Check data labels to see if categorical values are mislabeled.
4. **Count missing values.** Missing data can impact the analysis and skew the results.
5. **Check for numerical outliers.** Outliers in the data can cause problems and distort the results.
6. **Define valid data output and remove all invalid data values.** Invalid, incorrect, or incomplete data could result in a flawed analysis of the data.

Analyzing Quantitative Data

After the data is sufficiently cleaned and prepared, the HR analytics practitioner can then analyze the data. Analyzing data refers to the process of examining and interpreting data in order to extract meaningful insights and draw conclusions. This involves using various analytical techniques and tools to identify relationships, differences, patterns, and trends within the data. However, the choice of the most appropriate statistical tests to use in the analyses of quantitative data (numerical data) depends on the nature of the variables and scales of measurement.

Types of Variables

In HR research and analytics, "a variable can be defined as anything that can take on more than one value."[2] Variables are used to measure, manipulate, and control phenomena of interest in a research project, and there are many different types of variables to consider:

- **Independent variables** are variables that are manipulated or changed by the HR analytics practitioner in order to see their effect on the dependent variable.
- **Dependent variables** are variables that are being measured or observed by the HR analytics practitioner to determine the effect of the independent variable.
- **Categorical variables** can be classified into categories or mutually exclusive groups (e.g., gender, race/ethnicity).
- **Continuous variables** are numerical variables that can take on any value within a range (e.g., height, weight, and age).
- **Discrete variables** are numerical values that can only take on specific values, typically whole numbers (e.g., the number of employees in an organization).
- **Control variables** are variables that are held constant or controlled by the HR analytics practitioner to prevent them from influencing the results of the study.
- **Confounding variables** are a type of extraneous variables that are not directly controlled or manipulated by the HR analytics practitioner but can influence the relationship between the independent and dependent variables. Confounding variables need to be identified and controlled for.
- **Mediating variables** are variables that mediate the relationship between two other variables.
- **Moderating variables** are variables that influence the strength and direction of the relationship between two other variables.

Scales of Measurement

After identifying the variables, the next consideration when deciding which statistical test to use is the scale of measurement on a given HR analytics tool. The different data gathering tools and response alternatives discussed in Chapter 8 include open-ended, rating scale, multiple choice, binary, ranking, and checklist. Each of these tools and response types is associated with a specific scale of measurement, namely nominal, ordinal, interval, and ratio scales.[3]

The *nominal scale* is the first scale of measurement. An example of a nominal scale in HR analytics is employee gender, which can be classified into categories such as male, female, or nonbinary/third gender, among others. Another example of a nominal scale variable is employee job title or department, which can also be categorized into different groups without any inherent order or ranking. Nominal scales are useful for categorizing data for analysis, but they do not provide information about the magnitude of differences between categories.

The *ordinal scale* is the second scale of measurement. An example of an ordinal scale in HR analytics is a ranking scale used in employee performance evaluations. For instance, managers could rank employees on criteria such as teamwork, leadership, and communication. The rankings could be ordered from highest to lowest, indicating the relative position of each employee with respect to the others. This type of ordinal scale allows for comparisons between employees, but it does not provide information on the magnitude of differences between them.

The *interval scale* is the third scale of measurement, and the distinguishing characteristic is the equal distance between data points on the scale. An example of an interval scale is the five-point Likert-type scale, where respondents assume equal distances between neighboring numbers on the scale. Although labels are used to anchor the numbers on the scale, research has found that respondents focus on the numbers on the scale and assume equal distances between them.[4] There is some debate surrounding this type of data, with some arguing that Likert-type scales are ordinal levels of measurement. However, it is generally accepted to consider data from Likert-type scales as interval data since numerical values are assigned to each label on the scale.

The *ratio scale* is the final scale of measurement, characterized by the presence of an absolute zero on the scale.[5] An example of a ratio scale in HR analytics is employee salary, which is a quantitative variable with a true zero point and can be measured in meaningful units. A zero salary means that no money is being paid to the employee, and any value greater than zero indicates the amount of money being paid. In addition, salary can be compared using ratios, allowing for meaningful interpretations such as "Employee A earns twice as much as Employee B." However, the question arises whether anyone can have nothing of anything, even when it comes to the ratio scale of measurement.[6] While it is possible for an employee to collect no salary, it is unlikely that anyone can have zero intelligence, aptitude, or ability.

Statistical Tests Used in HR Analytics

Statistics is an HR analytics practitioner's best friend. Essentially, statistics describe a set of tools and techniques that are used for describing, organizing, and interpreting information or data.[7] Common descriptive statistics include:

- **Frequency distributions** describe how many times each value occurs in a dataset.
- **Percentiles** describe how a particular value compares to the rest of the data (e.g., 25th, 50th, and 75th percentiles).
- **Measures of central tendency** describe the central characteristics of values in a dataset (the mean, medium, and mode).
- **Measures of variability** describe the spread or dispersion of distribution of values in a dataset (the range, variance, and standard deviation).
- **Measures of shape** describe the shape of the distribution of values in a dataset (such as skewness and kurtosis).
- **Histograms** are a visual or graphical representations of frequency distributions that illustrate the number of values across different intervals.

Aside and apart from descriptive statistics, several other statistical tests are used in HR analytics. The most common include correlation, regression, and comparison tests. For example:

- **Correlation tests** are tests that look for an association between two or more variables of interest (e.g., Pearson correlation, Spearman correlation, and chi-square).
- **Regression tests** are tests that look for cause-and-effect relationships (e.g., simple linear regression, multiple linear regression, and logistic regression).
- **Comparison tests** are tests that look for differences between group means (e.g., paired t-test, independent t-test, ANOVA, and MANOVA).

Decision Tree Analysis

Decision tree analysis is a powerful data analysis tool that uses a tree-like model of decisions and their possible consequences. In decision tree analysis, a complex problem is broken down into smaller, more manageable parts that can be analyzed and solved more easily.

In HR analytics, decision tree analysis can be used to make predictions about various HR-related outcomes, such as employee performance, turnover, and job satisfaction. For example, a decision tree model can be built to predict the likelihood that an employee will leave the company based on factors such as their age, job title, tenure, salary, and performance ratings.

To use decision tree analysis for HR analytics, you would first need to collect and prepare the relevant data. This would involve identifying the variables that are most likely to influence the outcome you are interested in, and then collecting data on those variables from your HR systems or other sources.

Once you have the data, you can use a software tool such as SPSS to build a decision tree model. This involves selecting a suitable algorithm, configuring the model parameters, and then training the model on your data. Once the model is trained, you can use it to make predictions about future outcomes. For example, you might use the model to identify employees who are at high risk of leaving the company, and then take proactive steps to retain those employees.

Overall, decision tree analysis is a valuable tool for HR analytics that can enable smarter workforce decisions.

Advanced Statistical Procedures

Adept HR analytics practitioners such as industrial and organizational psychologists, statisticians, and data scientists also perform advanced analyses in the context of HR analytics. Some of these advanced procedures include:

- **Cluster analysis** is a method used to group similar objects or individuals into clusters based on their characteristics. In HR analytics, cluster analysis can be used to identify subgroups of employees with similar demographics, job characteristics, or performance ratings.
- **Principal components analysis** is a statistical technique used to identify underlying patterns in a dataset by reducing the number of variables and transforming them into a smaller set of components, known as principal components.[8] It is commonly used in exploratory data analysis to identify the most important variables in a dataset and reduce the dimensionality of the data.

* **Factor analysis** is a statistical technique used to identify underlying factors that explain patterns in a set of variables—specifically whether some variables correlated more strongly with some than others.[9] In the context of HR analytics, factor analysis can be used to identify underlying factors that influence employee engagement, job satisfaction, or other HR outcomes.
* **Structural equation modeling (SEM)** is a confirmatory statistical technique used to test and validate complex causal relationships among variables. SEM presents the results as a path diagram or graphical representation of the causal relationships in a hypothesized theoretical model (i.e., examines how well the data fits the model).[10] When it comes to HR analytics, structural equation modeling can be used to test theories about the drivers of employee engagement, performance, and other desired outcomes.
* **Meta-analysis** is a statistical technique used to synthesize the results of multiple studies on a particular HR topic and examine patterns and trends, such as the relationship between employee engagement and performance, or the effectiveness of different HR interventions. By pooling the results of multiple studies, meta-analysis can provide a more accurate and reliable estimate of the effect size and can identify factors and variables that affect the strength of the relationship between variables.[11]

Analyzing Qualitative Data

Not all data and information in the context of HR analytics is quantitative. As mentioned in the previous chapter, HR analytics practitioners gather data that is both quantitative and qualitative. Unlike quantitative data analysis involving the use of statistical methods to analyze numerical data, qualitative data analysis involves analyzing nonnumerical data such as interview transcripts, focus group feedback, open-ended survey responses, and other forms of unstructured data. In HR analytics, this may involve analyzing employee feedback and other qualitative data sources to gain insights into the employee experience and workplace culture. Qualitative data analysis typically involves methods such as thematic analysis, content analysis, and sentiment analysis to identify patterns and themes in the data:

- **Thematic analysis** involves identifying and analyzing patterns, themes, and categories in the data. HR analytics practitioners can use inductive or deductive approaches to generate themes and subthemes that capture the essence of the data.
- **Content analysis** involves examining the content of the data to identify recurring patterns or themes. HR analytics practitioners can use coding schemes to categorize the data and identify key concepts and ideas.
- **Sentiment analysis** involves natural language processing and machine learning to analyze text data, such as employee survey written comments or social media posts to identify the overall sentiment of the text as positive, negative, or neutral.

Other qualitative analysis methods include discourse analysis, grounded theory, narrative analysis, and phenomenological analysis. However, these methods are rarely used in the context of HR analytics work.

Both quantitative and qualitative data analysis play an important role in HR analytics. While quantitative analysis provides critical numerical insights into individual and organizational effectiveness, performance, and trends, qualitative analysis can provide a deeper understanding of employee experiences and perspectives. By combining both quantitative and qualitative analysis, HR analytics practitioners can obtain a more comprehensive and contextualized view of multiple forms of data and insights in order to make smarter workforce decisions.

Data Science and Data Mining

Not all HR analytics data can be gathered and analyzed through traditional quantitative and qualitative approaches. Increasingly, organizations are using a broader range of data science techniques to extract valuable insights from structured and unstructured data in the context of HR analytics.[12] Data science is an interdisciplinary field that includes various methods and tools, such as statistical modeling, data visualization, data mining, and AI and machine learning (ML) with specific subject matter expertise to uncover actionable insights.[13] For instance, data exploration and visualization techniques like histograms, scatterplots, and heat maps can help identify patterns, trends, and outliers in HR data.

Similarly, one of the most common data science techniques is *data mining*, which involves analyzing and extracting valuable information from large datasets from both structured and unstructured sources. Structured data refers to data that is organized in a predefined manner, such as data in a human resources information system (HRIS), database, or spreadsheet. It is easy to search, analyze, and process as it is stored in a tabular format with well-defined fields. Unstructured data, on the other hand, does not have a clear structure and is not organized in a predefined manner. Examples of unstructured data sources include social media activity, emails, and written comments from an employee or exit survey.[14] Analyzing and processing unstructured data requires a sophisticated toolset and advanced techniques to extract meaningful insights.

Predictive modeling is another data science technique that can predict employee behaviors, such as attrition, performance, and engagement. These models can help organizations identify employees who are at risk of leaving, candidates likely to succeed in a role, and effective interventions to improve employee engagement and performance. As mentioned in Chapter 7, *natural language processing* (NLP) is another popular data science approach that can analyze employee feedback, such as survey responses or social media posts, to understand employee sentiment and identify areas of concern. NLP can also analyze job postings and résumés to identify the most critical skills and qualifications for a specific role.[15]

Overall, HR analytics has increasingly relied on data mining techniques, which are powerful forms of secondary data gathering and statistical analysis that provide valuable HR insights. In addition, other data science approaches like predictive modeling and NLP can help organizations make informed decisions and improve their HR practices. As a result, organizations are increasingly hiring statisticians, mathematicians, data engineers, and data scientists to join HR analytic teams, all of whom bring an advanced analytical toolkit to the table such as SPSS, SAS, R, Python, SQL, Tableau, and Power BI, to name a few.

Theory-Driven and Data-Driven Analysis

As discussed in Chapter 6, there are two broad approaches to HR analytics. The *theory-driven* (deductive) approach to HR analytics involves starting with a theoretical framework or model and then testing hypotheses derived from that framework using data. In this approach, the HR analytics practitioner has a clear idea of the variables and relationships of interest and designs the data gathering tools and techniques accordingly. The goal is to confirm or disconfirm the theory, and the analysis is often quantitative and hypothesis driven.

On the other hand, a *data-driven* (inductive) approach to HR analytics involves starting with data and then using advanced technologies and techniques such as AI/ML algorithms to identify patterns and relationships in the data. In this approach, the HR analytics practitioner may not have a clear theoretical framework at the outset but instead allows the data to drive the analysis. The goal here is to discover new insights, trends, or patterns in the data that can inform workforce decision-making. The analysis is often exploratory and descriptive, and the HR analytics practitioner may use a range of methods.

It is important to note, however, that merely mining and modeling a huge dataset alone is akin to a fishing expedition, which can result in a lot of "noise and nonsense" and discovering spurious correlations and bogus patterns that are ultimately meaningless. Psychologists refer to this as a theory-free form of "dustbowl empiricism," while statisticians refer to this as the "Bonferroni principle," which essentially means that "if you look in more places for interesting patterns than your data can support, you are bound to find crap."[16] Therefore, it is crucial to strike a balance between theory-driven and data-driven approaches when conducting HR analytics work.

Making Sense of Disparate Data Sources

When it comes to HR analytics, organizations often struggle to make sense of their disparate data sources for both targeted workforce decisions and broader HR strategy (strategy is addressed Chapter 11). To address this challenge, organizations should perform a meta-analysis—an analysis of analysis—across select data sources. Here the term "meta-analysis" is used loosely and not in the traditional sense of combining results from multiple scientific studies and examining the effect sizes with advanced statistical procedures.[17] Instead, meta-analysis in the context of HR analytics is a practical approach to explore and understand multiple data sources in relation to each other. For instance, organizations can analyze individual

360-degree assessments alongside employee survey data, exit survey data, or actual turnover rates to identify patterns and inconsistencies. Meta-analysis can also help organizations determine if high-potential emerging leaders are leaving the organization for the same reasons each year, such as lack of advancement opportunities, few organizational leadership opportunities, low base pay relative to the market, or lack of decision-making authority (see Chapter 13). By performing a meta-analysis, organizations can make sense of their various data sources and uncover critical workforce insights. The complexity of this analysis largely depends on the nature of the data gathered, the expertise of the HR researcher, analyst, or data scientist, and the available resources and time.

Data Warehousing

Data warehousing is a more sophisticated and technologically driven approach to meta-analysis. It involves collecting, storing, and managing large volumes of data from various sources to support business intelligence and analytics activities.[18] In the context of HR analytics, data warehousing entails gathering and integrating various types of employee-related data, such as employee demographics, job performance, compensation, and engagement levels.

To achieve this, data warehouses for HR analytics collect data from multiple data sources, such as HRIS, applicant tracking systems (ATS), performance management tools, employee surveys, and other internal and external data sources. The extracted data is then transformed into a format that can be easily integrated into the data warehouse. This step involves cleaning and restructuring the data, removing duplicates, and converting data types as needed. Finally, the transformed data is loaded into the data warehouse, where it is integrated into appropriate tables while ensuring data quality for analysis, data visualization, and reporting. This process is referred to as *extract, transform, and load* (ETL). This is highlighted in Figure 9.1.

One of the significant benefits of data warehousing in HR analytics is that it enables organizations to analyze, visualize, and report key insights from employee data over time. By analyzing employee data over several years, organizations can identify changes in employee turnover rates, track employee engagement levels, and identify areas where learning and development are needed. Additionally, data warehousing enables organizations to conduct predictive analytics by using historical data to identify trends and predict future outcomes. By analyzing employee data, organizations can predict which employees are at risk of leaving the company and take proactive steps to retain them.

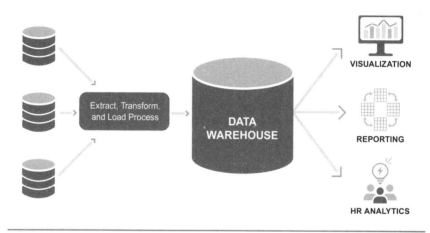

Figure 9.1   ETL Data Warehouse

As discussed throughout this book, there are a number of on-demand data aggregation and visualization platforms in the marketplace, such as One Model, which can help organizations aggregate their disparate data sources for real-time analyses, data visualization, and reporting. By collecting and analyzing employee data in a centralized location, organizations can gain valuable insights into their workforce and use that information to enable better business outcomes. Hence, data warehousing is an essential tool for organizations looking to leverage the power of HR analytics to make smarter workforce decisions.

Interpreting Data

Once the data is analyzed, the HR analytics practitioner must interpret the data in a meaningful way. Before any interpretation can be made, however, several important assumptions must be revisited. For example, the HR analytics practitioner should consider the following:

- Were the data gathering tools valid and reliable (as discussed in Chapter 8)?

- Was the sample representative of the broader employee population, if applicable?
- Was the data anomalous in any way?
- Were extreme scores or outliers evident?
- Was the data relatively complete without many missing responses?
- Is the data relatively free of bias?
- Is there any other reason to believe the data is not reliable?

Although many of these questions were addressed in the early steps of the HR analytics cycle, they are worth another look while interpreting the data. If the results are inconsistent with expectations (for example, the desired outcomes were not achieved), then these assumptions should be carefully examined to identify potential reasons.

In examining the data, the HR analytics practitioner must make sense of the data as a whole. The data from different tools or sources should not be interpreted in isolation. In general, the data can be analyzed with respect to:

- Individual items (open- and closed-ended)
- Comparisons to previously collected data or comparisons among work groups
- Research questions and hypotheses
- Factors and variables of interest
- Relationships among the factors and variables.

Additional data should be sought to corroborate or refute your interpretations. Furthermore, additional data may be needed to substantiate interpretations. The HR analytics practitioner has a responsibility to interpret the data and insights in a meaningful and ethical manner.

How to Avoid Crossing the Line

Ethical Outcome for Step 5: Ethical Analysis and Interpretation

To ensure ethical analysis and interpretation during Step 5 of the HR analytics cycle, consider the following guidelines:

1. **Balance theory-driven and data-driven approaches:** Strike a balance between theory driven (top-down) and data driven (bottom-up) approaches. Simply mining and modeling unstructured data without a clear theoretical framework can lead to spurious correlations and unreliable insights.

2. **Maintain data accuracy and integrity:** Use reliable measurement tools, clean and preprocess data properly, and employ robust analytical techniques to minimize biases and errors.

3. **Prevent unfair bias and discrimination:** Identify and address potential biases in data collection, analysis, and interpretation that may disproportionately affect certain demographics or protected characteristics.

When interpreting the data, keep the following ethical considerations in mind:

- **Avoid misrepresentation and distortion:** Present data accurately and transparently, without manipulating it to support a particular agenda or outcome.
- **Steer clear of overgeneralization and stereotyping:** Acknowledge data limitations and avoid making broad conclusions or assumptions that perpetuate unfair stereotypes or biases.
- **Be aware of biases in interpretation:** Recognize personal biases and strive for objectivity. Also, consider potential biases in the data itself and take steps to minimize their impact.
- **Consider alternative explanations:** Explore multiple perspectives and plausible hypotheses to gain a comprehensive understanding of the data and avoid bias.

By adhering to these ethical considerations, HR analytics practitioners can conduct data analysis and interpretation in a responsible, unbiased, and transparent manner.

CHAPTER 10

Step 6

Communicate Intelligence Results

Advanced analytics does not care who it annoys.

—James Sesil

The sixth step in the HR analytics cycle is crucial to the success of the entire process: communicating the intelligence results. As HR analytics is all about enabling workforce decisions, effective communication with stakeholders at every stage is essential. However, it's not just about engaging stakeholders; it's about meeting their information needs and tailoring your communication accordingly.

To achieve this, you need to identify your audience and their specific needs. Use a matrix like the one in Table 10.1 to help plan your communications. Once you have identified your audience, determine the purpose and goal of the communication in terms of specific objectives, political sensitivities, content, communication medium, timing, and sequencing for rollout.

Table 10.1 Communication Matrix Example

AUDIENCE	OBJECTIVES	AUDIENCE NEEDS	POLITICAL SENSITIVITIES	CONTENT OF THE MESSAGE	MEDIUM	TIMING AND SEQUENCING	FEEDBACK MECHANISM
CHRO							
Senior executives (C-suite)							
HR CoE/functional leaders							
Line managers							
Employees							
Others							

Next, design and develop content and materials that will effectively convey your message. This could include email content, presentation packages, and more. Prepare a master schedule of communication activities, including the timing and frequency of all communications, to ensure that you stay on track. Finally, construct evaluation tools to assess the effectiveness of your communication. This will help you continually improve your approach and ensure that stakeholders receive the insights they need to make informed workforce decisions.

This chapter highlights some practical tips in writing a formal HR analytics report and offers guidelines on delivering compelling presentations. Emphasis is placed on storytelling to provide context to the data and insight derived from HR analytics. By using stories to supplement the data, you can create a more compelling narrative, increase stakeholder engagement, and influence workforce decision-making. Lastly, ethical guidelines are shared to ensure that the insights shared and stories told are accurate and trustworthy.

The HR Analytics Report

The HR analytics report is a significant output of an HR analytics project, particularly large and complex ones, and is eagerly anticipated by stakeholders when it comes to the overall results, key insights, and recommendations. Typically, the report includes an executive summary, project background, research questions and hypotheses, insights and interpretation, and recommendations. Here are some suggestions for preparing a HR analytics report:

* Use a conversational writing style to ensure that the report is easy to read and comprehend.
* Organize and simplify the material by using text boxes, bullets, headings, subheadings, and transitions.
* Use visual aids, such as tables, charts, matrices, diagrams, and illustrations, to present the data and insights in meaningful formats.
* Define acronyms and abbreviations on the first mention and include them in a glossary.
* Avoid using technical terms; if necessary, explain them fully on the first mention and include them in the glossary.

The research design, including specific tools and techniques used and the data gathering schedule, should not appear in the main body of the report but rather in the appendices. It is crucial to allow stakeholders enough time to review the report. Therefore, you should distribute drafts to stakeholders in advance and schedule a formal group review to solicit feedback. This opportunity to provide feedback on the report, even in draft form, increases stakeholder buy-in and ownership of the HR analytics process and results. It is important to note that the HR analytics report is a formal communication tool and is best used to communicate a substantial amount of information to a broad audience.

Dashboards and Scorecards

Dashboards and scorecards are two commonly used tools for tracking and reporting on key HR metrics related to an organization's workforce. *Dashboards* provide a visual display of information that offers a quick and easy-to-understand overview of an organization's performance in real time.[1] In the context of HR analytics, a dashboard may display metrics related to employee engagement, turnover, diversity and inclusion, performance management, and other areas of interest. Dashboards use graphs, charts, and other visual aids to convey data and information at a glance, making them easy to read and interpret. This allows organizations to quickly identify trends and potential issues and take action to address them in a timely manner.

On the other hand, a *scorecard* is a more detailed report that provides a deeper level of analysis than a dashboard.[2] Scorecards focus on specific areas of interest, such as talent acquisition, talent development, or workforce planning. They include a mix of quantitative and qualitative data, such as employee surveys, performance metrics, and feedback from managers and other stakeholders. Scorecards track progress against specific goals or objectives and identify areas for improvement. They may also benchmark performance against industry standards or other organizations within and across industries.

Both dashboards and scorecards are important tools for HR analytics because they provide a way to measure and track progress in key areas of workforce management. By using these tools, organizations can identify areas of strength and weakness and make data-driven decisions to improve performance and achieve their goals. Furthermore, dashboards and scorecards can be customized to meet the specific needs of different stakeholders, such as HR leaders and line managers, making them a versatile tool for communicating insights and driving action throughout the organization.

HRIS software has evolved over the years to incorporate dashboard and data visualization capabilities that enable HR leaders to better manage and understand their workforce data. These capabilities include customizable dashboards, interactive charts, and graphs with drill-down capabilities, mobile access, and predictive analytics. In addition, specialized tools such as Tableau, Power BI, and QlikView are available to help HR analytics practitioners visualize and report their analytical insights.

Delivering Compelling Presentations

In the context of HR analytics, presentations are the most common vehicle of communication. These presentations can take various forms, including formal presentations for large or small stakeholder meetings, regular staff meetings, video- and audioconferences, and recorded presentations. Crafting a compelling presentation in the context of HR analytics requires thorough planning, a clear message, and an engaging delivery.

As mentioned earlier in this chapter, knowing your audience is vital. You need to tailor your presentation content to suit their needs, interests, and level of expertise. Additionally, it is essential to determine the purpose or objective of your presentation and what you want your audience to gain from it. This will help you focus your message and structure your presentation. It is important to use simple language, avoid technical terms, and incorporate visuals like charts, graphs, images, and infographics to support your message.

Storytelling can illustrate your points and create an emotional connection with your audience. Using examples and anecdotes that relate to your audience's experiences and interests, as well as the organization's history and culture can help engage your audience. When delivering your presentation, it is vital to engage your audience by asking questions, encouraging participation, and using interactive tools such as polls and quizzes to keep them engaged throughout the presentation.

Lastly, it is essential to end the presentation with a call to action. You should summarize the main points and end with a clear call to action that inspires your audience to take action on the data and insights you have presented. Crafting a compelling presentation requires careful planning, practice, and engaging delivery. It emphasizes the importance of telling a story about the data and visualizing the data in the context of the organization's most pressing problems and successes.[3]

Storytelling with Data

The use of storytelling can be a powerful method to communicate data-driven insights in both written and visual forms because it evokes emotions, which the brain processes differently than facts and data.[4] Cole Nussbaumer Knaflic, in her bestselling book *Storytelling with Data: A Data Visualization Guide for Business Professionals*, suggests that "there is a story in your data" and that HR analytics practitioners and communicators have the responsibility to "bring that story visually and contextually to life."[5] Storytelling is a critical business skill, in which HR analytics plays a significant role as a narrator, translator, and sense maker when it comes to communicating HR analytics data, insights, and recommendations. Therefore, storytelling with data involves eliminating noise and creating a narrative that brings the data to life, thus capturing stakeholders' attention on the essential insights and recommendations.

Data visualization is a crucial aspect of storytelling. It involves the graphical representation of data and information, using visual elements such as charts, graphs, maps, and infographics to present complex information in an easy-to-understand and visually appealing manner. The purpose of data visualization is to help stakeholders comprehend the significance of data by presenting it in a visual format that makes it easier to identify patterns, trends, and relationships between different variables. By employing data visualization techniques, HR analytics practitioners can analyze large and complex datasets, make data-driven decisions, and communicate their findings to key stakeholders in a clear and compelling way.

In recent years, the marketplace has been inundated with a plethora of sexy data visualization technologies and tools, leading to an overreliance on visual representation of data. While presenting data and information in visual and graphical formats can be a powerful means of conveying a story effectively and memorably, it is critical to adopt a balanced approach when communicating intelligence results. This involves incorporating a combination of data, narrative, and visualization.

In his compelling book *Effective Data Storytelling*, Brent Dykes advocates for a comprehensive approach that incorporates three distinct elements: data, narrative, and visuals.[6] The unique relationship between these elements plays a significant role in the storytelling process. For instance, when narrative is combined with data, it can help explain the insights effectively. When visuals are employed to represent data, they can elucidate to stakeholders insights that may not be apparent without charts and graphs. When narrative and visuals are used together, they can engage stakeholders emotionally and often entertain them. Therefore, "the skill of data storytelling is removing the noise and focusing people's attention on the key insights" according to Dykes.[7] In fact, the goal of storytelling with data is to appeal to stakeholder sensibilities, persuade them, and influence workforce decisions and strategies for action and change.

The Veracity of the Story Matters

In highly political organizations, HR analytics leaders may use storytelling as a way to tell executives what they want to hear or selectively present data and insights, which is commonly referred to as "cherrypicking." Cherry-picking refers to the practice of using data selectively to support one's position while disregarding other data that contradicts one's views. This practice is widespread and is not always intended to be malicious. We all engage in cherry-picking at times. However, in the context of HR analytics, cherry-picking can be abused to maintain the status quo and promote specific agendas.[8] It is crucial to consider the validity and ethicality of data-driven insights and how they are communicated and used. Further, sharing inaccurate or misleading insights can result in bad workforce decisions.[9] Therefore, HR analytics leaders must provide recommendations based on an ethical interpretation of data and insights and, when necessary, "speak truth to power." Consequently, the veracity of the story that HR analytics leaders tell matters in terms of enabling and maintaining leadership integrity and credibility.

Bring Me a Rock

Throughout my career, I've had the pleasure of collaborating with a variety of savvy senior executives and CHROs and colorful personalities. As noted in Chapter 5 (Step 1), stakeholders in HR analytics always have their own agenda—it is human nature. However, to avoid the endless game of "Bring Me a Rock," it's essential to establish trust with powerful stakeholders early in the HR analytics cycle.

Bring Me a Rock is a classic management game where a leader assigns a task to a subordinate but is never satisfied with the result. In the world of HR analytics, this game is a favorite among executives looking to flex their power and control the narrative over the data and evidence presented. The game typically starts with a powerful executive stakeholder requesting data and insights that support their preconceived ideas and strategies. The HR analytics leader then scurries off to gather the necessary data and evidence. The HR analytics leader brings back a shiny blue rock, but the senior executive demands a red one that's not too shiny. After multiple iterations and narratives, the HR analytics leader may reluctantly come back with misleading data or embellished facts that align with the executive's ideas and strategies, or out of frustration, may come back with evidence that completely refutes the executive's ideas and strategies, neither of which is a desirable outcome.

To steer clear of the Bring Me a Rock game, it's essential to build trust with stakeholders and have a clear understanding of their data and informational requirements early on. It's equally important to remain flexible and adaptable since data and information needs, as well as organizational change strategies, are likely to change and evolve. But don't let the endless pursuit of the ideal rock trip you up! Instead, remain focused on the HR analytics project priorities by answering the research questions and hypotheses posed in the early steps of the HR analytics cycle.

In summary, this chapter briefly outlined some practical guidelines and tips on writing a formal HR analytics report, delivering compelling presentations, and crafting engaging stories with data to influence workforce decisions in the context of communicating HR analytical insights. Additional tips were shared on how to steer clear of common political dynamics such as cherry picking and the classic Bring Me a Rock game. The remainder of the chapter outlines some ethical best practices to avoid crossing the line.

How to Avoid Crossing the Line

Ethical Outcome for Step 6:
Ethical Insights and Storytelling

In Step 6 of the HR analytics cycle, delivering ethical insights and stories is critical. To ensure this, follow these guidelines:

1. **Harness the power of storytelling:** Storytelling is a powerful approach to convey insights. However, it is important to ensure the accuracy and integrity of the story being told. HR analytics leaders should prioritize maintaining leadership integrity and credibility by delivering truthful and reliable narratives. In short, the veracity of the story matters.

2. **Avoid telling executives what they want to hear:** Storytelling should not be a way to appease or cater to the desires of executives. It is essential to provide objective insights, even if they challenge preconceived notions or decisions that have already been made.

3. **Avoid cherry-picking data:** It is unethical to selectively choose data and insights that only support a powerful stakeholder's agenda. HR analytics leaders should present a comprehensive and balanced view of the data, including both positive and negative findings.

4. **Provide recommendations based on ethical insights:** HR analytics leaders must offer recommendations that align with ethical principles and are supported by the insights derived from the data analysis. When necessary, they should be willing to speak truth to power and raise ethical concerns.

5. **Establish trust with powerful stakeholders:** Avoid getting caught in the Bring Me a Rock game, where stakeholders continuously request specific insights or data to suit their preferences. Building trust with powerful stakeholders from the beginning of the HR analytics cycle helps foster an environment of open communication and collaboration.

6. **HR analytics work doesn't end with visualizing, storytelling, and communicating the data and insights:** HR analytics leaders have

an ethical responsibility to play an active role in influencing HR strategy and workforce decisions (see Step 7 in Chapter 11).

By adhering to these guidelines, HR analytics leaders can deliver ethical insights and stories that provide value, maintain integrity, and contribute to informed decision-making within the organization.

CHAPTER 11

Step 7

Enable Strategy and Decision-Making

When we don't find the logical answer, we settle for a stupid one.
Ritual is what happens when we run out of rational.

—Dr. Gregory House[1]
(*House*, Season 7: "Small Sacrifices")

The final step of the HR analytics cycle is to enable HR strategy and decision-making. This is an important, yet curiously missing step in most HR analytics books, which typically conclude with visualizing, storytelling, and communicating the data and insights. Enabling strategy and decision-making and adding business value are the ultimate outcomes when it comes to an organization's HR analytics journey. It is supposed to close the loop of the HR analytics cycle. Unfortunately, this final step is frequently performed in isolation, sometimes covertly behind closed doors, with little input and influence from the HR analytics leader. Therefore, as mentioned in Step 1 of the HR analytics cycle (see

Chapter 5), it is vital to establish key relationships with powerful stake-holders, particularly with the CHRO, earlier on to ensure HR analytical insights inform the overarching, long-term HR strategy and short-term workforce decisions that arise.

Although HR strategy and decision-making are coupled together in this step, they differ in terms of scope and focus. HR strategy provides the overall architecture for managing human resources, while workforce decision-making is simply the process of making a choice—preferably one that is evidence-based, data-driven, and ethical. Therefore, in this chapter, a distinction is made between HR strategy and workforce decision-making as well as how workforce planning differs from broader HR strategy. Some common HR strategy models and frameworks are shared to provide context and background, including people-first and strategy-first approaches. A framework for strategic HR choices—the HR strategy axis—is introduced, which emphasizes the importance of formulating and executing an evidence-based and HR analytics-driven innovation strategy for strategic and sustainable competitive advantage. Further, a case is made to establish an HR analytics and strategy function to ensure a coordinate effort between HR analytics, strategy, and evidence-based decisions. Lastly, some practical tips are outlined to help HR leaders when it comes to ethical use and decisions based on insights derived from HR analytics.

HR Strategy

We have heard the proverbial mantra that behind every successful organization is a strategy that works. But what exactly is strategy? Strategy is a multidimensional concept that can be defined in many ways. Henry Mintzberg and colleagues describe strategy in terms of a plan, ploy, pattern, position, and perspective.[2] As a plan, strategy relates to leaders establishing the overall direction for the organization. As a ploy, strategy is all about maneuvering and outwitting competitors. As a pattern, strategy involves engaging in specific behaviors and consistent action to effectively implement the strategy. Strategy is also a position in terms of how an organization differentiates itself in the competitive marketplace. Lastly, strategy is a perspective that reflects an organization's culture and character (Does the organization see itself as an imitator, improver, or innovator when it comes to its people, products, and services?).[3] In summary, strategy involves asking intelligent questions; identifying strengths, weaknesses, opportunities, and threats (SWOT); knowing the right things at the right time; scenario planning; evidence-based decision-making; establishing priorities and goals; and effectively managing execution.

Despite these various methods and processes, strategy in the context of HR "refers to the processes, decisions, and choices organizations make regarding how they manage their people."[4] HR strategy tends to focus on aligning people policies, practices, and processes with the overall business strategy in order to achieve the organization's goals and objectives. HR strategy also assumes a resource-based view—the idea that organizations possess bundles of assets (people, processes, culture) that lead to strategic competitive advantage, which includes a distinctive set of capabilities and competencies that are hard to mimic. In a perfect world, HR strategy creation should be done in concert with the overall business strategy, although this rarely occurs in practice.

HR Strategy Versus Workforce Planning

It is important to distinguish between HR strategy and workforce planning, as these terms are often used interchangeably by those who specialize in strategic workforce planning. In their excellent book *Introduction to People Analytics*, Nadeem Kahn and Dave Millner describe workforce planning as "a process to ensure organizations have the resources needed to meet their business goals by proactively mapping, aligning, and forecasting current and future workforce capabilities." They further characterize workforce planning as "all about getting the right people, in the right roles, with the right skills, at the right place, at the right cost, at the right time to deliver the right results."[5] Indeed, workforce planning is a vital component of the overall HR strategy.

However, HR strategy has a broader scope and is driven by the CHRO. It goes beyond workforce planning and encompasses all strategic choices related to adopting best and next practices, and evidence-based HR programs and solutions. HR strategy involves a comprehensive approach to aligning HR practices with the organization's overall objectives and ensuring the effective management and development of its human capital beyond the identification of current and future workforce skills, competencies, and capabilities. In essence, HR strategy encompasses a broader range of strategic HR choices, including workforce planning, that cut across the entire employee and talent life cycle.

The HR Strategy Paradox

Organizational and HR leaders face various recurring paradoxes concerning HR strategy, structure, and systems. Some of these relate to deciding whether to adopt a centralized or decentralized model for HR, while others involve choosing between horizontal or vertical alignment to the business or building or buying various HR programs and practices. However, one of the most perplexing paradoxes is deciding whether to formulate a people-first or strategy-first HR strategy for the organization. While it is a well-known fact that human capital is the most important source of strategic and sustainable competitive advantage, not all individuals and positions have an equal strategic impact when it comes to moving the needle on desired business outcomes. Some people and positions can create rarity, value, and inimitability that are difficult for competitors to replicate, but others may not. This has resulted in two seemingly incompatible approaches to HR strategy, the people-first, and strategy-first approaches.

People-First Approach

Over two decades ago, Lynda Gratton, in her thoughtful and creative book *Living Strategy: Putting People at the Heart of Corporate Purpose*, contends that "people are our most important asset." However, for many in organizations, "people do not feel inspired, engaged, or free to voice their opinion."[6] Gratton argues that people differ from financial capital (money) and technology (machines) and therefore proposes three underlying tenets that should remain central in organizational life, that is, people (1) operate in time, (2) search for meaning, and (3) have a soul.[7] Most organizations struggle with or tend to disregard such philosophical concepts. Nonetheless, Gratton argues that each is essential to build the capabilities needed for organizational success. Moreover, she outlines nine capabilities that cut across these tenets, including[8]:

We Operate in Time
1. Vision capability
2. Scanning capability
3. Strategic capability

We Search for Meaning
4. Diagnostic capability
5. Systemic capability
6. Adaptive capability

We Have Soul

7. Emotional capability

8. Trust-building capability

9. Capability to build the psychological contract

The three tenets and nine capabilities are aspirational and come to life through a living strategy. Gratton outlines several critical elements at the content and process levels. Content elements of a living strategy include creating a vision and short- and long-term goals for the organization, understanding the current and future capabilities needed for success, and identifying a cluster of people process levers (recruitment and selection, performance management, rewards and recognition, learning and development). Process elements of a living strategy involve establishing broad stakeholder involvement across the organization, working back from a vision of the future, aligning business goals and the context in which people work, and inspiring commitment and action in terms of change.[9]

To create a living strategy in the context of HR and people, there is a sequence of steps:

1. Build a guiding coalition.

2. Imagine the future.

3. Understand current and future capability and identify the gap.

4. Map the system.

5. Model the dynamics.

6. Bridge into action.

Building on this six-step model, according to Gratton, enables the capabilities and competencies needed to drive organizational effectiveness and performance by putting people at the heart of the strategy.[10]

Strategy-First Approach

Over a decade ago, Brian Becker, Mark Huselid, and Richard Betty proposed a strategy-first approach for organizations to create and implement a differentiated workforce strategy in their book titled *The Differentiated Workforce*.[11] This approach calls for organizations to disproportionately invest in the strategic positions (jobs and roles) and top talent that align with their strategic capabilities for success in terms of strategy execution and business results. Rather than implementing a one-size-fits-all or generic HR strategy, a differentiated workforce strategy focuses on the strategic positions and roles, or the "A" positions needed to deliver the capabilities for success, as well as the portion of the workforce that is most likely to make the most significant strategic impact, such as A-level leaders and high-potential talent.[12]

A differentiated workforce strategy places strategy, not people, first. Specifically, it aligns to the most pressing problems facing line management in the organization and equips leaders with the necessary capabilities to execute the strategy. Capabilities refer to an organization's ability to achieve its strategic goals and objectives.[13] In contrast to traditional, people-centric HR strategy initiatives that typically place too much emphasis on the war for talent and delivering so-called HR best practices and other fads and trends for the workforce as a whole, a differentiated workforce strategy targets workforce investments where they are likely to add the greatest value and strategic return. It relies heavily on the notion of workforce or talent segmentation discussed in Chapter 8. For instance, a differentiated workforce strategy is a strategic approach that focuses on the most critical jobs and roles and workforce segment that is likely to make the most significant strategic impact (the 20 percent of the workforce that generates 80 percent of the business value). Hence, a differentiated workforce strategy recognizes that not all jobs, roles, and people are equal when it comes to strategy execution and value creation.

If an organization hopes to cultivate a unique source of strategic and sustainable competitive advantage, then merely implementing an undifferentiated, one-size-fits-all approach makes little sense. Yet, organizations frequently benchmark and copy what other organizations do when it comes to HR best practices and the latest fads and trends. To be fair, it may not be possible to implement a differentiated workforce strategy all at once. Indeed, a genuine HR transformation is no easy undertaking, and can take considerable time to implement. Therefore, a differentiated workforce strategy must be implemented incrementally over time. The following stages represent this journey, according to Becker and his colleagues:[14]

- **Stage 1: One-size-fits-all.** Represents a workforce strategy that is aligned with external HR best practices instead of the organization's strategy (low-impact differentiation).
- **Stage 2: Generic fit.** Typically involves selecting two or three types of workforce strategies to align or fit with two or three types of generic organizational strategies (low to moderate-impact differentiation).

- **Stage 3: Differentiated by strategic capability.** A workforce strategy differentiated based on the talent requirements of strategic capabilities (moderate- to high-impact differentiation).
- **Stage 4: Differentiated by jobs within strategic capabilities.** Represents a workforce strategy differentiated based on "A" positions, jobs, and roles within strategic capabilities (high-impact differentiation).

In summary, there are several key steps an organization must take to formulate and implement a differentiated workforce strategy, including:

1. Clarifying and aligning the organization's strategic capabilities with the workforce strategy.
2. Identifying strategic positions ("A" positions, jobs, and roles) in those capabilities.
3. Placing "A" players in "A" positions, jobs, and roles.
4. Establishing leadership accountability for workforce success (e.g., the line manager's HR role).
5. Designing an HR architecture for a differentiated workforce (e.g., workforce philosophy, workplace culture, the structure of the HR function).
6. Developing workforce measures to track and monitor progress (e.g., workforce and HR scorecards).

The strategy paradox is not really an either-or choice between a people-first or strategy-first approach for an organization. The two approaches are complementary and consistent with each other. For example, Gratton's concept of a living strategy, which is humanistic in its orientation, emphasizes aligning business goals with people's work and jobs. It also requires a strong commitment and a bias for action in formulating strategies for change. Furthermore, a living strategy places people at the heart of the capabilities needed for organizational success, making it a business strategy with people at its core. Additionally, a living strategy is agile and adaptable, allowing for workforce differentiation for strategic and sustainable competitive advantage. While Becker and his colleagues prioritize strategy over people, they acknowledge that without people, there would be little organizational capability for success, no matter how much automation and augmentation an organization invests in. Hence, both the people-first and strategy-first approaches recognize the importance of human capital in organizational success.

Smarter (and Stupider) Workforce Decisions

As discussed, HR strategy refers to the long-term plans, decisions, and choices made by an organization to effectively manage its human resources in a way that supports its overall business. HR strategy also involves making smarter workforce decisions. While HR strategy and decision-making are related, they differ in scope and focus. Workforce decision-making refers to the process of making choices, some of which are smart choices, while others, bluntly speaking, may be stupid choices. Smarter workforce decisions are choices based on HR analytical insights, supported by the best available evidence from multiple sources, and consider both the unintended consequences and ethical implications of these choices. Conversely, stupid workforce decisions tend to be based on prior experiences, opinions, current fads, and trends. Such decisions typically involve dubious and unethical choices.

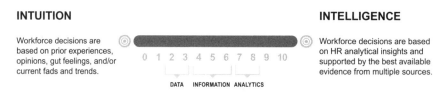

INTUITION

Workforce decisions are based on prior experiences, opinions, gut feelings, and/or current fads and trends.

0 1 2 3 4 5 6 7 8 9 10

DATA INFORMATION ANALYTICS

INTELLIGENCE

Workforce decisions are based on HR analytical insights and supported by the best available evidence from multiple sources.

Figure 11.1   HR Intelligence Value Chain

Source: Adapted from Salvatore V. Falletta, "HR Intelligence: Advancing People Research and Analytics," *International HR Information Management Journal* 12, no. 3 (2008): 21–31; and Kathryn Dekas, "People Analytics: Using Data to Drive HR Strategy and Action," September 27, 2011, video, YouTube, https://www.youtube.com/watch?v=l6ISTjupi5g.

The HR Intelligence Value Chain, as shown in Figure 11.1, illustrates the importance of moving beyond intuition to intelligence in making smarter and ethical workforce decisions that lead to responsible change and good outcomes. The HR Intelligence Value Chain provides a practical framework with which to move the needle when it comes to developing HR analytics capabilities and creating an evidence-based and data driven culture. While the goal is to move up the value chain from intuition to intelligence, the HR Intelligence Value Chain is not prescriptive when it comes to the technologies and tools needed for HR analytics success. Instead, the chosen technologies and tools should be determined by the

HR analytics team rather than what industry analysts, consultants, and HCM technologists suggest, or other competitors possess. Lastly, the HR Intelligence Value Chain emphasizes the notion of evidence-based HR and use of the best scientific evidence when it comes to making smarter workforce decisions and adopting HR practices.

HR Strategy Models and Frameworks

When it comes to HR strategy and workforce decision-making, there is no shortage of models, frameworks, and guidelines on the topic. Gratton's notion of a living strategy and Becker, Huselid, and Betty's conception of a differentiated workforce strategy were already discussed. Other models and frameworks that warrant mention include Dave Ulrich's HR Model that identifies four roles that HR professionals play: strategic partner, change agent, administrative expert, and employee champion.[15] In addition, there are several causal chain models that depict specific links between business strategy, HR strategy, HR practices, HR outcomes, individual and organizational performance, and financial performance, respectively. Causal chain models are very popular among academics and practitioners but tend to be oversimplifications of reality.[16] More complex linkage models have emerged in the literature such as the Service Profit Chain that depicts the relationship between internal service quality (workplace culture, competencies, and capabilities), employee satisfaction, retention, and productivity and its causal connection to customer satisfaction and loyalty, and in turn revenue growth and profitability.[17]

Newer models and frameworks for HR strategy and decision-making are available today. For example, Boudreau and Ramstad introduced their HR decision science approach and LAMP (logic, analytics, measures, and process) framework to improve human capital decisions and drive strategic change and organizational effectiveness.[18] More recently, and as discussed earlier in Chapter 4, the notion of evidence-based HR advocates the practice of making HR decisions through the conscientious, explicit, and judicious use of the best available evidence from multiple sources of information.[19]

Today, some of the large consulting firms such as McKinsey and Company have identified several shifts in innovation that are driving new emerging "HR operating models" at leading organizations including:

1. **Ulrich+:** This model is an agile adaptation of the classic Ulrich HR Model with HR business partners having greater role and decision rights in executing programs and practices from centers of expertise (CoEs).
2. **Employee experience (EX) driven:** This model focuses on gaining strategic competitive advantage by creating a world-class EX journey.
3. **Leader-led:** This model empowers frontline leaders and discontinues outmoded policies and practices that get in the way of innovation and responsiveness.
4. **Agile:** This model calls for fewer HR business partners who serve as advisors to senior executives, while CoEs focus on HR analytics, HR strategy, workforce planning, DEI, and the like.
5. **Machine-powered:** This model relies on automation and AI-powered tools for improved decision outcomes.[20]

The Ulrich HR model and similar variants are still the most prevalent models in use today, although many organizations are increasingly adopting EX-driven, leader-led approaches, and/or agile approaches. Time will tell whether more organizations adopt machine-powered HR operating models in which most HR decisions and processes are automated with AI-powered tools and capabilities. Similarly, Josh Bersin has been observing the transformative trends in HR strategy and recently called for a shift from traditional HR operating models to an "HR operating systems" approach. The latter considers that "everything in HR is interconnected," and as such, HR needs to do a much better job at cultivating agility and creativity, developing cross-functional HR professionals' expertise, integrating of products and services, focusing on business problems, and investing in HR analytics, among other key areas.[21]

All the models and approaches discussed in this chapter represent a complementary approach for enabling strategy and decision-making in the context of HR. No single model or framework is necessarily superior to another, nor comprehensive and complete enough to encompass all of the factors and variables that lead to desired business outcomes. The choice of model for a given organization ultimately depends on its overarching strategy, sector and industry, and values and culture, as well as the HR function's familiarity and comfort level with a particular model or framework. With that in mind, the following section introduces an alternative and relatively simple framework for strategic HR choices: the HR strategy axis.

The HR Strategy Axis

The term *strategy creation* is distinct from traditional strategic HR planning. Strategy creation involves the formulation of something creative, innovative, or new. Conversely, strategic planning tends to focus on analyzing and evaluating all the consequences associated with selecting and implementing proven solutions or best-known methods. While there is nothing wrong with adopting best-in-class solutions from other organization, copycatting and leveraging what everyone else does rarely leads to strategic and sustainable competitive advantage in terms of differentiation as discussed earlier. Instead, HR should drive an appropriate level of innovation as part of their overall HR strategy to differentiate their organization for competitive advantage. Therefore, in addition to the HR decision-making frameworks and approaches mentioned earlier, the HR Strategy Axis shown in Figure 11.2 is useful as a relatively simple framework to guide strategic HR choices with respect to evidence-based management and workforce decision-making and investments in organization.

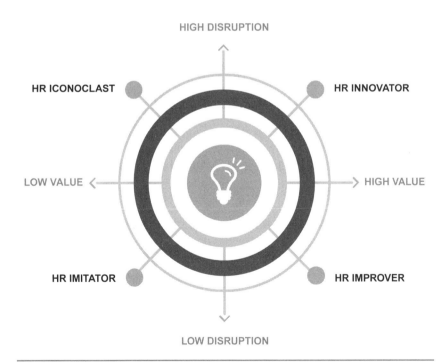

Figure 11.2   The HR Strategy Axis

The HR Strategy Axis depicts four types of strategic HR choices—HR Imitator, HR Improver, HR Innovator, and HR Iconoclast—in a Cartesian fashion in terms of business value and an organization's tolerance for disruption. Typically, organizations tend to operate as an *HR Imitator* but strive for incremental improvement that is aligned with and responsive to their overall business strategy (*HR Improver*). Over the past two decades, HR has showed little change in terms of implementing innovative HR strategies (high involvement HR policies, practices, and processes), which has been characterized as a sort of "stubborn traditionalism" affecting the profession.[22] While some extol the value of imitation and copying other organizations' ideas and practices, Cascio and Boudreau suggest that organizations should engage in prudent risk-taking and innovation and use practical frameworks to help explore and balance HR risk mitigation and uncertainty with HR risk-taking and opportunity.[23] It stands to reason that a business strategy that seeks competitive advantage (differentiation relative to cost) necessitates an evidence-based and HR analytics-driven innovation strategy. Therefore, organizations committed to evidence-based management and differentiating their HR practices, policies, and processes to attract, development, engage, and retain top talent for strategic competitive advantage need to weigh the potential rewards and risks associated with their strategic HR choices and human capital investments.

Sometimes It's OK to "Blow Stuff Up!"

HR Iconoclast is also depicted as a strategic HR choice in the HR Strategy Axis. Although HR Iconoclast is characterized as highly disruptive and low in terms of business value, there may be situations and circumstances in which this strategic choice is appropriate. HR Iconoclast is all about radical HR transformation, and frankly, when it is time to "blow stuff up!" Organizational and HR leaders alike, unfortunately, play lip service when it comes to HR transformation and radical change, and in turn typically make small, incremental, or symbolic changes. However, when an organization makes a commitment and choice to think and act like an HR Iconoclast, it is willing to dismantle the entire HR architecture, break all of the rules, throw out the HR playbook, and start from scratch.

Companies such as Google are a clear example of a true HR Iconoclast. Google had to think outside of the box and act like an HR Iconoclast first (low value, high disruption) as they navigated the design of their people operations model and architecture in order to become the evidence-based and HR analytics–driven innovator we are all familiar with today. Arguably, it is easier to think and act like an HR Iconoclast when an organization is a new venture or startup. Startup organizations are able to implement an evidence-based and HR analytics–driven innovation strategy from the start, whereas larger, established organizations have a much more challenging and complex HR transformation to navigate. However, this shouldn't dissuade or discourage strategic and data-driven HR leaders within larger organizations from pushing the proverbial envelope when it comes to HR transformation and radical change when needed.

Too frequently, larger organizations default to small, symbolic, or ritualized changes for incremental improvements (*HR Improver*), which doesn't amount to any sustainable change or strategic competitive advantage. Unfortunately, "ritual is what happens when we run out of rational," according to Dr. Gregory House of the *House* television series—but here is where HR analytics come in. Proactive evidence-based and ethical HR analytics arms strategists and decision makers with the knowledge and insights to make smarter workforce decisions for their organizations.

HR Analytics Role in HR Strategy and Decision-Making

As mentioned, the primary purpose of HR analytics is to inform HR strategy and decision-making. The data and insights derived from HR analytics should play a central role in influencing HR strategy, decision-making, and the strategic choices organizational leaders make when it comes to adopting evidence-based HR practices. Unfortunately, this is not always the case in many organizations. HR analytics has been characterized as having "input into HR strategy" but "not playing a central role" in its formulation. Along these lines, research has revealed an unfortunate state of affairs when it comes to the relationship between HR analytics and strategy. Specifically, HR analytics was largely described as an exhaustive data gathering exercise (a data dump), whereby "preconceived notions" or "after the fact" HR strategies and decisions drove the actual data requirements, when ideally, it should be the other way around.[24] In short, HR analytics has a long way to go. More often than not, data and analytics are used to support decisions that have already been made rather than to question the current path of HR strategy and planning within large organizations.

The idea of using data to make decisions changes the power dynamics in an organization. For example, a powerful and/or narcissistic leader would probably prefer to make decisions based upon his or her opinions and intuition rather than relying on facts and figures (i.e., evidence).[25] Similarly, James Sesil explains in his book *Applying Advanced Analytics to HR Management Decisions* that those in positions of power might have fragile egos and be primarily concerned with advancing their own agenda rather than dealing with actual facts.[26] Indeed, further work is needed in terms of elevating the status and legitimacy of HR analytics and its influence on HR strategy and decision-making.

The beauty of advanced analytics, according to Sesil, is that it "does not care who it annoys."[27] While speaking truth to power can be risky (and a little fun), we need to recognize that HR analytics is both art and science. That is, we shouldn't abandon our intuition and well-seasoned expertise. Analytics and the role of quantitative and qualitative data have their obvious limitations.[28] For example, a purely analytical and dispassionate approach to workforce decisions is a recipe for organizational analysis paralysis. Likewise, making critical HR decisions based solely on prior experience, intuition, gut feelings, and/or fads and trends could have disastrous effects. Therefore, we need to balance the art and the science of HR analytics by adopting a strategic approach while raising the bar in terms of evidence-based HR and ethics.

The HR Analytics and Strategy CoE

In terms of elevating the status and legitimacy of HR analytics and its influence on HR strategy, it is recommended that HR analytics be merged with an organization's HR strategy function rather than being embedded in operations, technology, or some other CoE. In many organizations, a dedicated HR strategy function doesn't exist. Politically, some organizations prefer this arrangement in that all HR business partner groups, CoEs, and functional leaders have an equal role and responsibility in driving HR strategy and execution rather than a centralized function. However, organizations should establish a dedicated HR analytics and strategy CoE to address the gap between HR analytics, strategy and execution, and evidence-based decision-making. This critical function should be part of the overall HR function and report directly to the CHRO rather than being buried deep in the bowels of a single HR function or CoE such as HR technology and operations. Moreover, the HR analytics and strategy leader should serve in a dual role as the chief of staff for the CHRO. Hence, the establishment of an "HR Analytics and Strategy" CoE would be ideal and ensure a coordinated effort between HR analytics, advanced research and experimentation, strategy and execution, smarter workforce decisions, and the adoption of evidence-based practices while ensuring ethical HR analytics activities. It would also ensure the likelihood of closing the loop with key stakeholders as part of the overall HR analytics cycle.

How to Avoid Crossing the Line

Ethical Outcome for Step 7:
Ethical Use and Decisions

Ensuring ethical use and decision-making is of utmost importance in HR analytics work. To effectively close the loop in this final step, consider the following guidelines:

1. **Stick to the intended purpose:** Avoid using HR analytical data and insights for purposes other than their original intended purpose. Similarly, ensure that HCM technologies, AI-powered platforms, and HR analytics practices are used ethically and in alignment with their intended purpose.

2. **Influence HR strategy and workforce decisions:** HR analytics leaders have an ethical responsibility to play a significant role in shaping HR strategy and workforce decisions. They should leverage their insights and expertise to drive positive change and promote ethical practices within the organization.

3. **Integrate HR analytics with overall business and HR strategy:** Rather than embedding the HR analytics function within HR operations or technology centers of expertise (CoEs), organizations should establish a dedicated "HR Analytics and Strategy" CoE that reports directly to the chief human resources officer (CHRO). This integration ensures that HR analytics is aligned with and supports the overall strategy (demonstrated in Chapter 12).

4. Embrace evidence-based management: The HR profession is often influenced by fads and trends. To make ethical decisions and take appropriate actions, it is critical to adhere to evidence-based management principles. This involves adopting science-based HR programs, practices, and solutions that have been proven effective and reliable.

By following these guidelines, HR analytics practitioners can uphold ethical standards, contribute to informed decision-making, and foster a culture of evidence-based and ethical practices within the organization.

In Part III, guidelines for starting and scaling the HR analytics function are discussed including how to structure and position the HR analytics function for success and the role, competencies, and characteristics of the HR analytics leader, as well as composition of the broader HR analytics team. In addition, three case studies using the HR analytics cycle as an organizing framework are featured. Finally, I share some concluding thoughts regarding the future of evidence-based and ethical HR analytics.

PART III

Capabilities, Cases, and a Clarion Call

CHAPTER 12

Starting and Scaling the HR Analytics CoE

Here's the new org chart, maybe you're on it and maybe not.

—Catbert, *Dilbert*'s evil HR Director

There is no shortage of perspectives and opinions on how to start and scale the HR analytics function. Several colleagues in the HR analytics community share their views on this matter, which differ depending on their disciplinary background, experience in the field of HR, and overall perspective. Therefore, this chapter presents my thoughts as a social, behavioral, and organizational scientist; educator and consultant; a former HR research and analytics leader for a Fortune 100 company; and a former CHRO at a large global firm.

First, I will delve into the ideal placement and positioning of the HR analytics function within an organization to ensure its success. Second, I will explore the essential competencies, characteristics, and responsibilities of an effective HR analytics leader. In addition, I will highlight several common missteps that CHROs should be mindful of in their efforts to attract, engage, and retain a highly qualified HR analytics leader. Lastly, I will outline the diverse roles and composition of the broader HR analytics team.

187

Positioning HR Analytics for Success

Throughout this book, I have emphasized that HR analytics must reside squarely within the HR organization and report directly to the CHRO to maintain its ethical and evidence-based approach and to ensure good governance, stewardship, accountability, and strategic influence. As discussed in Chapter 1, some argue that HR analytics should be situated within an enterprise-wide business intelligence function and report to line management outside of the HR function.[1] However, this is a strategic battle the HR profession, particularly the CHRO, cannot afford to lose. After all, a strategic and savvy CHRO and HR analytics leader would never allow it to reside outside of HR.

When it comes to starting and scaling HR analytics, a critical consideration is its positioning within the HR organization. Proper placement is essential for effective governance, stewardship, and accountability. To achieve this, the HR analytics function should be established as a standalone center of expertise (CoE), reporting directly to the CHRO. This allows it to serve all HR functional areas and CoEs, as well as the overall business, impartially. Burying HR analytics in the HR hierarchy within a single CoE, such as HR technology and operations, learning and development, or compensation and benefits, would be a mistake. This placement would inevitably cause HR analytics to become overly focused on the specific HR functional area or CoE it is situated in. For instance, if HR analytics is embedded in the learning and development group, it would likely concentrate solely on learning measurement, evaluation, and ROI. Similarly, if placed within the HR technology and operations team, it would likely be swamped with ad hoc data fetching and reporting requests (as discussed in Chapter 6) and constantly chasing the next AI-powered platform.

To ensure equitable service to the entire HR organization, it is essential that the HR analytics function is positioned at the highest level, preferably reporting directly to the CHRO. This close proximity would enable the HR analytics team to be intimately involved in HR strategy and execution, effectively addressing the most critical business challenges throughout the organization. However, if a direct reporting relationship with the CHRO is not possible, an alternative option would be to have the HR analytics CoE report to the head of talent management, as long as the HR analytics leader has unrestricted access to the CHRO, other HR leaders, and C-suite executives.

HR Analytics (and Strategy)

In line with the recommendations in Chapter 11, the HR analytics CoE and its leader should be closely connected to the overall HR strategy, focusing on the entire employee life cycle. An optimal approach would be to establish an "HR Analytics and Strategy" CoE where the HR analytics leader serves as the CHRO's chief of staff, facilitating strategy and planning in collaboration with the broader HR leadership team as advocated for in Chapter 11. This setup ensures a coordinated effort between HR analytics, advanced research and experimentation, strategy execution, and the adoption of evidence-based practices while maintaining ethical HR analytics activities (Figure 12.1).

Figure 12.1 HR Analytics and Strategy CoE

By positioning the HR analytics as a stand-alone CoE at a high level and integrating it closely with HR strategy, organizations can maximize the benefits derived from data-driven insights. This arrangement encourages alignment with the strategic priorities and most pressing business problems, enables smarter workforce decisions, ensures ethical HR analytics outcomes, and promotes the adoption of evidence-based HR practices across the organization.

Are We There Yet?

A decade ago, research estimated that over 75 percent of Fortune 1000 firms have an individual or group dedicated to HR research and analytics, and nearly a third of these dedicated HR research and analytics functions report directly to the CHRO, suggesting that HR analytics capabilities are strategically positioned in terms of organizational structure and influence.[2] More recently, a report by Insight222 revealed that HR analytics is growing in importance, and their research found that 90 percent of HR analytics leaders now report to the CHRO or one level down. While this is a promising trend, the majority of the HR analytics leaders (69 percent) still report "one level down" into a HR functional or CoE leader, whereas only 21 percent report directly to the CHRO.[3]

In examining current HR analytics job postings, it becomes apparent that HR analytics leadership opportunities may not be as strategically positioned as one might hope. For instance, Richard Rosenow, VP of people analytics strategy at One Model, generously compiled and curated a list of 309 HR analytics positions for the HR analytics community.[4] A cursory analysis reveals that approximately 13 percent ($n = 41$) of these positions are at the leadership level (VP, senior director, or director). The majority of these HR analytics leadership roles reside within HR, but they are often found in areas such as HR technology, operations, or compensation. A small number of them are part of talent acquisition/recruiting CoEs. Each of these 41 roles is either embedded in and/or reports to an HR functional area or a specific CoE leader, as opposed to the CHRO. Notably, none of the 41 leadership roles explicitly indicated a direct reporting relationship to the CHRO.

In a recent conversation with Richard Rosenow, he posited that one's perspective on HR analytics leadership roles could influence their understanding of accountability and the reporting relationship to the CHRO.[5] For instance, if a head of people analytics reports to an HR Technology or Operations CoE leader, who should be considered the true HR analytics leader? Is it the HR analytics practitioner with an advanced degree in social, behavioral, and organizational science, data science, or business intelligence, who leads and spearheads HR analytics capabilities and work, or is it the HR Technology or Operations CoE leader? If it's the latter, then HR analytics effectively reports directly to the CHRO.

As a social, behavioral, and organizational scientist and former head of HR research and analytics, I must admit that I neither share nor agree with this perspective. For instance, it would be akin to having a reporting relationship in which the CHRO reports to the CFO, in which case, would the CFO effectively be the CHRO for the organization? Nonetheless, Rosenow does raise a thought-provoking point. This viewpoint might shed light on the current trends reported by Insight222 concerning the reporting relationship to the CHRO or "one level down." However, if we believe that the HR analytics leader should possess the appropriate background and credentials, then one could argue that there is still significant progress to be made in terms of where HR analytics is positioned within the organizational chart and who should be at its helm.

The HR Analytics Leader

In terms of starting and scaling HR analytical capabilities, organizations tend to be enticed into procuring R, Python, and the latest HCM technology and AI/ML powered platforms with sexy data visualization tools, and subsequently hire a low-level HR analyst to operate these tools without clarity about their HR analytics vision, strategy, and the capabilities and outcomes they hope to achieve. Therefore, it is highly recommended that organizations bring in a well-qualified HR analytics leader with the right disciplinary background and skill set before investing in any technological or analytical resources. A highly trained HR analytics leader with a strategic HR perspective can pave the way by establishing the overall HR analytics vision, strategy, and capabilities for success.

Who Should Lead the HR Analytics Function?

The leadership of an HR analytics CoE within an organization is a complex role that requires a broad range of skills from multiple disciplines, including business management, HR, organizational behavior, economics, finance, statistics, data science, and computer engineering. While organizations are increasingly opting for data scientists or business intelligence professionals for this role, it's important to consider the unique expertise required to interpret HR analytical insights ethically and accurately.

HR analytics leaders need not only technical and statistical skills but also a deep understanding of individual, group, and organizational behavior. This understanding is typically found in professionals from social, behavioral, and organizational science backgrounds. These individuals are equipped with both strong analytical skills and HR experience, placing them in an advantageous position over data scientists or business intelligence professionals who may lack the necessary HR experience. Furthermore, professionals from the social, behavioral, and organizational sciences tend to prioritize an ethical approach and humanistic orientation.[6] This is vital to establishing an ethical ecosystem within the organization and ensuring that the practices and technologies employed align with ethical standards and the ethics charter adopted by the organization. The field of HR, like many professions, is underpinned by strong ethical norms and principles. HR professionals are expected to foster fairness and justice, as outlined in the Code of Ethics for the Society for Human Resource Management. Similarly, the American Psychological Association (APA) requires psychologists to abide by the principle of "First, Do No Harm."[7]

A recent study has expanded on the application of the APA's ethical principles in nonclinical settings, such as industrial and organizational psychology.[8] This study has highlighted areas for improvement in terms of applied psychology that are related to HR analytics, including organizational assessments, research practices, data management, professional interactions, business practices, and proactive ethical behavior. Moreover, disciplines such as industrial and organizational psychology have long-established, regularly updated ethical codes, unlike newer fields such as data science or business intelligence. For instance, the APA has formed a task force to revise their ethical codes in response to technological advancements impacting psychology and HR analytics practices.[9]

Alongside ethical considerations, HR analytics leaders need to be committed to evidence-based management. Professionals from social, behavioral, and organizational sciences are trained to use multiple sources of information, including scientific research findings. They are less likely to adopt untested practices or procure dubious AI/ML technologies that could pose risks to the organization or harm to employees. They are also more likely to engage in theory-driven HR analytics practices, involving active research and experimentation with hypothesis testing, rather than simply searching for patterns in the data or fishing for possibly spurious correlations. Therefore, organizations should ideally look for a leader for their HR analytics function who has a background in social, behavioral, and organizational sciences. This individual should also have HR or management consulting experience, along with effective leadership skills and competencies. This combination will ensure that the HR analytics function is led with both technical proficiency and a deep understanding of organizational behavior, ethics, and evidence-based management.

Critical Competencies and Characteristics of the HR Analytics Leader

There are several competencies and characteristics that an HR analytics leaders should possess. So, what exactly are competencies? Competencies are "underlying characteristic[s] of an individual that [are] causally related to criterion-referenced effective and/or superior performance."[10] In plain terms, a competency can be a technical or behavior skill, an attribute, or an attitude. Competencies are measurable characteristics of an individual that are related to success at work. They can be visible such as skills and knowledge or hidden such as motives, traits, and self-concept (a person's attitudes, values, and self-image).[11]

When it comes to the HR analytics leadership role, some of the most important and obvious competencies and characteristics include the following:

* Business acumen
* Stakeholder engagement
* Leadership skills
* Strategic thinking
* Creativity and innovation
* Communication and influence skills
* Listening skills
* Self-awareness
* Collaboration and relationship-building skills
* Politically savvy
* Integrity and trust
* Data analysis and interpretation
* Presentation and storytelling skills
* Continuous learning and adaptability

There are several additional competencies that warrant our attention and exploration: an evidence-based orientation, an ethical mindset, courage, compassion, a sense of humor, and a humble ego. Let's delve into each of these attributes in more detail to gain a better understanding of their significance in the professional context.

Evidence-Based Orientation

HR analytics leaders must possess an evidence-based HR orientation, as highlighted in Chapter 4. They should rely on various forms of evidence, including scientific research findings, to make informed decisions.

Additionally, they should actively foster a culture of data-driven decision-making and have a significant influence on critical workforce decisions and HR strategic choices. It's important to emphasize that the work of HR analytics leaders doesn't end with communicating analytical insights. They have a responsibility to ensure the adoption of evidence-based programs, practices, and solutions derived from those insights. Despite investing time and resources in developing top-tier HR analytics capabilities, organizational leaders sometimes succumb to passing fads and trends. Therefore, HR analytics leaders play a vital role, not only in the area of HR analytics, but also in promoting the adoption of scientifically grounded programs, practices, and solutions.

Ethical Mindset

In addition to an evidence-based orientation, this book emphasizes the importance of adopting an ethical approach to HR analytics. As discussed in Chapter 4, HR analytics faces an ethical crossroad, requiring HR analytics leaders and their teams to adopt a principled approach and establish an ethical ecosystem. As organizations enhance their HR analytics capabilities, it is imperative for HR analytics leaders to cultivate an ethical mindset as a fundamental competency and prioritize ethical outcomes throughout the HR analytics cycle. By doing so, HR analytics leaders must display the courage to avoid crossing the "creepy line."

Courage

Courage is frequently discussed as a critical characteristic and skill for HR leaders to exhibit in their work, particularly when it matters most. Indeed, HR analytics leaders must be able and willing to take bold and principled actions, facing fears, taking risks, and standing up for what is right, even in the face of adversity. It involves displaying bravery, conviction, and a willingness to step outside of one's comfort zone to address tough issues or pursue important goals. As mentioned in Chapters 10 and 11, HR analytics leaders may need to speak truth to power when necessary.

Compassion

Compassion refers to the practice of demonstrating empathy and understanding. Compassionate HR analytics leaders genuinely care about people and actively listen to others to understand their perspectives, emotions, and challenges. Moreover, compassionate HR analytics leaders are keenly aware of ethical and privacy concerns in the workplace. Along these lines, they are mindful of the HR analytics practices they engaged in and AI/ML powered platforms and HCM technologies their organizations adopt.

Sense of Humor

Having a sense of humor is vital, particularly for HR analytics leaders. Nobody wants to collaborate with or be led by someone who lacks humor and comes across as dull. HR analytics leaders should embody a positive and constructive sense of humor. They should be capable of engaging in self-deprecating behavior and sharing laughter with others. Infusing a touch of sarcasm and cynicism can effectively highlight certain points during meetings and presentations. However, HR analytics leaders must exercise caution and sensitivity to ensure that their humor is inclusive and respectful. Humor serves as a powerful tool for influencing and storytelling, but it should always be wielded with good taste in mind.

Humble Ego

Exhibiting any semblance of ego in the workplace presents an intriguing paradox for HR leaders in general. C-level executives effortlessly showcase their ego, expertise, opinions, and privileges throughout the organization. However, when it comes to HR leaders in general and HR analytics leaders in particular, there is an expectation of being "egoless." After all, HR analytics leaders should understand their place within the organizational hierarchy. As such, these skilled leaders have mastered the art of selflessness, tactfully channeling their ideas through the voices of others.[12] This prompts us to question what it is about the role of HR analytics leaders—their access to the organization's data, expertise, educational credentials, and backgrounds—that threatens those in positions of power.

Nevertheless, I believe it is unrealistic and unfair to expect HR analytics leaders to completely suppress their sense of self, competence, and ambitions. Instead, HR analytics leaders should embrace the concept of a humble ego. This entails recognizing and enacting one's own courage, strengths, and abilities without displaying arrogance or boastfulness. A humble ego involves acknowledging and valuing the contributions of others, being receptive to feedback and learning, and approaching situations with humility and a willingness to collaborate. Therefore, HR analytics leaders should lean in with their well-earned competence and confidence while maintaining a humble perspective.

Ten Ways to Lose an HR Analytics Leader

According to a recent article published by the Society for Human Resource Management (SHRM), the role of the HR analytics leader is experiencing rapid growth in the United States. This indicates a shift in perception, as HR is increasingly recognized as a strategic function, leading to the emergence of specialized positions such as "HR analytics managers" and "employee experience" managers.[13] Despite this positive trend, organizations often make costly mistakes when it comes to attracting, selecting, and retaining top HR analytics leadership talent.

Experienced and highly qualified HR analytics leaders carefully evaluate job position descriptions, paying attention to certain warning signs that can deter top candidates. To ensure a successful recruitment and hiring process, the CHRO and the organization should consider avoiding the following 10 missteps when posting a job position for an HR analytics leader and throughout the interview process. These missteps also have significant implications for engaging and retaining HR analytics leaders once they are onboard.

1. **Ambiguous reporting relationship:** Clearly outline the reporting structure for the HR analytics leader, including their placement within the organization, reporting lines, the number of levels separating them from the CHRO, and the extent of their access to senior executives.

2. **Overemphasis on metrics, data reporting, and data visualization:** While these aspects are important, it is critical to highlight the broader role of advanced HR research and experimentation, evidence-based management, and the HR analytics leader's contribution to shaping the overall HR strategy in collaboration with the CHRO and other HR leaders. Focusing solely on metrics and reporting may indicate a limited view of HR analytics and may dissuade top HR analytics leadership talent.

3. **Overly prescriptive about technologies and tools:** While it's acceptable to mention existing systems like the HRIS, including an exhaustive list of specific technologies and tools in the job description can raise concerns for HR analytics leaders. They might question their involvement in selecting the HR digital

stack and the necessary technologies and tools for achieving HR analytics success.

4. **Undervaluing advanced degrees, credentials, and experience:** Avoid underestimating the importance of education, credentials, and experience by setting minimal requirements, such as a bachelor's degree and a few years of experience. HR experience and social, behavioral, and organizational science expertise shouldn't be optional but required. Tailor expectations to the organization's size, complexity, and HR analytics capabilities. This approach attracts qualified talent with advanced degrees, credentials, and extensive HR analytics experience, ensuring that their expertise is recognized and valued.

5. **Simultaneously posting and hiring subordinate HR analytics positions:** Hold off on posting and hiring additional HR analytics practitioners until a qualified HR analytics leader is in place. Seasoned leaders prefer to have a hand in building their team, including crafting job positions and participating in the hiring process.

6. **Predetermined HR research and analytics agenda:** Rather than predefining the agenda, it is advisable to empower the HR analytics leader to actively participate in shaping the HR research and analytics agenda in collaboration with key stakeholders after they are hired. While it is reasonable to highlight general needs and expectations through the job description or during the interview process, embracing flexibility and promoting a co-creative approach is vital. This allows the HR analytics leader to leverage their expertise, insights, and understanding of the organization's unique challenges to develop an HR research and analytics agenda that aligns with strategic goals and objectives of the business.

7. **Excessive focus on novel data sources and passive data gathering:** A strong HR analytics leader may perceive an overemphasis on novel data sources and passive data-gathering as a red flag. It implies a preference for these approaches over traditional data sources and active data-gathering and analysis methods. It may also suggest a lack of recognition for the leader's role in establishing the vision, core capabilities, and HR research and analytics agenda.

8. **Overuse of the term "storytelling":** While storytelling can effectively communicate HR analytical insights, be cautious about excessive use of the term in job descriptions. Savvy HR analytics leaders interpret it as a code for telling executives what they want to hear, potentially indicating a culture where data, insights, and stories are cherry-picked to support specific agendas.

9. **Relying on AI-powered video interviewing tools:** Senior HR analytics leaders, who possess a comprehensive understanding of the underlying mechanisms at work in AI-powered video interviewing tools, find them both annoying and demeaning (see Giorgio's story in Chapter 3). They may even question their validity, reliability, and the organization's culture and business ethics. Therefore, it is advisable to refrain from using these tools when evaluating candidates for senior executive roles in general and HR analytics leadership positions in particular as they might be inclined to discourage their usage once hired.

10. **Lack of integration between HR analytics and workforce/HR strategy:** HR analytics leaders with extensive experience expect to play an active role in shaping the HR strategy. Ideally, HR analytics should be closely linked to the workforce/HR strategy (beyond just workforce planning) and report directly to the CHRO. If HR analytics is disconnected from the strategy and only embedded in HR technology and/or operations, it could be seen as a potential red flag in terms of influencing HR strategy and workforce decisions.

By avoiding these missteps, organizations can attract, engage, and retain top HR analytics leadership talent and foster a successful HR analytics and strategy function.

Building the HR Analytics Team

Once a well-qualified HR analytics leader is hired, they should take the initiative to onboard themselves and actively engage with key stakeholders. This engagement should involve discussions about the organization's existing capabilities, overall strategy, and pressing business problems. By collaborating with stakeholders, the HR analytics leader can identify strategic HR analytics priorities and expectations.

Moreover, the HR analytics leader should start thinking about various strategic areas to build the HR analytics CoE and its capabilities. These areas include establishing an effective governance model and structure, defining the mission and brand of the HR analytics function, designing a strategic operating model, considering the formation of an ethics and privacy council, and building the HR analytics team, among other relevant aspects as discussed in Chapter 5.

Regarding the composition of the HR analytics team, the newly appointed leader will likely inherit existing team members. However, they should also assess the future competencies and roles required for the team's success. Conducting a capability and competency gap analysis would help the HR analytics leader pinpoint both the technological capabilities and human resources necessary to round out the HR analytics team. Depending on the size and complexity of the organization as well as the nature and scope of the HR analytics work, the composition of the HR analytics team should include some combination of the following roles:[14]

- HR analytics leader
- Communications specialists
- Data analysts
- Data engineers
- Data management and security specialists
- Data scientists
- Data storytellers
- Employee experience professionals
- Employee surveys and sensing specialists
- Ethics and privacy specialists
- Evidence-based HR experts
- HR analytics consultants
- HR analytics interpreters and translators
- HR digital technologists
- HR strategists
- Data and insights interpreters and translators
- Product and platform owners
- Social, behavioral, and organizational scientists
- Workforce planning professionals

Starting Small and Scaling Up

To successfully embark on an HR analytics journey, organizations should begin small and gradually scale their capabilities. Follow the HR analytics cycle, as described in Chapters 5 through 11 in this book and outlined as follows (also see Figure 12.2), to ensure a systematic and effective approach.

Step 1: Determine stakeholder requirements. Collaborate with key stakeholders to identify their needs, conduct a strategic analytics diagnostic, frame business problems or opportunities, and establish realistic and ethical expectations.

Step 2: Define HR research and analytics agenda. Once stakeholder requirements are gathered, define the HR research and analytics agenda. Conduct a root cause analysis, generate research questions and hypotheses, and ensure ethical considerations. Start with a quick-win project and refine the agenda as you scale up.

Step 3: Identify data sources. Identify potential data sources, including public/private, traditional/novel, structured/unstructured, and HR/non-HR related data. Address data ownership, privacy concerns, and the rewards and risks of using novel data sources or AI technology.

Step 4: Gather data. Collect data through various methods, such as tracking key HR metrics, segmenting talent in the HRIS, conducting employee surveys and/or implementing an employee listening system, administering assessments, benchmarking, and responsibly leveraging passive data-gathering approaches and AI-powered tools.

Step 5: Analyze and transform data. Analyze data quantitatively using basic descriptive statistics and qualitatively by coding major themes from interviews, focus groups, and employee sentiment. Organize data by workforce segments and perform meta-analysis across multiple data sources. As you scale, consider building a data warehouse and using data aggregation technology.

Step 6: Communicate intelligence results. Move beyond traditional reporting by presenting strategic insights and interpretations. Tell a compelling data-driven story that relates to the organization's culture and challenges. Balance visualization with narrative and data, and encourage stakeholders to challenge insights while avoiding cherry-picking. Explore data visualization technologies and innovative reporting tools as you expand.

Step 7: Enable strategy and decision-making. Drive evidence-based HR decision-making by ensuring that insights inform workforce decisions, aligning data with HR strategy efforts, and grounding HR program and practice adoption decisions in scientific evidence, while promoting ethical and responsible use of data and insights.

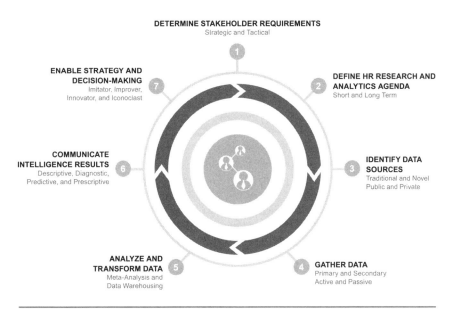

Figure 12.2 The HR Analytics Cycle

By embracing the HR analytics cycle and starting small while building on successes, organizations of any size and industry can develop robust HR analytics capabilities over time.

CHAPTER 13

The HR Analytics Cycle in Action

---

*I'm not a genius. I'm just a
tremendous bundle of experience.*

—R. Buckminster Fuller

ase studies play an essential role in generating comprehensive and contextualized information, advancing our understanding of HR analytics within specific contexts or situations. By delving into real-world complexities, case studies provide a deeper grasp of the subject matter and offer valuable insights for further exploration and continuous learning. They serve as practical examples, enabling practitioners to apply HR analytics effectively in their organizations.

In this chapter, three case studies that exemplify the practical application of the HR analytics cycle are presented. The seven-step framework of the HR analytics cycle serves as the organizing structure for each case. By showcasing real-world scenarios, I hope to inspire readers to apply the HR analytics cycle in their own organizational settings. While there is an attempt to maintain a consistent structure across the cases, it is important to acknowledge that each case is unique in terms of style and content.

Case 1: Business Unit Employee Survey Initiative at a Fortune 100 Firm

In this case, we delve into a Fortune 100 firm operating in the high-technology industry. The focus is on an employee survey initiative that was conducted within their product development organization. Through the HR analytics cycle, we explore how the organization utilized data-driven insights from a model-driven employee survey to gain a deeper understanding of their workforce and make informed decisions to improve employee satisfaction and engagement.

Organizational Profile

ABC Corporation, a Fortune 100 company in the high technology industry, operates globally. With a workforce of over 150,000 employees, ABC empowers customers worldwide to drive innovation and deliver value to their own clients.

Background

In contrast to many technology companies, ABC not only develops technology solutions but also uses their own technologies internally. While technology adoption is not a major challenge for ABC, their significant growth through numerous acquisitions poses unique business challenges. These acquisitions have strengthened their product offerings, accelerated innovation, improved customer responsiveness, and expanded partnership opportunities. However, ABC acknowledges the importance of effective onboarding, employee integration, continuous learning and development, and optimizing engagement and performance to retain critical talent and sustain their competitive edge.

Within the corporate HR function, there are several centers of expertise (CoEs), including the Talent Management and Development (TMD) CoE. TMD is responsible for training and learning, leadership and executive development, coaching, organization development and change, talent management, and HR analytics on a global scale. Acting as a CoE and business partner to ABC's global business units, TMD has initiated strategic initiatives focusing on evidence-based HR, HR analytics, and employee engagement, performance, and retention. To lead these initiatives, TMD established the HR analytics group, comprising industrial and organizational psychologists, HR analysts, data scientists, and project managers. This team fosters an evidence-based and data-driven culture to help enable HR strategy and decision-making processes.

Step 1: Determine Stakeholder Requirements

To enhance their HR analytics capabilities, the HR analytics group partnered with HR Intelligence—a research, advisory, and consulting group specializing in human capital research, workforce surveys, HR analytics and strategy, organizational effectiveness, talent management, workplace culture, and the future of work. As part of this collaboration, ABC was interested in designing and administering an organizational culture and effectiveness survey specifically designed for the product development business unit worldwide. Instead of conducting a global employee survey of the entire company, ABC opted for business unit–specific surveys to obtain targeted insights. At the time of this case, they were also exploring employee listening technologies as part of their overall HR analytics strategy and core capabilities.

Once the contract was finalized, HR Intelligence and the HR analytics group at ABC engaged in multiple working sessions with key stakeholders to outline the specific deliverables and desired outcomes for the employee survey project. These sessions involved influential stakeholders, including the senior executive of the business unit, who held a vested interest in understanding the unit's culture, identifying key drivers of employee engagement, and addressing concerns about organizational health and potential culture dilution resulting from recent acquisitions.

Further working sessions were conducted with essential TMD team members, including the head of the HR analytics group at ABC. The principal consultants from HR Intelligence collaborated with the client to frame the business problem within the context of ABC's rapid growth through acquisitions and the business unit's senior executive's concerns about culture dilution and employee disillusionment and dissatisfaction. It was collectively agreed that a formal strategic analytics diagnostic was not necessary for this project, as the strategic nature of the employee survey itself would serve as the diagnostic tool. Ethical considerations were thoroughly discussed, and stakeholders emphasized the importance of maintaining employee anonymity and confidentiality throughout the project. They also requested that all data and insights be reported at the aggregate level only.

By addressing stakeholder concerns and ensuring the ethical handling of data, HR Intelligence and the HR analytics group established a solid foundation for the employee survey project. This collaborative approach would enable a comprehensive assessment of the business unit's culture, identify engagement drivers, and provide insights to guide strategic decision-making while upholding the confidentiality and privacy of participating employees.

Step 2: Define HR Research and Analytics Agenda

After gathering stakeholder requirements, the HR research and analytics agenda for this project was established with relative ease. The project aimed to conduct a strategic assessment of organizational culture, effectiveness, and employee engagement, while identifying key variables that influence employee engagement and other critical business outcomes. The primary objective was to obtain data-driven insights that would inform priority areas for change and improvement within the organization.

An important aspect of the project was to assess the statistical and predictive validity of the Organizational Intelligence Model (OI model) that served as the framework for the employee survey (Figure 13.1).[1]

The OI model consisted of 11 variables arranged in a top-down causal chain, making tentative assertions about cause-and-effect relationships. The model depicts environmental inputs influencing the organization from the outside, while the strategic drivers (leadership, strategy, and culture) form a reciprocal relationship within the organization, represented by a Venn diagram. The organizational capability and execution variables directly affect employee engagement and performance outputs, serving as the primary drivers of organizational effectiveness. It is worth noting that the strategic factors (leadership, strategy, and culture) also influence employee engagement indirectly, through the primary drivers.

Detailed descriptions of each variable in the OI model can be found in Table 13.1.[2]

Environmental Inputs

LEADERSHIP

STRATEGY

CULTURE

Organizational Capability and Execution: Key Indices

1 Structure and Decision Rights

2 Information and Technology

3 Direct Manager

4 Measures and Rewards

5 Growth and Development

Employee Engagement

Performance Outputs

Figure 13.1 Organizational Intelligence Model

Table 13.1 Variable Descriptions of the Organizational Intelligence Model

VARIABLE	DESCRIPTION
Environmental Inputs	The outside conditions or situations that affect the organization (e.g., government policy, competitive intelligence, customer feedback, the economy).
Strategy	The means by which an organization intends on achieving its objectives and goals with respect to improving or innovating for competitive advantage.
Leadership	The most senior level of executives (VP and above) in the organization.
Culture	The underlying values, beliefs, and norms that drive team and organizational behavior.
Structure and Decision Rights	The structure is how the organization is designed (i.e., levels, roles, responsibilities, and accountabilities) to execute on the strategy, whereas decision rights refer to the extent to which the right decisions are made by the right people.
Information and Technology	The business systems, practices, and capabilities that facilitate and reinforce people's work (e.g., communication, IT infrastructure, knowledge sharing).
Direct Manager	The relative quality and effectiveness of an employee's direct manager or supervisor.
Measures and Rewards	Measures refer to the ways in which individual and team performance and accomplishments are measured and managed. Rewards are the monetary and nonmonetary incentives that reinforce people's behavior and actions, including advancement and promotion.
Growth and Development	The practices, resources, and opportunities available for employee skill development and enhancement, including development planning, training and learning, stretch assignments, and career paths.
Employee Engagement	Employee engagement involves the cognitive, emotional, and behavioral relationship employees have with their jobs, coworkers, direct managers, and organizations, and the effort and enthusiasm they put into their daily work (i.e., the extent to which employees contribute their discretionary energy and effort on behalf of the organization they serve).
Performance Outputs	The outcomes and indicators of individual and organizational achievement and results.

This project involved exploring the following research hypotheses related to the relationships between the variables and their impact on employee engagement and organizational effectiveness:

H$_1$: Leadership will be positively related to employee engagement.

H$_2$: Strategy will be positively related to employee engagement.

H$_3$: Culture will be positively related to employee engagement.

H$_4$: Structure and Decision Rights will be positively related to employee engagement.

H$_5$: Information and Technology will be positively related to employee engagement.

H$_6$: Direct Manager will be positively related to employee engagement.

H$_7$: Measures and Rewards will be positively related to employee engagement.

H$_8$: Growth and Development will be positively related to employee engagement.

By structuring the project around these research objectives and hypotheses, the team could systematically investigate and analyze the factors influencing employee engagement within the business unit at ABC Corporation. This approach ensured a data-driven and evidence-based assessment of the organization's culture and effectiveness while validating and refining the OI model for future employee survey efforts.

Step 3: Identify Data Sources

To proceed with our project, the next step involved identifying the appropriate data sources required to address the overarching research questions and hypotheses. Employee surveys are considered a traditional data source in the context of HR analytics, providing highly structured data, except for the written comments. Additionally, we leveraged employee data extracted from ABC's HR information systems (HRIS), such as employee email addresses.

In line with the principles of evidence-based management, we adopted a comprehensive approach by gathering and reviewing multiple sources of information. This included an extensive review of relevant literature on employee and organizational surveys, as well as organizational diagnostic models. Moreover, we delved into scholarly research encompassing topics such as organizational culture, effectiveness, behavior, and psychology. By incorporating diverse sources of information, we strengthened the validity and depth of our survey project, ensuring a robust foundation for our analysis and conclusions.

Step 4: Gather Data

As mentioned, the OI model and concomitant survey instrument were used. The survey included 52 questions/items using a five-point Likert-type "agreement" scale, in addition to a few customized items and demographic questions, as well as an open-ended question for each of the 11 variables (survey categories) in the model. An email invitation with an embedded URL to the survey was successfully delivered to all employees in the business unit ($n = 5,474$). The survey remained open for three weeks, and three email reminders were sent in an effort to increase the response rate. In total, 3,007 participants completed the survey, which was a 55 percent response rate.

Step 5: Analyze and Transform Data

To illustrate the value of the model-driven employee survey conducted at ABC, we present the following data and insights in a descriptive, predictive, and prescriptive fashion.

Descriptive Survey Analytics

In order to analyze the survey data and assess the reliability of the instrument, several types of analyses were conducted: item analysis, conceptual analysis, comparative analysis, and content analysis

As part of the item analysis, cross-tabulations were performed for each item and variable in the model by senior leader within the product development business unit. Customized reports were generated for each senior leader, providing descriptive statistics such as means and sample sizes for their segment of analysis, as compared to the entire business division. However, the specific items and associated data were not disclosed in this case to maintain the confidentiality of ABC's survey results and protect the proprietary nature of the survey instrument.

In the conceptual analysis, descriptive statistics including means, standard deviation, and reliability (internal consistency) were calculated on each of the 11 variables in the OI model. These results can be found in

Table 13.2. The alpha coefficients for each variable in the OI model and the survey as a whole were high, measuring 0.70 and above. These coefficients indicate that the instrument is sufficiently reliable.[3]

Table 13.2 Descriptive Statistics by Survey Variable

SURVEY VARIABLE	ITEMS	M	SD	N	ALPHA
Environmental Inputs	1–2	3.90	0.84	3,007	0.81
Leadership	3–7	3.56	0.85	3,007	0.90
Strategy	8–12	3.62	0.77	3,007	0.86
Culture	13–19	3.57	0.83	3,007	0.91
Structure and Decision Rights	20–24	3.56	0.81	3,007	0.85
Information and Technology	25–28	3.55	0.78	3,007	0.76
Direct Manager	29–33	3.74	0.94	3,007	0.92
Measures and Rewards	34–40	3.08	0.63	3,007	0.76
Growth and Development	41–43	3.45	0.85	3,007	0.72
Employee Engagement	44–49	3.59	0.89	3,007	0.89
Performance Outputs	50–52	3.67	0.82	3,007	0.80

Predictive Survey Analytics

To examine the relationship between the key variables in the OI model and employee engagement, correlation analyses were conducted. Pearson correlation coefficients (r) were calculated to determine the strength and direction of the associations between the variables. The results revealed significant positive correlations between all variables in the survey. Consistent with expectations, the primary drivers were found to be positively related to *employee engagement*. Specifically, *structure and decision rights* ($r = .67$, $p < 0.01$), *information and technology* ($r = .63$, $p < 0.01$), *direct manager* ($r = .56$, $p < 0.01$), *measures and rewards* ($r = .63$, $p < 0.01$), and *growth and development* ($r = .61$, $p < 0.01$) exhibited significant positive correlations with *employee engagement*. Notably, there was a significant correlation between *employee engagement* and *performance outputs* ($r = .69$, $p < 0.01$). These findings suggest that employee engagement can serve as an indicator of individual and organizational effectiveness, performance, and other desired outcomes, in addition to its well-established role as a mediating variable.

To test the hypotheses regarding the antecedents of employee engagement as depicted in the OI model, multiple regression analyses were conducted. Each measure of employee engagement was simultaneously regressed on all five primary drivers. The results, presented in Table 13.3, indicate that the primary drivers accounted for a significant amount of the variance in *employee engagement* ($R^2 = .55$, $p < 0.001$). Specifically, *structure and decision rights* ($R^2 = .25$, $p < 0.01$), *measures and rewards* ($R^2 = .23$, $p < 0.001$), *information and technology* ($R^2 = .21$, $p < 0.001$), and *growth and development* ($R^2 = .19$, $p < 0.001$) emerged as significant predictors of *employee engagement*. These findings support H_4, H_7, H_5, and H_8 respectively. Surprisingly, the *direct manager* variable, as a primary driver, had no influence on *employee engagement* ($R^2 = -.005$, $p < .811$).

Table 13.3 Multiple Regression Analysis Predicting Employee Engagement

STRATEGIC FACTORS (SECONDARY DRIVERS)	
VARIABLE	**EMPLOYEE ENGAGEMENT**
Leadership	.30***
Strategy	.21***
Culture	.33***
R^2	.56***
PRIMARY DRIVERS	
Structure and Decision Rights	.25**
Information and Technology	.21***
Direct Manager	−.005
Measures and Rewards	.23***
Growth and Development	.19***
R^2	.55***

Notes: *p < 0.05; **p < 0.01; ***p < 0.001; and values in table are standardized B coefficients

The strategic factors (i.e., secondary drivers) also accounted for a significant amount of the variance in *employee engagement*. For example, *leadership* was found to be a significant predictor of *employee engagement* (R^2 = .30, p < 0.001), as were *strategy* (R^2 = .21, p < 0.001) and *culture* (R^2 = .33, p < 0.001). These results provide support for H_1, H_2, and H_3, suggesting that these strategic factors play a significant role in shaping employee engagement within the organization.

In addition to the quantitative analysis, content analysis was performed on the open-ended survey items. The resultant data was reviewed and analyzed for major themes. This information was useful in providing context around the results of the quantitative analysis.

Prescriptive Analytics

Overall, the findings from the correlation and regression analyses provided valuable insights into the relationships between the variables in the OI model and employee engagement. They confirm the importance of the primary and secondary drivers in influencing employee engagement and highlight the specific variables that have the greatest potential impact as a lever for change. These results contribute to the understanding of the factors that drive employee engagement and can inform prescriptive interventions and initiatives aimed at enhancing engagement levels within the organization.

Step 6: Communicate Intelligence Results

The senior leadership team of the business division at ABC was presented with both quantitative and qualitative data, along with corresponding insights. To effectively communicate the findings, a storytelling approach was employed, emphasizing the organization's culture and addressing its current challenges. The principal consultants from HR Intelligence utilized a combination of visualizations, narratives, and data to convey the results. Overall, the data and insights were well received by the stakeholders. However, they expressed some surprise at the limited impact of the *direct manager* variable on *employee engagement* in terms of the predictive analytical insights. Notably, the *measures and rewards* variable received the lowest aggregate mean score of 3.08, which wasn't too surprising given that employees at ABC have not received a merit-based pay raise in a few years.

Step 7: Enable Strategy and Decision-Making

The action planning at the business unit level focused on four variables from the OI model: *leadership, structure and decision rights, measures and rewards,* and *growth and development.* These variables were identified as significant predictors of *employee engagement.* Surprisingly, the *direct manager* variable had little to no impact on *employee engagement,* contrary to the prevailing and popular belief that it is all about the direct manager when it comes to moving the needle on employee engagement.[4]

However, these findings can be explained by considering the specific workplace culture, structure, and decision-making processes within the business unit. The survey qualitative data revealed that mid-level managers felt powerless in their roles, lacking the authority to make day-to-day decisions, reward and recognize their team members, and provide growth and development opportunities. Employees in the written comments expressed frustration with the limited power their managers had in addressing their needs and expectations, particularly in areas like measures and rewards. These issues were attributed to the senior leadership's sole authority and accountability over budgetary decisions when it came to pay and bonuses, and the limited time for any growth and development opportunities at ABC.

As a result of this project, initiatives are underway to decentralize decision rights and budgetary authority to mid-level managers. A careful review of rewards and incentive practices is being conducted to align them with employee expectations. Efforts are also being made to provide employees with the necessary time and resources to fully benefit from growth and development opportunities at ABC.

Case 2: Advanced HR Analytics for Psychological Safety Improvement at Tamura Corporation

Contributing authors for this case:
Peter Romero, University of Cambridge, Psychometrics Centre
Haruka Asai, Tamura Corporation
Hiraku Nakanishi, Institution for a Global Society
Akiyo Tsuchimoto, Institution for a Global Society

The second case centers around an advanced HR analytics project conducted at Tamura Corporation, a Japanese company. Using cutting-edge data science methods and techniques, the organization aimed to establish and enhance psychological safety within their teams. The innovative approaches employed, the insights gained from the analysis, and the subsequent actions taken to foster a culture of psychological safety in the workplace are explored.

Organizational Profile

Headquartered in Japan, Tamura Corporation is a leading global supplier for the environmental and renewable energy industry. Tamura Corporation's consolidated revenue exceeded $769,102 million in 2022. Tamura Corporation operates principally along three global lines of business: electronic components, electronic chemicals and factory automation systems, and information equipment. With a workforce of approximately 4,440, of which 1,200 are based in Japan, Tamura Corporation supplies their customers with best-in-class products.

Background and Cultural Context

The Japanese labor market and organizations face specific challenges that set them apart from other industrialized nations. First, despite efforts by the government to digitally transform the Japan toward "Society 5.0" in alignment with the ongoing Fourth Industrial Revolution, there is a lower level of digitalization in the working environment, leading to a reliance on manual administrative work. Second, outdated models and practices still govern workplace decision-making. For instance, recruitment and hiring at most traditional Japanese corporations are organized based on the time of hire and tenure rather than functional or departmental groups. Tenure also heavily influences pay raises, advancement, and promotion opportunities. Third, Japanese culture emphasizes collectivism, where standing out can lead to pressure and scrutiny from both management and peers. Annual health checks are mandatory, whose outcomes are given to the HR department and are potentially visible to supervisors. Managers often organize after-work drinking and socializing, and nonparticipation might yield negative impact on employees' evaluation. Despite some progress, women remain underrepresented, and there is a tendency for employees to avoid collective action and hesitate to share innovative ideas. This collectivism is evident in Japanese psychometrics, with discussions about central tendency errors and a preference for forced-choice instruments. The leniency effect is also observed in 360-degree feedback systems. Furthermore, Japanese companies often operate on a membership system rather than an employment system, leading to uncertain career pathways and opaque decision-making processes. Last, Japanese work environments are known for being high-stress and psychologically unsafe, prioritizing university prestige and academic performance over other qualifications. This stress begins in schools with highly competitive acceptance tests and continues into the workforce, with long hours and lack of sleep becoming common in some companies despite being legally prohibited.

In the light of this traditional workplace culture and aligned with Society 5.0, Tamura Corporation identified the improvement of their working environment as a driver for their increasing market leadership, wherefore they display dedicated focus toward a consequent deployment of people analytics and psychometric instruments. As part of this initiative, their HR analytics leadership realized that a project for improving psychological safety might further enhance their competitive edge. As a scientific advisor for the Institution for a Global Society (IGS), a people analytics and assessment company that was selected for this project, I provided psychometric consultancy services for the client organization.

Step 1: Determine Stakeholder Requirements

During this project, our primary engagement was with stakeholders in the human resources and general affairs department, with the general manager as executive sponsor and their representative of HR analytics serving as our main point of contact and overall project lead. This provided us with operational leverage and strategic insights. Our mission was to explore innovative approaches to establish and raise awareness of practices for psychological safety within the organization. Through discussions with strategic HR leaders and a thorough review of the scientific literature, we identified managerial behavior as the key driver of psychological safety within teams. Consequently, we proposed linking "safety behaviors" to promotions into leadership positions as a lever for change. Previously, the organization's practice was to identify future leaders solely based on individual performance, without considering the impact on others or their ability to serve as network leaders.

Given the influence of our main point of contact and the strategic importance of the project, managing powerful and influential stakeholders was relatively straightforward. We focused on creating a prominent project that would promote HR analytics at the strategy table and transfer technical capabilities from external data scientists to the internal HR analytics team. Anticipating resistance to changes in the leadership selection process, we adopted a phased approach. We initially targeted a small group of "influencers" from senior management with strong ties to HR. They were invited to participate in a survey on psychological safety and a criterion-based 360-degree feedback instrument. The results were used to gather their feedback and secure their support. Based on their input, we refined the survey and expanded it to a larger group of senior leaders, gaining additional support along the way.

Although we did not have a formal governance model, ethical considerations were central to our operations. First, we ensured anonymity in the process, allowing teams to provide feedback on their managers without fear of reprisal. Second, access to raw data was limited to a select few within HR, and once data collection was complete, the results were aggregated, and the underlying data was deleted. Third, data was stored in a secure location with restricted access. All procedures adhered to Japanese regulations regarding the handling of personal information.

Step 2: Define HR Research and Analytics Agenda

We aligned the project with the overall strategy of innovation, creativity, and maintaining the highest quality in an increasingly global market that prioritizes sustainability, fairness, and flexibility in line with the Sustainable Development Goals. As part of the top-down process, we focused on creating and fostering managerial competencies based on inductive analysis. Instead of conducting a strict root-cause analysis, we held deep brainstorming sessions to gain a deeper understanding of macro-cultural factors influencing micro-systemic behavioral clusters, moderated through leadership behaviors. From these sessions, it became clear that leadership behavior was the driving force behind the transformational process and its impact on team psychological safety. Consequently, the main goal of the project emerged as the identification and establishment of leadership behaviors that promote psychological safety, leading to improved team performance, productivity, individual psychological flexibility, and creativity.

Our research question revolved around the possibility of fostering an organizational shift toward more freedom and a culture of excellence and high performance within the constraints of a strict Japanese culture. We hypothesized that leaders enabling their employees by allowing them to behave more freely and develop agency, with psychological safety as the social lubricant, would lead to a cultural shift once a critical mass of managers with new behaviors was reached. Additionally, we hypothesized that business outcomes would improve in the mid-term, with a delay reflecting corporate inertia. These hypotheses were derived from existing literature and theoretical in nature. To better understand the unique expression within the organization, we recognized the need for bottom-up behavioral data as well.

The HR research and analytics agenda of the project was shared top-down, then with all other stakeholders, and finally with all participating leaders. This iterative and cascading approach ensured that sufficient information and interest in the project was widely shared. To ensure ethical research questions and hypotheses, we maintained a productive and generative attitude toward our task. Our objective was not to pinpoint culprits but to identify best-performers and derive a set of universal competencies instrumental in unlocking psychological safety. To address biases, we analyzed HR data prior to the project, identifying potential problematic predictors that needed to be controlled or excluded, such as gender, rural background, or attendance at prestigious universities.

Step 3: Identify Data Sources

During the qualitative brainstorming phase, information on availability of data and its potential interpretation was collected by IGS in an unstructured format, primarily in the form of text notes organized as mind maps, which were used to better understand the situation at Tamura and prepare meetings with the project lead. Discussions resulted in the need to generate additional data that better represents psychological traits and systemic behavioral interaction. Subsequently, the main data sources included a commercial survey on psychological safety, namely SafetyZone, by ZEN-Tech, a consulting firm specializing in organizational and human resource development, and a 360-degree feedback instrument from IGS that uses AI to combat rater bias—GROW360. The HR database was solely used for descriptive analysis to understand potential predictors and exclude biases and was not used further in the project. Recognizing the limited availability of internal data, the focus was on generating and combining new data from two additional sources: cognitive and affective descriptions of psychological safety and behavioral data.

GROW360, a criterion-oriented feedback system, provided concrete and observable behavioral data, utilizing rubrics and a forced-choice Likert scale. SafetyZone, a dedicated tool for psychological safety, also employed a Likert-type scale. As a result, all collected data was structured. Both tools are well-established in the Japanese market and come with robust benchmarking and normative data.

As the data was specifically produced for the project, ownership concerns did not arise. Furthermore, precautions were taken to ensure data confidentiality. The data was stored in a restricted-access drive accessible only to selected HR employees. Rater responses were aggregated and then deleted at both IGS and ZENTech, whereby the latter only provided results for teams with at least three members to protect individuals. At IGS, notes from the brainstorming sessions were manually anonymized and deleted after project finalization. Predictors that could potentially have adverse impact were solely used for fairness control and subsequently deleted to ensure the universality of results.

Considerable attention was given to evaluating the rewards and risks associated with the deployment of external tools that generated additional data. Particularly with GROW360, which employed anti-bias algorithms fine-tuned with machine learning, the algorithm was thoroughly explained before deployment, and bias-reduced results were compared against raw scores.

To enhance the validity of the approach, the primary focus of the project was on developmental purposes. Only after achieving success in this area were the results considered for assessment. The AI-driven anti-bias algorithms proved beneficial in addressing responses influenced by social desirability bias. However, since the items varied in their alignment with real-life behaviors within the organization based on different positions, focus group sessions and interviews were additionally conducted to define the ultimate behaviors accurately.

Step 4: Gather Data

The research design, while having some elements of an experimental approach, cannot be considered a strict experimental study due to the lack of control groups and the absence of a double-blind study design. Instead, the goal was to influence the organization and create a pull-effect using the AIDA model from marketing, which involved capturing stakeholders' *attention*, generating *interest* through word-of-mouth communication, creating a sense of *desire* through top-down influencers and promoting exclusivity, and ultimately driving *action*.

Data collection primarily involved two online tools: a psychological safety questionnaire and a criterion-oriented 360-degree feedback instrument. This constituted primary research, aimed at understanding the relationship between behavioral criteria and psychological safety responses. Secondary research was also conducted, involving consultations with organizational scholars and studying relevant literature and best-practice reports from credible business sources. Additional demographic data from the internal HR database and official labor statistics were used to gain insights into potential under- or overrepresentation of specific groups within the workforce.

However, no additional social media data was gathered due to concerns of discretion, the absence of an internal social network, and the limited usefulness of available data from platforms such as LinkedIn, Facebook, and Twitter in terms of Japanese culture (e.g., an employee having an active LinkedIn account is considered an act of disloyalty and betrayal).

Step 5: Analyze and Transform Data

In the early stages of this project, the primary tool utilized by the client was a spreadsheet program for data management. Data scientists from IGS employed Python on JupyterLab, utilizing libraries such as pandas, numpy, and seaborn for subsequent analysis. Collaboration with members of the client's HR department was instrumental in providing qualitative insights and aiding in the interpretation of results from their perspective.

Following the outcomes obtained from the psychological safety instrument, teams were categorized into high and low safety groups. Subsequently, the 360-degree feedback results from the respective team managers were compared and subjected to significance testing for differences. The approach encompassed both bottom-up methodologies, employing statistical machine learning techniques, as well as top-down approaches integrating managerial and theoretical insights. The procedure entailed a relatively straightforward process combining quantitative analysis with qualitative perspectives. For example:

1. Creation of synthetic variables based on relevant theoretical concepts from the literature.
2. Implementation of a Random Forest algorithm to analyze all predictors and classify teams as either top or bottom in terms of psychological safety.
3. Evaluation of the correlation between the outcome and each predictor, utilizing measures such as Pearson's r and Euclidean distance correlation.
4. Application of maximal information coefficient and log-odds-ratio techniques, specifically on discretized predictors, to uncover additional insights.
5. Utilization of factor analysis to reduce the dimensionality of the predictors, considering the intercorrelations among psychological factors (employing nonorthogonal rotation).
6. Selection of predictors that consistently emerged as significant across multiple methods, while also incorporating client feedback and theoretical considerations for refinement.
7. Iterative binary regression analysis, incorporating predictors identified in the previous steps, leveraging insights from factor analysis, literature, and considering the practical feasibility for driving future change processes. This stage required a blend of scientific rigor and artistic decision-making, as finding the optimal selection of predictors that were both highly significant and aligned with client stakeholders' acceptance was critical.

To capture a comprehensive understanding of the organization, we employed a combination of bottom-up and top-down analysis. This approach allowed us to incorporate valuable insights from both individual-level data (360-degree feedback for managers) and team-level data (psychological safety). Control variables such as team numbers and divisions were included to account for focal phenomena and ensure fairness throughout the analysis process. It is important to note that the entire analysis was conducted manually, without the use of any specific platform or data warehouse.

In order to protect individual privacy, results from team members were aggregated, a practice that was clearly communicated and agreed upon by participating managers who recognized the significance of the project. While the official analysis focused on the overall organization without specific segmentation, IGS intended to take additional internal precautions to control against potentially stigmatizing variables such as gender, country origin, and attending a top university, wherever this data was available. However, this was not possible in most cases, thus these were excluded due to insufficient sample sizes for statistical relevance as were variables related to high-potential cohorts and top performers. These measures were implemented to ensure fairness and eliminate biases that could impact the accuracy of the results.

Step 6: Communicate Intelligence Results

The outcomes of the analysis were presented to participating managers through a dashboard-like report, which provided them with an overview of their individual strengths, areas for development, and their relative position compared to their peers. The main purpose of the dashboard was to guide managers in improving their current behaviors and actions to enhance psychological safety within their teams. For the overall organization, the identified behavioral characteristics were communicated as essential criteria for new managerial appointments. This approach was positively accepted, as the research background and rationale were thoroughly explained, emphasizing the importance of the project.

Data visualization was conducted using Python libraries such as matplotlib and seaborn for the data scientists, while Visual Basic for Applications was used within the spreadsheet program to generate and distribute the feedback dashboards to HR employees. The goal was to maintain an evidence-oriented and technical approach, highlighting the project's significance. Although storytelling was minimized during the process, it was used in the initial rounds to gain executive support.

Throughout the entire process, the data science team collaborated closely with the HR analytics team. In addition to analyzing the results, the interpretation phase focused on fine-tuning the findings into more concrete behaviors beyond the criterion-oriented items from GROW360. This involved conducting interviews with teams demonstrating high levels of psychological safety, using the STARL technique (situation-task-action-result-learning) from behavior-based interviewing. The goal was to extract relevant behaviors and understand the underlying values and cognitions to align with the organization's mental model.

While the actions and analytical methods were well-accepted and considered credible, there was significant resistance to the concept of "psychological safety," particularly from technical managers. Recognizing the need for better initial explanation, further workshops and training will be provided to foster greater acceptance and understanding of the concept among stakeholders.

Step 7: Enable Strategy and Decision-Making

First, a set of identified behaviors was extracted and distributed among managers for rating their subordinates. Displaying above-average competency scores in the annual review became a prerequisite for promotion into a leadership position. This information was communicated throughout the organization to facilitate the desired cultural bottom-up change, leveraging the existing collectivist culture.

Second, regular surveys and feedback rounds were implemented to encourage managers to review their daily managerial behavior and engage in self-reflection. The feedback format used was derived from the STARL method, emphasizing behavior-based feedback. This approach is entirely data-driven, derived from the analytical process described earlier. After the project, the existing data was further analyzed to generate additional synthetic variables based on client experiences and leadership and coaching literature. This enriched the portfolio of behaviors available for managers to define their personal strategies.

The HR analytics team placed a strong emphasis on the ethical use of data for smarter workforce decision-making. They fully disclosed the derived managerial behaviors to all managers, providing detailed explanations of how each behavior relates to psychological safety. Precautions were taken to ensure the data could not be used to identify individuals. Additionally, the team made connections to existing scientific literature in terms of evidence-based HR and provided references for further reading to interested individuals. Storytelling techniques were employed once again to help managers visualize the impact of psychological safety on their own behaviors and to foster empathy with their employees.

Case 3: A Global Study on Employee Engagement Drivers and Talent Management Practices for HR Professionals

This final case shares the findings of the largest study to date on employee engagement drivers and talent management practices for HR professionals worldwide.

Organizational Profile

This study was conducted in partnership with Drexel University, a top 100 Carnegie Research I institution, based in Philadelphia, Pennsylvania, and HRCI', a global leader in experiential education headquartered in Alexandria, Virginia. HRCI is the premier credentialing and learning organization for the human resources profession. For 50 years, HRCI has set the global standard for HR expertise and excellence through their commitment to the development and advancement of businesspeople in the people business. HRCI develops and offers world-class learning, as well as the administration of eight global certifications, and is dedicated to helping professionals achieve new competencies that drive business results.[5]

Background

In the wake of global talent shortages, the Great Resignation phenomenon, and the media-driven concept of "quiet quitting," employee engagement has experienced a significant decline. Gallup's recent article estimates that this decline began in 2020 and has been steadily worsening ever since. For instance, in 2021, only 34 percent of workers described themselves as engaged in their jobs, marking a decline from 36 percent in 2020. This represents the first drop in over a decade.[6] These trends are particularly concerning when considering the current talent crisis and widespread attrition, as highlighted by *Fortune* and the Institute of Corporate Productivity (i4CP) in a joint survey conducted among organizational leaders and HR professionals.[7]

What is even more troubling is the tendency of senior leadership to adopt a "one-size-fits-all" approach to addressing employee engagement. Compounding the issue is the constant pivoting when it comes to desired outcomes promoted by LinkedIn influencers and thought leaders, calling for newfangled and nebulous concepts such as employee experience, employee fulfillment, and employee thriving. Merely measuring employee engagement or any other desired outcome is insufficient. It is critical for organizations to identify the underlying factors, resources, characteristics, conditions, or employee value propositions that matter most by various talent segments.[8]

In recent years, the HR profession has increasingly embraced evidence-based and data-driven practices. Leading organizations are developing advanced HR analytics capabilities, including strategies for measuring and managing employee engagement, generating critical insights into the workforce and various talent segments (e.g., high-potentials, high-performers), employing data visualization and storytelling techniques, and more.[9] Despite the ongoing data science revolution, there remains limited knowledge about the employee engagement of HR professionals and the extent to which organizations prioritize talent management for this critical segment. After all, HR professionals play a pivotal role in designing and implementing talent management practices within their organizations. However, talent management initiatives often neglect HR professionals, either excluding them altogether or involving them only as an afterthought.

Over the past few years, HR professionals have borne the brunt of stress and burnout, as they operate on the front lines of the global talent crisis.[10] A recent study concluded that being an HR professional has become more challenging than ever, with a talent war raging to secure highly skilled HR talent.[11] In summary, these trends emphasize the significance of HR professionals as a talent segment deserving of attention and investment.

Step 1: Determine Stakeholder Requirements

This research project was a collaborative effort between Drexel University and HRCI, the leading credentialing and learning organization for the human resources profession. The principal researcher engaged in productive discussions with representatives from HRCI to present the proposed research project, seeking their approval and support to survey their extensive global membership, consisting of over 130,000 HR professionals. The involvement of HRCI and their members as key stakeholders adds significant value to this study. Furthermore, the participants in this research study are HR professionals from around the world, ensuring a diverse and representative sample.

Beyond HRCI and the participating HR professionals, there are several other important stakeholders in this project. Business leaders across industries have a vested interest in the findings, as the research aims to shed light on critical aspects of the HR profession. Additionally, HR professionals themselves, as well as various professional and industry associations, will find the study report informative and relevant to their work. Lastly, media outlets play a significant role in disseminating the study's outcomes to a wider audience, amplifying its impact and facilitating knowledge sharing within the HR community and beyond.

Step 2: Define HR Research and Analytics Agenda

Following fruitful discussions with HRCI and aligning with their overall expectations, the HR research and analytics agenda for this project was carefully developed. The primary objective of the study was to obtain valuable insights into the key determinants (factors, resources, and employee value propositions) influencing employee engagement, specifically among HR professionals. The research also explored potential variations in these engagement drivers across different talent segments and demographic variables and sought to evaluate the extent to which organizations implement talent management practices specifically targeted at HR professionals.

The following research questions were formulated to guide the study:

1. What are the primary factors, resources, and employee value propositions that significantly impact employee engagement among HR professionals?
2. To what extent do these engagement drivers differ among various talent segments within the HR profession?
3. How do demographic variables, such as age, gender, and race/ethnicity, influence the engagement drivers among HR professionals?
4. What is the level of implementation of talent management practices specifically tailored for HR professionals within organizations?

Step 3: Identify Data Sources

The next step was to identify the data sources that would effectively address our overarching research questions. Survey research is a well-established and reliable approach and a traditional source of information. We also used the data available from HRCI's membership database, which enabled us to identify participants for our study.

In line with the principles of evidence-based management, we conducted an extensive review of relevant research literature focusing on employee engagement. This encompassed a thorough exploration of the concept of employee engagement itself, as well as its antecedents and consequences. We also delved into scholarly research concerning talent management, ensuring a comprehensive understanding of this topic and its implications.

Regarding employee engagement, we identified it as a multidimensional concept, comprising cognitive, emotional, and behavioral domains. Cognitive engagement refers to employees' thoughts, encompassing their rational commitment to and beliefs about the organization. Emotional engagement relates to employees' feelings toward their organizations, reflecting their emotional attachment and connection to their jobs, direct managers, coworkers, and the organization as a whole. The behavioral domain pertains to employees' actions, capturing the discretionary energy and effort they put forth on behalf of the organizations they serve (Figure 13.2).

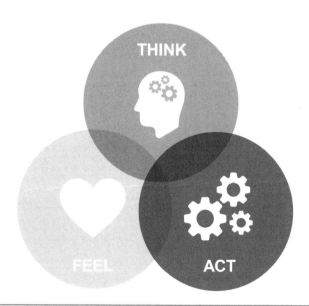

Figure 13.2 Employee Engagement: A Multidimensional Concept

To measure employee engagement in this study, we opted to use a well-established employee engagement scale. The Employee Engagement Scale was developed by Dr. Brad Shuck, a professor of human resources and organization development at the University of Louisville and cofounder and chief data officer at OrgVitals—a leading SaaS-based platform specializing in measuring employee engagement, workplace culture, and more. By employing this scale, we ensured a robust and reliable measurement of employee engagement throughout our research endeavor. Shuck and his colleagues define employee engagement "as a positive, active, work-related psychological state operationalized by the maintenance, intensity, and direction of cognitive, emotional, and behavioral energy."[12]

Step 4: Gather Data

The study employed a nonexperimental cross-sectional design to examine the research objectives. The population for this study was derived from the extensive database of HR professionals within HRCI. To ensure a diverse representation of organizations across various sectors and industries, an email invitation containing a survey URL was sent to a broad cross-section of HR professionals.

The survey used a reliable and valid six-item scale to measure cognitive, emotional, and behavioral engagement. Respondents were asked to rate their agreement on a five-point Likert-type scale, as previously mentioned. The survey included a comprehensive list of potential factors, resources, and employee value propositions known to drive employee engagement. Integrated talent management practices were also explored through customized questions. To gain insights into participants' career goals, aspirations, and demographics, additional questions were included (e.g., HR function, job level, gender, ethnicity/race, generational cohort). A few open-ended questions were also included to gather participants' thoughts and perspectives on the topic.

To promote and generate interest in the survey, a snowball sampling approach was employed. The survey was widely shared across various LinkedIn groups within the global HR community. The survey remained open for a duration of four weeks, and three email reminders were sent to encourage participation. Ultimately, a total of 2,032 HR professionals completed the survey, contributing valuable insights to the study.

Step 5: Analyze and Transform Data

In this project, SPSS was used to analyze the survey responses. Descriptive statistics, including means, standard deviation, frequencies, and percentages, were calculated to provide an overview of the data. Various graphs and charts were created to visualize the results. Qualitative data underwent analysis and coding to identify major themes.

Overall, HR professionals reported moderate to high levels of engagement, with an average engagement score of 3.86 (see Table 13.4).

Table 13.4 The Employee Engagement Scale

THE EMPLOYEE ENGAGEMENT SCALE©	
1. I am very focused when I am working at my job.	3.88
2. I give my job responsibilities a lot of attention.	4.23
3. Working at my job has a great deal of personal meaning to me.	3.83
4. I feel a strong sense of belonging to my workplace.	3.46
5. I really push myself to work beyond what is expected of me at my job.	3.86
6. I work harder than expected to help my company be successful.	3.88
Overall Mean Score	**3.86**

Source: Shuck, B. (1-7762123109). *The Employee Engagement Scale (6 questions).* Washington, DC: U.S. Copyright Office.[13]

For simplicity, participants providing a rating of 4 or 5 on the five-point Likert-type scale were classified as "engaged." On average, approximately 70 percent of the HR professionals were engaged. These results are relatively favorable, especially when considering the downward trend reported by Gallup for the overall workforce.[14] It indicates that the majority of HR professionals are exhibiting discretionary energy and effort in their organizational roles.

Regarding key demographic variables, overall engagement levels among HR professionals did not significantly differ based on generational cohort and gender. However, there was a notable difference in engagement levels between Black or African American HR professionals (62 percent engaged) and Caucasian HR professionals (72 percent engaged), with a

10 percentage point gap. No significant differences were observed among other racial or ethnic groups.

In this study, mid-level managers (managers/supervisors and directors) exhibited lower levels of engagement compared to individual contributors and executives (VP and above) (Figure 13.3). These findings align with previous research indicating that mid-level managers often face higher workloads and are caught in challenging positions. This phenomenon, known as the "disillusioned middle," has been observed in mid-career professionals[15] and mid-level managers in general.[16] It is worth noting that the category of CEO/presidents in this study refers to either the most senior executives of consulting firms or those who identified themselves as self-employed working as external HR and/or management consultants.

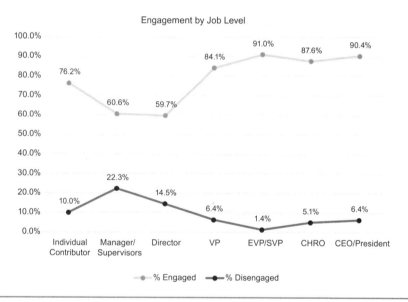

Figure 13.3 Engagement by Job Level

Below are the engagement scores by HR functional area, presented in rank order:

1. External consultant: 84.2% ($n = 100$)
2. Equal employment opportunity/HR compliance: 78.0% ($n = 22$)
3. Human resource planning/strategy: 74.9% ($n = 147$)
4. Staffing including talent acquisition/recruitment: 74.8% ($n = 134$)

5. HR/people/workforce/talent analytics: 73.0% ($n = 81$)
6. HRD, learning, talent development, and/or organization development: 72.6% ($n = 174$)
7. Employee and labor relations: 71.5% ($n = 149$)
8. Performance management and appraisal systems: 71.2% ($n = 18$)
9. Compensation and benefits/total rewards: 70.5% ($n = 137$)
10. HR business partner/generalist: 69.7% ($n = 977$)
11. Human capital technology, digital HR, and/or HRIS: 68.7% ($n = 33$)
12. Health, safety, security, and risk management: 66.6% ($n = 15$)
13. HR operations, services, and administration: 61.6% ($n = 43$)
14. DEI and belonging: 16% ($n = 2$)

Please note that these percentages reflect the engagement scores for each respective HR functional area, and the accompanying "n" represents the sample size for each area.

Upon analyzing these results, it is encouraging to observe that HR planning and strategy, as well as HR analytics practitioners, demonstrate high levels of engagement. Conversely, the DEI and belonging functional area shows the lowest level of engagement. However, it is important to note that this group consists of only two respondents, making it difficult to draw meaningful conclusions from this limited sample size.

Comparatively, HR operations, services, and administration, along with health, safety, security, and risk management, exhibit relatively lower levels of engagement compared to other HR functional areas. It is important to note the substantial representation of HR business partners/generalists in this study, accounting for approximately 48 percent of all respondents ($n = 977$). This group displayed an engagement rate of over 69 percent. HR business partners/generalists play a diverse and multifaceted role, often lacking the support of a center of expertise (CoE) or shared service function, especially in smaller to mid-sized organizations. They serve as the backbone of the HR profession and act as a comprehensive barometer for overall employee engagement among HR professionals in this study.

Engagement Drivers

Employee engagement is influenced by a multitude of factors, resources, and employee value propositions. Several key drivers have been identified in research:

- Trust and integrity
- Nature of the job
- Line of sight between individual performance and company performance
- Career growth opportunities
- Pride about the company
- Coworker/team members
- Employee development
- Personal relationship with one's manager
- Pay fairness
- Personal influence
- Well-being

These drivers were identified by The Conference Board as critical factors impacting employee engagement.[17]

More recently, Glint identified seven factors that enable individuals to perform at their best in the workplace:[18]

- Meaningful work
- Career growth
- Empowerment
- Belonging
- Recognition
- Leadership
- Fulfilling work relationships

While these factors capture the general aspects of employee engagement, they represent the "usual suspects" and may not fully address the specific needs and preferences of critical talent segments such as high-performers, high-potentials, current leaders, and aspiring leaders. Therefore, to comprehensively examine employee engagement drivers, this study incorporated a list of 57 drivers sourced from the employee engagement literature. This approach ensured that the research considered a wide range of drivers that are relevant and applicable to various talent segments within the organization.

Respondents were asked to rate the extent to which each driver has an impact on their own engagement (i.e., what matters most for HR professionals). While the usual suspects are evident for all individual respondents as a whole (see Table 13.5), the combination of drivers differs significantly by talent segment (see Tables 13.6 and 13.7).

Table 13.5   What Matters Most for HR Professionals

RANK	WHAT MATTERS MOST FOR HR PROFESSIONALS (N = 2,032)	MEAN
1	Ethical Workplace/Work Environment	4.54
2	Trust and Integrity in the Leadership	4.51
3	Compassionate Leader/Manager Behavior	4.35
4	Meaningful Work	4.32
5	Immediate Manager/Supervisor Quality	4.29
6	Workplace Culture	4.29
7	Work-Life Balance	4.26
8	Coworker/Team Member Quality	4.23
9	Wellness and Well-Being Programs/Interventions	4.22
10	Relationship with Immediate Manager/Leader	4.21
11	Job Fit	4.17
12	Access to Information/Sharing Information	4.17
13	Total Compensation/Enumeration	4.17
14	Vacation/Personal Time Off	4.16
15	Senior Leadership Quality	4.15
16	Remote Work/Flexible Arrangements	4.14
17	Decision-Making Authority/Decision Rights	4.09
18	Relationships with Coworkers/Team Members	4.07
19	Job Security	4.05
20	Fair and Accurate Performance Appraisal/Evaluation System	4.05
21	Organizational Performance/Effectiveness/Success	4.05
22	Pride About the Organization	4.02
23	Learning and Development Opportunities	4.01
24	Advancement and Promotion Opportunities	3.98
25	Team Climate	3.96

While the usual suspects play a role in moving the needle on employee engagement for senior HR leaders (such as CHRO, EVP, SVP, and VP), they often serve as secondary drivers for this specific talent segment. Senior HR leaders prioritize factors that align more closely with their strategic responsibilities and senior leadership roles. Key factors that matter most to senior HR leaders include ethics, trust, and integrity, alongside decision-making authority and access to budget and resources. They also place significance on the organizational structure, recognizing its impact on their ability to effectively carry out their roles. These factors intuitively make sense for senior leaders, as having decision-making autonomy and ample resources are vital for their success.

Additionally, the positioning of senior HR leaders within the organizational hierarchy holds importance in terms of strategic alignment, influence, and legitimacy. For instance, senior HR leaders generally prefer to have a direct reporting relationship with the CEO or the C-suite. This positioning contributes to their ability to drive strategic initiatives and have a broader organizational impact. In summary, the primary drivers that matter most to senior HR leaders extend beyond the popular notion that employee engagement is all about the quality and effectiveness of the immediate manager.[19] Senior HR leaders require a broader range of drivers that aligns with their unique responsibilities and influence within the organization.

Table 13.6   What Matters Most for Senior HR Leaders

RANK	WHAT MATTERS MOST FOR SENIOR HR LEADERS (N = 337)	MEAN
1	Trust and Integrity in the Leadership	4.68
2	Ethical Workplace/Work Environment	4.60
3	Decision-Making Authority/Decision Rights	4.49
4	Access to Budget/Fiscal Resources	4.45
5	Organizational Structure	4.43
6	Senior Leadership Quality	4.41
7	Meaningful Work	4.40
8	Compassionate Leader/Manager Behavior	4.38

(continued)

Table 13.6 What Matters Most for Senior HR Leaders *(continued)*

RANK	WHAT MATTERS MOST FOR SENIOR HR LEADERS (N = 337)	MEAN
9	Workplace Culture	4.38
10	Immediate Manager/Supervisor Quality	4.38
11	Relationship with Immediate Manager/Leader	4.35
12	Coworker/Team Member Quality	4.32
13	Job Fit	4.26
14	Positional Authority	4.26
15	Access to Information/Sharing Information	4.24
16	Organizational Leadership Opportunities (opportunities to lead a business unit, function, or department with significant mission and charter ownership, human resource responsibility, fiscal/budgetary accountability, and decision rights)	4.23
17	Direct Reports Quality	4.23
18	Wellness and Well-Being Programs/Interventions	4.19
19	Pride About the Organization	4.18
20	Organizational Performance/Effectiveness/Success	4.16
21	Directly Leading and Managing People	4.16
22	Team Climate	4.14
23	Relationships with Coworkers/Team Members	4.12
24	Executive Visibility	4.12
25	Personal Influence	4.10

Participants in the study were surveyed regarding their aspirations to assume a senior executive or C-level position in their HR career. They were also asked to complete a concise five-item Achievement/Ambition Scale, developed by researchers at the University of Pennsylvania.[20] Data analysis identified a subset of respondents (n = 648) who displayed both C-level aspirations and a high ambition and achievement orientation.

As anticipated, this particular group of HR professionals identified a distinct set of engagement drivers that align with their career aspirations. These drivers include advancement and promotion opportunities, job title, decision-making authority/decision rights, organizational leadership opportunities, executive visibility, and total compensation. While the usual suspects of engagement drivers are still evident, they assume a secondary role for HR professionals on the fast track to the executive suite. These individuals prioritize factors that support their journey toward senior leadership positions.

It is essential to acknowledge that the study did not determine whether any of the respondents in this group were classified as high-performers or high-potentials within their respective organizations. Nonetheless, the results demonstrate that engagement drivers are likely to differ across various talent segments who share similar characteristics, values, preferences, and career goals and aspirations. This suggests that engagement strategies need to be tailored to the specific needs and aspirations of different talent segments within the HR profession.

Table 13.7 What Matters Most for "Aspiring HR Leaders"

RANK	WHAT MATTERS MOST FOR "ASPIRING HR LEADERS" (N = 648)	MEAN
1	Advancement and Promotion Opportunities	4.71
2	Ethical Workplace/Work Environment	4.52
3	Trust and Integrity in the Leadership	4.49
4	Job Title (EVP, VP, Director)	4.43
5	Decision-Making Authority/Decision Rights	4.42
6	Meaningful Work	4.41
7	Compassionate Leader/Manager Behavior	4.38
8	Wellness and Well-Being Programs/Interventions	4.37
9	Total Compensation/Enumeration	4.35
10	Workplace Culture	4.34
11	Work-Life Balance	4.31

(continued)

Table 13.7   What Matters Most for "Aspiring HR Leaders" *(continued)*

RANK	WHAT MATTERS MOST FOR SENIOR HR LEADERS (N = 337)	MEAN
12	Organizational Leadership Opportunities (opportunities to lead a business unit, function, or department with significant mission and charter ownership, human resource responsibility, fiscal/budgetary accountability, and decision rights)	4.29
13	Executive Visibility	4.27
14	Coworker/Team Member Quality	4.26
15	Job Fit	4.26
16	Senior Leadership Quality	4.21
17	Vacation/Personal Time Off	4.21
18	Remote Work/Flexible Arrangements	4.20
19	Access to Information/Sharing Information	4.20
20	Learning and Development Opportunities	4.19
21	Fair and Accurate Performance Appraisal/Evaluation System	4.14
22	Immediate Manager/Supervisor Quality	4.13
23	Organizational Performance/Effectiveness/Success	4.10
24	Pride About the Organization	4.09
25	Relationships with Coworkers/Team Members	4.06

Do the Cobbler's Children Have Shoes?

In addition to measuring employee engagement among HR professionals, the study also sought to evaluate the extent to which organizations engage in talent management practices for both HR and non-HR employees. Participants were asked to rate the level of implementation of these practices in their respective organizations.

Overall, HR professionals reported that their organizations implement talent management practices to a moderate extent (Figure 13.4). The study examined 13 specific talent management practices, and there is a general similarity between the engagement of non-HR employees and HR employees across eight talent management practice areas. These areas include leadership development, structured mentoring, coaching for growth and development, HR analytics, workforce planning, workforce segmentation, and employee surveys and sensing. In terms of these practices, the level of engagement and implementation appears to be relatively equivalent for both HR and non-HR employees as mentioned.

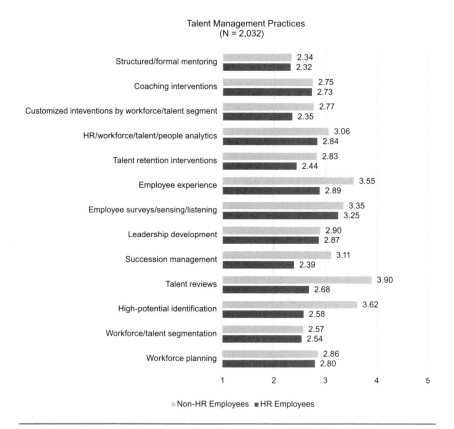

Figure 13.4   Talent Management Practices (Non-HR Employees vs. HR Employees)

These findings suggest that organizations recognize the importance of talent management practices and are applying them in a comparable manner for HR and non-HR employees. This parity underscores the significance of fostering growth, development, and effective leadership across all segments of the workforce, regardless of their role within the organization.

However, respondents indicated significant disparities in certain critical talent management practices, namely:

1. Talent reviews
2. High-potential identification
3. Succession management
4. Talent retention interventions
5. Employee experience
6. Customized interventions by workforce/talent segment

While HR professionals reported receiving growth and development opportunities and participating in various organization-wide practices, they expressed a notable absence in the most critical talent management practices related to career advancement and leadership succession. These findings suggest that the "cobbler's children have no shoes" where HR professionals themselves may be overlooked when it comes to managing top HR talent.

One respondent shared the following comments, which encapsulate the perplexing and concerning consensus and sentiment regarding talent management for HR professionals.

Our company implemented an integrated talent management program about six years ago. The HR business partner team works closely with the Talent Enablement CoE to facilitate an annual talent review process for each business division and function. Since I've been with the company, we have not held a single talent review process for the HR organization. . . . When I asked about this, I was told that talent management is for the business—not HR.

—Director, human resources, at a midsize
bio-technology firm

Step 6: Communicate Intelligence Results

The study's findings and results were compiled into a comprehensive report and shared with HRCI, the partnering organization. Additionally, the principal researcher and key staff members at HRCI organized a LinkedIn Live event, focusing on the employee engagement aspect of the study. The event attracted a substantial audience, with over 1,500 attendees interested in the topic. Moving forward, there are plans to share the results pertaining to the extent of talent management practices for HR employees within organizations. This will further contribute to the dissemination of valuable insights among professionals in the HR community.

Furthermore, this case being published in this book serves as a means to widely distribute the study's results to the broader HR analytics community and contribute to the collective knowledge and understanding of employee engagement and talent management practices for HR professionals in the context of HR analytics.

Step 7: Enable Strategy and Decision-Making

Measuring employee engagement alone is insufficient if we fail to identify what truly matters to employees across different talent segments, including HR professionals. Organizations committed to talent management should replace generic, one-size-fits-all practices with strategies tailored to individuals' unique strengths, motivations, career aspirations, and values.[21]

In recent years, there has been a prevalent and popular belief that employee engagement is primarily influenced by managers. However, more recently, there has been a tendency to overlook the importance of talent segmentation and specific drivers of engagement. Instead, there is a growing emphasis on broad, all-encompassing concepts such as employee experience and workplace culture, as well as the introduction of new factors like employee fulfillment and employee thriving.[22] While these areas are undoubtedly important, placing sole focus on these concepts may allow the C-suite to avoid implementing a differentiated talent management and employee engagement strategy tailored to distinct talent segments. This prompts important questions: Whom are we truly designing the employee experience and workplace culture for? What may be an exceptional employee experience and workplace culture for the general workforce may fail to meet the needs of an organization's top talent, leading to disengagement and undesired attrition. Moreover, the introduction of new concepts like employee fulfillment and employee thriving may suggest that organizations can sidestep the responsibility of providing certain drivers or employee value propositions that the C-suite doesn't agree with simply by creating new desired outcomes.

As HR professionals, we have the responsibility to aim higher and advocate for a flexible yet targeted set of drivers and employee value propositions (EVPs) for different talent segments. While creating a positive employee experience and workplace culture is important, it is unlikely to retain high-potentials, aspiring leaders, or individuals with career ambitions unless organizations design and deliver the right mix of rewards and resources that align with the specific needs of critical talent segments. Recent i4CP research confirmed that burnout was the top reason for employee attrition, followed by a lack of advancement opportunities, compensation, and the insistence on remote employees returning to the workplace.[23] Yet, organizations curiously ignore unpopular or inconvenient factors and continue offering the same conventional EVPs when designing their strategies.

This research, which focuses on HR professionals, supports the need for a differentiated talent management and employee engagement strategy, avoiding a one-size-fits-all approach. It also provides a compelling business case for talent segmentation, regular measurement of employee engagement, and, most importantly, the identification of the drivers and EVPs that matter most to critical talent segments. Currently, AI-powered employee listening and sensing platforms do not encompass the full range of employee engagement drivers. Therefore, customized and bespoke surveys are imperative.

Moreover, this research illuminates the existing state of engagement among HR professionals, revealing that nearly 70 percent of them are actively engaged. However, the increasing prevalence of stress and burnout poses a significant threat to the long-term sustainability of these engagement levels.

Additionally, the research highlights clear gaps in HR professionals' involvement in critical talent management activities. Despite their instrumental role in designing and implementing integrated talent management practices, HR professionals themselves often receive insufficient attention, which is both perplexing and problematic. HR professionals make substantial contributions to delivering business value, fostering a positive employee experience, and shaping workplace culture. Consequently, they deserve the same level of support and focus that they provide to others.

Bright Future,
Dark Future?

*The optimist proclaims that we live in the best of all
possible worlds, and the pessimist fears that this is true.*

—James Branch Cabell

"The future is now" is a powerful statement that encapsulates the essence of embracing the present while considering the potential outcomes and developments that lie ahead. It represents an active and forward-thinking mindset, one that acknowledges the ever-evolving trends, technologies, and societal shifts that shape our current reality and future path.

Drawing from my experience as a social, behavioral, and organizational scientist; educator; consultant; former HR research and analytics leader; and a former CHRO, and after writing this book, I find myself deep in contemplation about what lies ahead for HR analytics. As transformative changes and technological advancements unfold, the burning question emerges: Will HR analytics have a bright future or a dark future? However, before we can even attempt to answer this question, it is important to recognize the wide range of viewpoints regarding the ethical implications of HR analytics.

In my observation and for the sake of simplicity, there are three broad camps within the HR analytics community—the optimists, the pessimists, and the realists.

The Optimists

Optimists within the HR analytics community enthusiastically advocate for the positive aspects and potential benefits of HR analytics, all while conscientiously addressing ethical concerns through robust governance, transparency, and responsible data usage. They possess a forward-thinking mindset, focusing on what is achievable, what *can* be done, and the possibilities that HR analytics can unlock, often overlooking the question of what *should* be done.

However, optimists firmly uphold values, ethics, and privacy as guiding principles. They genuinely believe that HR analytics can act as a catalyst for positive transformation and remain a force for good in the workplace. By emphasizing the importance of implementing strong governance structures, ensuring transparency in data practices, and maintaining ethical standards, optimists strive to harness the power of HR analytics ethically and responsibly in a way that benefits both the organization and the workforce.

The Pessimists

On the other hand, pessimists bring attention to the ethical paradoxes and pitfalls associated with HR analytics. They raise valid concerns regarding privacy infringements, opaque practices, data misuse, and biased decision-making, whether by humans or AI systems. Pessimists acknowledge the emergence of a quantified employee agenda, potentially creepy practices, and stress the need for caution and the implementation of country-specific legislation to effectively tackle these challenges. Pessimists wouldn't necessarily consider themselves Luddites, but they are not big fans of the technological advancements and workforce surveillance that is running amok in the workplace.

Pessimists argue that despite the well-intentioned efforts of the HR analytics community, there is a risk that human nature and profit-driven motives will likely prevail and overshadow ethical considerations.

Therefore, they advocate for the necessity of regulatory measures to prevent potential harm. Recognizing the potential impact on individuals, pessimists emphasize the importance of safeguards and guidelines to protect privacy, promote transparency, and ensure unbiased decision-making within HR analytics practices. By highlighting the ethical complexities involved, pessimists seek to foster a critical dialogue and encourage the responsible use of HR analytics practices and technologies.

The Realists

Realists take a pragmatic approach when it comes to HR analytics, recognizing both the potential benefits and ethical considerations at hand. They approach the situation by thoroughly evaluating the rewards and risks of engaging in certain HR practices. Realists understand the importance of ethical considerations, such as safeguarding data privacy, mitigating biases, and promoting transparency and trust. However, they may be open to pushing the boundaries of what some may perceive as the "creepy line" to benefit the organizations they serve, even if it is at odds with their own professional and personal values and ethics.

Realists strongly advocate for the implementation of safeguards and guidelines to navigate the complex ethical landscape surrounding HR analytics. They acknowledge that HR analytics can generate both positive and negative outcomes. By leveraging the potential of HR analytics, realists strive to harness its power in a way that strategically benefits their organizations, even if the benefits for employees may not be immediately apparent. Optimists, pessimists, and realists within the HR analytics community are not mutually exclusive camps. They merely represent broad perspectives, each shedding light on the ethical concerns associated with HR analytics. The future, therefore, presents a spectrum of possibilities—both bright and dark.

In short, optimists envision a bright and promising future where HR analytics facilitates informed workforce decisions, positive change, and innovation. Conversely, pessimists fear that without proper safeguards, we will likely face ethical transgressions and a dark, dystopian future. Realists advocate for a pragmatic and balanced approach to ensure the success of HR analytics. They are more comfortable with the ethical shades of gray and the quantified employee agenda when it comes to HR analytics practices and new and emerging technologies.

Shifting Ethical Norms

The HR community faces a significant challenge in ensuring that HR analytics remains ethical and a force for good due to the constantly shifting ethical norms. These norms represent changes in societal and cultural standards, influencing what is considered morally acceptable or unacceptable behavior. These changes can shape laws, regulations, and societal behaviors as they reflect the values and concerns of a particular time.

Over the years, I have had thought-provoking and some alarming conversations with HCM technology entrepreneurs and individuals in the HR analytics community who embrace a form of moral or ethical relativism. They argue for a reassessment of ethical norms in response to evolving societal values and expectations. For example, one technology entrepreneur proudly claimed that privacy expectations in the workplace will fundamentally change in the next decade, continuously evolving with each new generation entering the workforce. This perspective raises concerns and represents a clarion call for those of us who uphold humanistic values and strive to adhere to a professional code of ethics that transcends personal or cultural biases.

The idea of reevaluating ethical norms based on changing societal values can be disconcerting, especially when it comes to HR analytics practices that directly impact people's lives. Those of us who prioritize human well-being and ethical conduct in our work find it challenging to accept the notion that ethical standards should be subject to constant reinterpretation.

While we acknowledge the importance of adapting to societal progress and evolving ethical dilemmas, we believe that a strong foundation of enduring humanistic values and unwavering adherence to professional codes of ethics is necessary to responsibly navigate the complexities of HR analytics work. By upholding these principles, we can strive for a balance between innovation and the preservation of fundamental human rights in the workplace, ultimately creating an environment that promotes the well-being and dignity of individuals.

As discussed throughout this book, the HR analytics community stands at an ethical crossroad, and the choices made now will determine whether HR analytics remains a positive force for good. It remains to be seen whether the HR analytics community will avoid crossing the line and where technologies and practices we employ become troubling. As discussed in Chapter 4, organizations and HR analytics practitioners may choose to tread a precarious path, teetering on the "creepy line," by engaging in questionable and potentially creepy HR analytics practices. To ensure that HR analytics remains a force for good, we must prioritize cultivating an ethical mindset, establishing an ethical ecosystem, and considering the ethical outcomes we aim to achieve throughout our HR analytics journey. How we navigate the ethical gray areas, address creepy analytics, and adapt to ever-shifting norms will define our professional values and ethics for years to come.

In conclusion, I believe that both a bright and a dark future lie ahead for HR analytics. The different perspectives on the ethical concerns surrounding HR analytics provide valuable insights, with optimists, pessimists, and realists offering distinct viewpoints. While I do not possess prophetic abilities or claim to be a futurist, it is difficult to overlook human nature. Considering this, I maintain an optimistic outlook regarding the potential benefits of HR analytics for organizations. However, I hold a more cautious stance when it comes to the advantages it may bring to employees. The future is now upon us, presenting both opportunities and challenges, compelling us to navigate the ethical landscape of HR analytics with care, consideration, and compassion.

NOTES

INTRODUCTION

1. Alec Levenson, *Strategic Analytics: Advancing Strategy Execution and Organizational Effectiveness* (Oakland: Berrett-Koehler Publishers, 2015).
2. Nigel Guenole, Jonathan Ferrar, and Sheri Feinzig, *The Power of People: Learn How Successful Organizations Use Workforce Analytics to Improve Business Performance,* (Pearson Education, 2017).
3. Jonathan Ferrar and David Green, *Excellence in People Analytics: How to Use Workforce Data to Create Business Value* (London: Kogan Page, 2021).
4. Salvatore V. Falletta, "HR Intelligence: Advancing People Research and Analytics," *International HR Information Management Journal* 12, no. 3 (2008): 21–31.

CHAPTER 1

1. Janet H. Marler and John W. Boudreau, "An Evidence-Based Review of HR Analytics," *International Journal of Human Resource Management* 28, no. 1 (2017): 3–26, https://doi.org/10.1080/09585192.2016.1244699.
2. Sjoerd van den Heuvel and Tanya Bondarouk, "The Rise (and Fall?) of HR Analytics: A Study into the Future Application, Value, Structure, and System Support," *Journal of Organizational Effectiveness: People and Performance* 4, no. 2 (2017): 157–178, https://doi.org/10.1108/JOEPP-03-2017-0022.
3. Salvatore V. Falletta and Wendy L. Combs, "The Organizational Intelligence Model in Context: A Comparative Analysis Case Study," *OD Practitioner* 50, no. 1 (2018): 22–29.
4. Mark A. Huselid, "The Science and Practice of Workforce Analytics: Introduction to the HRM Special Issue," *Human Resource Management* 57, no. 3 (2018): 679–684, https://doi.org/10.1002/hrm.21916.
5. Jonathan Ferrar and David Green, *Excellence in People Analytics: How to Use Workforce Data to Create Business Value* (London: Kogan Page, 2021), 3.
6. Nigel Guenole, Jonathan Ferrar, and Sheri Feinzig, *The Power of People: Learn How Successful Organizations Use Workforce Analytics to Improve Business Performance* (Pearson Education, 2017), 17.
7. Huselid, "The Science and Practice of Workforce Analytics."
8. Edward E. Lawler III, Alec Levenson, and John W. Boudreau, "HR Metrics and Analytics: Use and Impact," *Human Resource Planning* 27 (2004): 27–35.

9. Martin R. Edwards, Andy Charlwood, Nigel Guenole, and Janet Marler, "HR Analytics: An Emerging Field Finding its Place in the World Alongside Simmering Ethical Challenges," *Human Resource Management Journal* (2022): 1–11, https://doi.org/10.1111/1748-8583.12435.

10. Thomas Rasmussen and Dave Ulrich, "Learning from Practice: How HR Analytics Avoids Being a Management Fad," *Organizational Dynamics* 44, no. 3 (2015): 236–242, https://doi.org/10.1016/j.orgdyn.2015.05.008.

11. Eden B. King, Scott Tonidandel, Jose M. Cortina, and Alexis A. Fink, "Building Understanding of the Data Science Revolution and I-O Psychology," in *Big Data at Work: The Data Science Revolution and Organizational Psychology*, eds. Eden B. King, Scott Tonidandel, Jose M. Cortina, and Alexis A. Fink (New York: Routledge, 2016), 1–15.

12. Laurie Bassi, "Raging Debates in HR Analytics," *People & Strategy* 34, no. 2 (2011): 14–18.

13. Salvatore V. Falletta and Wendy L. Combs, "The HR Analytics Cycle: A Seven-Step Process for Building Evidence-Based and Ethical HR Analytics Capabilities," *Journal of Work-Applied Management* 13, no. 1 (2021): 51–68, https://doi.org/10.1108/JWAM-03-2020-0020.

14. Salvatore V. Falletta, "In Search of HR Intelligence: Evidence-Based HR Analytics Practices in High Performing Companies," *People & Strategy* 36, no. 4 (2014): 28–37.

15. Lawler III, Levenson, and Boudreau, "HR Metrics and Analytics: Use and Impact."

16. Marler and Boudreau, "An Evidence-Based Review of HR Analytics."

17. Lawler III, Levenson, and Boudreau, "HR Metrics and Analytics: Use and Impact."

18. Salvatore V. Falletta, "HR Intelligence: Advancing People Research and Analytics," *International HR Information Management Journal* 12, no. 3 (2008): 21–31.

19. Bassi, "Raging Debates in HR Analytics."

20. Scott Mondore, Shane Douthitt, and Marisa Carson, "Maximizing the Impact and Effectiveness of HR Analytics to Drive Business Outcomes," *People & Strategy* 34, no. 2 (2011): 20–27.

21. Marler and Boudreau, "An Evidence-Based Review of HR Analytics."

22. Van den Heuvel and Bondarouk, "The Rise (and Fall?) of HR Analytics."

23. Aizhan Tursunbayeva, Stefano Di Lauro, and Claudia Pagliari, "People Analytics: A Scoping Review of Conceptual Boundaries and Value Propositions," *International Journal of Information Management* 43 (2018): 224–247, https://doi.org/10.1016/j.ijinfomgt.2018.08.002.

24. Roslyn Vargas, Yuliya V. Yurova, Cynthia P. Ruppel, Leslie C. Tworoger, and Regina Greenwood, "Individual Adoption of HR Analytics: A Fine Grained View of the Early Stages Leading to Adoption," *International Journal of Human Resource Management* 29, no. 22 (2018): 3046–3067, https://doi.org/10.1080/09585192.2018.1446181.

25. Alec Levenson, "Using Workforce Analytics to Improve Strategy Execution," *Human Resource Management* 57, no. 3 (2018): 685–700, https://doi.org/10.1002/hrm.21850.

26. Huselid, "The Science and Practice of Workforce Analytics."

27. Derrick McIver, Mark L. Lengnick-Hall, and Cynthia A. Lengnick-Hall, "A Strategic Approach to Workforce Analytics: Integrating Science and Agility," *Business Horizons* 61, no. 3 (2018): 397–407, https://doi.org/10.1016/j.bushor.2018.01.005.

28. Vicenc Fernandez and Eva Gallardo-Gallardo, "Tackling the HR Digitalization Challenge: Key Factors and Barriers to HR Analytics Adoption," *Competitiveness Review* 31, no. 1 (2021): 162–187, https://doi.org/10.1108/CR-12-2019-0163.

29. James C. Ryan, "Retaining, Resigning and Firing: Bibliometrics as a People Analytics Tool for Examining Research Performance Outcomes and Faculty Turnover," *Personnel Review* 50, no. 5 (2021): 1316–1335, https://doi.org/10.1108/PR-12-2019 -0676.

30. John Boudreau and Wayne Cascio, "Human Capital Analytics: Why Are We Not There?" *Journal of Organizational Effectiveness: People and Performance* 4, no. 2 (2017): 119-126. https://doi.org/10.1108/JOEPP-03-2017-0021.

31. Jac Fitz-enz, *The New HR Analytics: Predicting the Economic Value of Your Company's Human Capital Investments* (New York: AMACOM, 2010), 4.

32. Laurie Bassi, Rob Carpenter, and Dan McMurrer, *HR Analytics Handbook* (Amsterdam: Read Business, 2010), 11.

33. Gene Pease, *Optimize Your Greatest Asset—Your People: How to Apply Analytics to Big Data to Improve Your Human Capital Investments* (Hoboken: John Wiley & Sons, 2015), 19.

34. Erik van Vulpen, *The Basic Principles of People Analytics* (AnalyticsinHR.com, 2016), 11.

35. "SHRM Foundation Report: Use of Workforce Analytics for Competitive Advantage," *SHRM*, 2016, https://www.shrm.org/foundation/ourwork/initiatives /preparing-for-future-hr-trends/Documents/Workforce%20Analytics%20Report .pdf.

36. Martin R. Edwards and Kirsten Edwards, *Predictive HR Analytics: Mastering the HR Metric* (London: Kogan Page, 2016), 2.

37. Jean Paul Isson and Jesse S. Harriott, *People Analytics in the Era of Big Data: Changing the Way You Attract, Acquire, Develop, and Retain Talent* (Hoboken: Wiley, 2016), 8.

38. Guenole, Ferrar, and Feinzig, *The Power of People*, Preface.

39. "CIPD Factsheet on People Analytics," Chartered Institute of Personnel and Development, 2022, https://www.cipd.org/en/knowledge/factsheets/analytics -factsheet/.

40. Mike West, *People Analytics for Dummies* (Hoboken: John Wiley & Sons, 2019), 12.

41. Ferrar and Green, *Excellence in People Analytics*, 5.

42. Alec Levenson and Alexis Fink, "Human Capital Analytics: Too Much Data and Analysis, Not Enough Models and Business Insights," *Journal of Organizational Effectiveness: People and Performance* 4, no. 2 (2017): 145–156, https://doi.org/10 .1108/JOEPP-03-2017-0029.

43. Laszlo Bock, *Work Rules! Insights from Inside Google That Will Transform How You Live and Lead* (New York: Twelve, 2015), 357.

44. Bock, *Work Rules!*, 357.

45. William A. Schiemann, Jerry H. Seibert, and Mark H. Blankenship, "Putting Human Capital Analytics to Work: Predicting and Driving Business Success," *Human Resource Management* 57, no. 3 (2018): 795–807, https://doi.org/10.1002 /hrm.21843.

46. J. McK. Cattell, "Mental Tests and Measurements," *Mind* 15, no. 59 (1890): 373–381, https://doi.org/10.1093/mind/os-XV.59.373.

47. William McDougall, *An Introduction to Social Psychology* (London: Methaen, 1908).
48. Walter D. Scott, *Increasing Human Efficiency in Business* (New York: Macmillan, 1911).
49. Frederick Winslow Taylor, *The Principles of Scientific Management* (New York: Harper & Brothers, 1911).
50. Hugo Munsterberg, *Psychology and Industrial Efficiency* (Boston: Houghton Mifflin, 1913).
51. Edward L. Thorndike, "Intelligence and Its Uses," *Harper's Magazine* 140 (1920): 227–235.
52. Carl G. Jung, *Psychological Types* (Princeton: Princeton University Press, 1971).
53. Rensis Likert, "A Technique for the Measurement of Attitudes," *Archives of Psychology* 22, no. 140 (1932): 5–55.
54. Elton Mayo, *The Human Problems of an Industrial Civilization* (New York: The Macmillan Company,1933).
55. Kurt Lewin, "Action Research and Minority Problems," *Journal of Social Issues* 2, no. 4 (1946): 34–46, https://doi.org/10.1111/j.1540-4560.1946.tb02295.x.
56. Robert L. Thorndike, *Personnel Selection: Test and Measurement Techniques* (New York: John Wiley & Sons, 1949).
57. Douglas W. Bray and Donald. L. Grant, "The Assessment Center in the Measurement of Potential for Business Management," *Psychological Monographs* 80, no. 17 (1966): 1–27, https://doi.org/10.1037/h0093895.
58. Don R. Bryant, Michael J. Maggard, and Robert P. Taylor, "Manpower Planning Models and Techniques: A Descriptive Survey," *Business Horizons* 16, no. 2 (1973): 69–78.
59. David A. Nadler, *Feedback and Organization Development: Using Data-Based Methods* (Reading, MA: Addison-Wesley, 1977); Janine Waclawski and Allan H. Church, eds., *Organization Development: A Data-Driven Approach to Organizational Change* (San Francisco: Jossey-Bass, 2002).
60. Jac Fitz-enz, "Measurement Imperative," *Personnel Journal* 57, no. 4 (1978): 193-195.
61. George Gallup, "Employee Research: From Nice to Know to Need to Know," *Personnel Journal* 67, no. 8 (1988): 42–43; Allen I. Kraut, ed., *Organizational Surveys: Tools for Assessment and Change* (San Francisco: Jossey-Bass, 1996); Allan H. Church and Janine Waclawski, *Designing and Using Organizational Surveys: A Seven-Step Process* (San Franciso: Jossey-Bass, 2001).
62. Jac Fitz-Enz, "Benchmarking: HR's New Improvement Tool," *HR Horizons* 107 (1992): 7–12; Ellen F. Glanz and Lee K. Dailey, "Benchmarking," *Human Resource Management* 31, no. 1–2 (1992): 9–20, https://doi.org/10.1002/hrm.3930310102.
63. Jack Edwards, John C. Scott, and Nambury S. Raju, *The Human Resources Program-Evaluation Handbook* (Thousand Oaks: Sage, 2003); Donald L. Kirkpatrick, *Evaluating Training Programs: The Four Levels* (San Francisco: Berrett-Koehler, 1998); Jack J. Phillips, *Return on Investment in Training and Performance Improvement Programs* (Houston: Gulf Publishing, 1997); Darlene Russ-Eft and Hallie Preskill, *Evaluation in Organizations: A Systematic Approach to Enhancing Learning, Performance, and Change* (New York: Basic Books, 2001).
64. Robert S. Kaplan and David P. Norton, "The Balanced Scorecard: Measures That Drive Performance," *Harvard Business Review* 70, no. 1 (1992): 71–79; Brian E.

Becker, David Ulrich, and Mark A. Huselid, *The HR Scorecard: Linking People, Strategy, and Performance* (Boston: Harvard Business School Press, 2001).

65. Rob Briner, "Evidence-Based Human Resource Management," in *Evidence-Based Practice: A Critical Appraisal*, eds. Liz Trinder and Shirley Reynolds (London: Blackwell Science, 2000), 184–211; Jeffrey Pfeffer and Robert I. Sutton, *Hard Facts, Dangerous Half-Truths, and Total Nonsense: Profiting from Evidence-Based Management* (Boston: Harvard Business School Press, 2006); Denise M. Rousseau, "Is There Such a Thing as Evidence-Based Management?" *Academy of Management Review* 31, no. 2 (2006): 256–269, https://doi.org/10.5465/AMR.2006.20208679.

66. John W. Boudreau and Peter M. Ramstad, *Beyond HR: The New Science of Human Capital* (Boston: Harvard Business School Press, 2007); Wayne F. Cascio and John W. Boudreau, *Investing in People: Financial Impact of Human Resource Initiatives* (Upper Saddle River, NJ: Pearson, FT Press, 2008).

67. Falletta, "HR Intelligence: Advancing People Research and Analytics."

68. Herbert Read, "Review of *A Coat of Many Colours: Occasional Essays*," *Poetry Quarterly* 7, no. 4. Winter 1945.

69. Rodney L. Lowman, "Douglas W. Bray (1918–2006): Career and Personal 'Life Themes,'" *Psychologist Manager Journal* 11, no. 1 (2008): 185–199, https://doi.org/10.1080/10887150801967720.

70. Jac Fitz-enz, *How to Measure Human Resources Management* (New York: McGraw-Hill, 1984).

71. Kaplan and Norton, "The Balanced Scorecard"; Becker, Ulrich, and Huselid, *The HR Scorecard*.

72. Briner, "Evidence-Based Human Resource Management."

73. Falletta, "HR Intelligence: Advancing People Research and Analytics."

74. John W. Boudreau and Peter M. Ramstad, "Talentship and the New Paradigm for Human Resource Management: From Professional Practices to Strategic Talent Decision Science," *Human Resource Planning* 28, no. 2 (2005): 17–26.

75. Pfeffer and Sutton, *Hard Facts, Dangerous Half-Truths, and Total Nonsense*.

76. Thomas H. Davenport and Jeanne G. Harris, *Competing on Analytics: The New Science of Winning* (Boston: Harvard Business School Press, 2007).

77. Cascio and Boudreau, *Investing in People*.

78. Fitz-enz, *The New HR Analytics*; Bassi, Carpenter, Dan McMurrer, *HR Analytics Handbook*.

79. Thomas H. Davenport, Jeanne Harris, and Jeremy Shapiro, "Competing on Talent Analytics," *Harvard Business Review* 88, no. 10 (2010): 52–58.

80. Falletta, "In Search of HR Intelligence."

81. Allan H. Church and Subhadra Dutta, "The Promise of Big Data for OD: Old Wine in New Bottles or the Next Generation of Data-Driven Methods for Change," *OD Practitioner* 45 (2013): 23–31.

82. Josh Bersin, "The Geeks Arrive in HR: People Analytics Is Here," *Forbes*, February 1, 2015, https://www.forbes.com/sites/joshbersin/2015/02/01/geeks-arrive-in-hr-people-analytics-is-here/.

CHAPTER 2

1. Viktor Mayer-Schönberger and Kenneth Cukier, *Big Data: A Revolution That Will Transform How We Live, Work, and Think* (Boston: HarperCollins, 2013).

2. James Somers, "Torching the Modern-Day Library of Alexandria," *Atlantic*, April 20, 2017, https://www.theatlantic.com/technology/archive/2017/04/the-tragedy-of-google-books/523320/.
3. Mayer-Schönberger and Cukier, *Big Data*.
4. James Bennet and Eric Schmidt, "Eric Schmidt at Washington Ideas Forum 2010," October 1, 2010, YouTube video, 24:32, https://www.youtube.com/watch?v=CeQsPSaitL0.
5. Bennet and Schmidt, "Eric Schmidt at Washington Ideas Forum 2010."
6. Shoshana Zuboff, *The Age of Surveillance Capitalism: The Fight for a Human Future at the New Frontier of Power* (New York: Hachette Book Group, 2019).
7. Zuboff, *The Age of Surveillance Capitalism*.
8. Josh Bersin, "Quantified Self: Meet the Quantified Employee," *Forbes*, June 25, 2014, https://www.forbes.com/sites/joshbersin/2014/06/25/quantified-self-meet-the-quantified-employee/?sh=3f92055bc5fe.
9. Mary B. Young, "Going Public on HR Data Privacy: Implications for Human Capital Analytics and Strategic Workforce Planning," *The Conference Board*, last modified February 26, 2013, https://www.conference-board.org/publications/going-public-on-HR-data-privacy.
10. Arvind Narayanan, "How to Recognize AI Snake Oil," Princeton University, Department of Computer Science, January 16, 2021, video, 1:36:53, https://www.cs.princeton.edu/news/how-recognize-ai-snake-oil.
11. Narayanan, "How to Recognize AI Snake Oil."
12. Taylor Clark and Nicholas Garbis, "Keep It Real and Ethical: What You Need to Know About AI and ML in HR," *One Model*, 2022, https://www.onemodel.co/whitepapers/ethics-of-ai-ml-in-hr.
13. Cynthia Rudin and Joanna Radin, "Why Are We Using Black Box Models in AI When We Don't Need To? A Lesson from an Explainable AI Competition," *Harvard Data Science Review* 1, no. 2 (2019), https://doi.org/10.1162/99608f92.5a8a3a3d.
14. Adam Zewe, "In Machine Learning, Synthetic Data Can Offer Real Performance Improvements," *MIT News*, November 3, 2022, https://news.mit.edu/2022/synthetic-data-ai-improvements-1103.
15. Jeffrey Dastin, "Amazon Scraps Secret AI Recruiting Tool That Showed Bias Against Women," *Reuters*, October 10, 2018, https://www.reuters.com/article/us-amazon-com-jobs-automation-insight-idUSKCN1MK08G.
16. Tomas Chamorro-Premuzic, *I, Human: AI, Automation, and the Quest to Reclaim What Makes Us Unique* (Boston: Harvard Business Review Press, 2023).
17. Chris Butler, CEO, One Model, interview by Salvatore Falletta, November 22, 2022.
18. Rudin and Radin, "Why Are We Using Black Box Models in AI When We Don't Need to?"
19. Butler, interview by Salvatore Falletta.
20. Edward Snowden, *Permanent Record* (New York: Metropolitan Books, 2019).
21. "Future of Work: What Is Meant by the Future of Work?," *SHRM*, accessed May 22, 2023, https://www.shrm.org/resourcesandtools/pages/future-of-work.aspx.
22. "Future of Work," SHRM.
23. John W. Boudreau, "Robots Don't Get Sick," *USC's Marshall Center for Effective Organizations*, September 15, 2020, https://ceo.usc.edu/2020/09/15/robots-dont-get-sick/.

24. Ravin Jesuthasan and John W. Boudreau, *Work Without Jobs: How to Reboot Your Organization's Work Operating System* (New York: MIT Press, 2022).

CHAPTER 3

1. Mary B. Young and Patty Phillips, "Big Data Doesn't Mean 'Big Brother,' " *The Conference Board*, Report No. R-1582-15-RR, 2015, https://www.conference-board.org/publications/publicationdetail.cfm?publicationid=2954.
2. Don Peck, "They're Watching You at Work," *Atlantic*, December 2013, http://www.theatlantic.com/magazine/archive/2013/12/theyre-watching-you-at-work/354681.
3. Chris Broderick, Nicholas Bremner, Carolyn Kalafut, Allen Kamin, and Richard Rosenow, "Leveraging Passive Data: From Creepy to Cool" (panel presentation), Society for Industrial and Organizational Psychology Conference, Boston, MA, April 19–22, 2023.
4. Lisa Frye, "Reviewing Employee Emails: When You Should, When You Shouldn't," SHRM, May 15, 2017, https://www.shrm.org/resourcesandtools/hr-topics/employee-relations/pages/reviewing-employee-e-mails-when-you-should-when-you-shouldnt.aspx.
5. Jack Morse, "Yes, Your Boss Can Read Your Gmail Drafts (and That's Not All)," *Mashable*, October 9, 2019, https://mashable.com/article/gmail-g-suite-privacy.
6. Peck, "They're Watching You at Work."
7. Saul Hansell, "Google's Answer to Filling Jobs Is an Algorithm," *New York Times*, January 3, 2007, https://www.nytimes.com/2007/01/03/technology/03google.html.
8. Broderick et al., "Leveraging Passive Data: From Creepy to Cool."
9. Heather Krause, "Introduction to Proxy Variables," *We All Count*, June 12, 2020, https://weallcount.com/2020/06/12/introduction-to-proxy-variables/.
10. *Silence of the Lambs* (transcript of movie), accessed June 20, 2023, http://www.script-o-rama.com/movie_scripts/s/silence-of-the-lambs-script-transcript.html.
11. "The Pretender," IMDb, accessed June 20, 2023, https://www.imdb.com/title/tt0115320/.
12. Dibeyendu Ganguly, "Taming the Beast: Psychometric Profiling, Demographic Regression Models, and Predictive Algorithms," *Economic Times*, February 23, 2007.
13. Frank J. Cavico, Bahaudin G. Mujtaba, Stephen C. Muffler, and Marrisa Samuel, "Wellness Programs in the Workplace: An Unfolding Legal Quandary for Employers," *International Journal of Occupational Health and Public Health Nursing* 1, no. 1 (2014): 5–50.
14. Cavico et al., "Wellness Programs in the Workplace."
15. Rachel Emma Silverman, "Bosses Tap Outside Firms to Predict Which Workers Might Get Sick," *Wall Street Journal*, February 17, 2016, https://www.wsj.com/articles/bosses-harness-big-data-to-predict- which-workers-might-get-sick-1455664940.
16. Peter High, "Former Google HR Chief Laszlo Bock Aims to Revolutionize People Management with Humu," *Forbes*, September 9, 2019, https://www.forbes.com/sites/peterhigh/2019/09/09/former-google-hr-chief-laszlo-bock-aims-to-revolutionize-people-management-with-humu.
17. Daisuke Wakabayashi, "Firm Led by Google Veterans Uses A.I. to 'Nudge' Workers Toward Happiness," *New York Times*, December 31, 2018, https://www.nytimes.com/2018/12/31/technology/human-resources-artificial-intelligence-humu.html.

18. Mareike Möhlmann, "Algorithmic Nudges Don't Have to Be Unethical," *Harvard Business Review*, April 22, 2021, https://hbr.org/2021/04/algorithmic-nudges-dont -have-to-be-unethical.

19. Möhlmann, "Algorithmic Nudges Don't Have to Be Unethical."

20. "Pump and Dump Schemes," Security and Exchange Commission, accessed May 21, 2023, https://www.investor.gov/introduction-investing/investing-basics /glossary/pump-and-dump-schemes.

21. "Employee Survey Consortium Meeting," anonymous member in discussion with author, May 2013.

22. Manuel Valdes, "Job Seekers Getting Asked for Facebook Passwords," *Yahoo Finance*, March 20, 2012, https://finance.yahoo.com/news/job-seekers-getting -asked-facebook-080920368.html.

23. Amy Traub and Sean McElwee, "Bad Credit Shouldn't Block Employment: How to Make State Bans on Employment Credit Checks More Effective," *Demos*, February 25, 2016, https://www.demos.org/research/bad-credit-shouldnt-block -employment-how-make-state-bans-employment-credit-checks-more.

24. Cathy O'Neil, *Weapons of Math Destruction: How Big Data Increases Inequality and Threatens Democracy* (New York: Crown Publishers, 2016).

25. Zachary S. Smith, "Scraping Data from LinkedIn Profiles Is Legal, Appeals Court Rules," *Forbes*, April 18, 2022, https://www.forbes.com/sites/zacharysmith/2022 /04/18/scraping-data-from-linkedin-profiles-is-legal-appeals-court-rules/?sh= 703f2db42a9c.

26. Bernard Marr, "The Amazing Potential of Voice Analysis," *Forbes*, August 8, 2016, https://www.forbes.com/sites/bernardmarr/2016/08/08/the-amazing-potential-of -voice-analytics/?sh=7b0b1ed54f77; Tomas Chamorro-Premuzic and Seymour Adler, "Should Your Voice Determine Whether You Get Hired?," *Harvard Business Review*, April 20, 2015, https://hbr.org/2015/04/should-your-voice-determine -whether-you-get-hired.

27. Chamorro-Premuzic and Adler, "Should Your Voice Determine Whether You Get Hired?."

28. Midam Kim, "Think Leader, Think Deep Voice? CEO Voice Pitch and Gender," *Academy of Management Proceedings*, 2022, https://doi.org/10.5465/AMBPP.2022 .17778abstract.

29. Josh Bersin, "Privacy and Ethics in People Analytics," *In Focus*, SHRM Executive Network, 2020, 1–8, https://www.shrm.org/executive/resources/pages/privacy -and-ethics-in-people-analytics-.aspx.

30. Katie Johnston, "A Milton Resident's Lawsuit Against CVS Raises Questions About the Use of AI Lie Detectors in Hiring," *Boston Globe*, May 22, 2023, https://www .boston.com/news/the-boston-globe/2023/05/22/milton-residents-lawsuit-cvs-ai -lie-detectors/.

31. Carmen Fernández-Martínez and Alberto Fernández, "AI and Recruiting Software: Ethical and Legal Implications," *Paladyn, Journal of Behavioral Robotics* 11 (2020): 199–216, https://doi.org/10.1515/pjbr-2020-0030.

32. Fernández-Martínez and Fernández, "AI and Recruiting Software."

33. "EEOC Hearing Explores Potential Benefits and Harms of Artificial Intelligence and Other Automated Systems in Employment Decisions," U.S. Equal Employment Commission, January 31, 2023, https://www.eeoc.gov/newsroom/eeoc -hearing-explores-potential-benefits-and-harms-artificial-intelligence-and-other.

34. Joseph J. Lazzarotti and Rob Yang, "California Draft Regulations Would Curb Employer Use of Artificial Intelligence," *SHRM*, April 25, 2022, https://www.shrm .org/resourcesandtools/legal-and-compliance/state-and-local-updates/pages/cal -draft-regulations-employer-use-of-artificial-intelligence.aspx.

35. Guoying Zhao and Xiaobai Li, "Automatic Micro-Expression Analysis: Open Challenges," *Frontiers in Psychology* 10 (2019), https://doi.org/10.3389/fpsyg.2019 .01833.

36. Zhao and Li, "Automatic Micro-Expression Analysis: Open Challenges."

37. "Giorgio" (head of people analytics), in discussion with the author, May 18, 2023.

38. "Biometrics," Department of Homeland Security, accessed May 22, 2023, https:// www.dhs.gov/biometrics.

39. Andrea North-Samardzic, "Biometric Technology and Ethics: Beyond Security Applications," *Journal of Business Ethics* 167, no. 3 (2020): 433–450. https://doi.org /10.1007/s10551-019-04143-6.

40. North-Samardzic, "Biometric Technology and Ethics: Beyond Security Applications."

41. Aaron Holmes, "Employees at Home Are Being Photographed Every 5 Minutes by an Always-on Video Service to Ensure They're Actually Working—and the Service Is Seeing a Rapid Expansion Since the Coronavirus Outbreak," *Business Insider*, March 23, 2020, https://www.businessinsider.com/work-from-home-sneek -webcam-picture-5-minutes-monitor-video-2020-3?op=1.

42. Kirstie Ball, "Electronic Monitoring and Surveillance in the Workplace," Publications Office of the European Union, Luxembourg, 2021, doi:10.2760/5137, JRC125716, https://publications.jrc.ec.europa.eu/repository/handle/JRC125716.

43. Broderick et al., "Leveraging Passive Data: From Creepy to Cool."

44. Mark C. Perna, "Why 78% of Employers Are Sacrificing Employee Trust by Spying on Them," *Forbes*, March 3, 2022, https://www.forbes.com/sites/markcperna/2022 /03/15/why-78-of-employers-are-sacrificing-employee-trust-by-spying-on-them.

45. "S.262 – Stop Spying Bosses Act," Congress.gov, February 2, 2023, https://www .congress.gov/bill/118th-congress/senate-bill/262?s=1&r=23.

46. KnackApp, accessed May 23, 2023, https://knackapp.com/.

47. KnackApp.

48. Tomas Chamorro-Premuzic, Dave Winsborough, Ryne A. Sherman, and Robert Hogan, "New Talent Signals: Shiny New Objects or a Brave New World," *Industrial and Organizational Psychology* 9, no. 3 (2016): 621–640.

49. Peck, "They're Watching You at Work."

50. Ben Waber, *People Analytics: How Social Sensing Technology Will Transform Business and What It Tells Us About the Future of Work* (Upper Saddle River, FT Press, 2013).

51. Waber, *People Analytics*.

52. Tom Flanagan, "Company Under Fire for Installing Timers Over Employees' Toilets," *Yahoo! News*, October 20, 2020, https://au.news.yahoo.com/company-under -fire-timers-on-employees-toilets-044236716.html.

53. Joshua Rhett Miller, "This Tech Company Will Start Microchipping Their Workers," *New York Post*, July 24, 2017, https://nypost.com/2017/07/24/this-tech -company-will-start-microchipping-their-workers/.

54. Camille Caldera, "Fact Check: Americans Won't Have Microchips Implanted by End of 2020," *USA Today*, August 1, 2020, https://www.usatoday.com/story/news /factcheck/2020/08/01/fact-check-americans-will-not-receive-microchips-end -2020/5413714002/.

55. "Genetic Information Discrimination," U.S. Equal Employment Commission, accessed May 25, 2023, https://www.eeoc.gov/genetic-information-discrimination.

56. "Genetic Information Discrimination."

57. Antonio Regalado, "DNA Tests for IQ Are Coming, But It Might Not Be Smart to Take One," *MIT Technology Review*, April 2, 2018, https://www.technologyreview .com/2018/04/02/144169/dna-tests-for-iq-are-coming-but-it-might-not-be-smart -to-take-one/.

58. Catherine Bliss, *Social by Nature: The Promise and Peril of Sociogenomics* (Palo Alto: Stanford University Press, 2018).

59. Neal Stephenson, *Snow Crash* (New York: Bantam Books, 1992).

60. Eric Ravenscraft, "What Is the Metaverse, Exactly?," *Wired*, June 15, 2023, https:// www.wired.com/story/what-is-the-metaverse/.

61. Ravenscraft, "What Is the Metaverse, Exactly?."

62. Sheera Frenkel and Kellen Browning (2021), "The Metaverse's Dark Side: Here Come Harassment and Assaults," *New York Times*, December 30, 2021, https:// www.nytimes.com/2021/12/30/technology/metaverse-harassment-assaults.html.

63. Tatum Hunter, "Surveillance Will Follow Us into 'the Metaverse,' and Our Bodies Could Be Its New Data Source," *Washington Post*, January 13, 2022, https://www .washingtonpost.com/technology/2022/01/13/privacy-vr-metaverse/.

64. Bill Gates, "Year in Review: Reasons for Optimism After a Difficult Year," *Gates-Notes*, December 7, 2021, https://www.gatesnotes.com/About-Bill-Gates/Year-in -Review-2021.

65. Nicholas Thompson and Nira A. Farahany, "Ready for Brain Transparency?," World Economic Forum, January 19, 2023, video, https://www.weforum.org /events/world-economic-forum-annual-meeting-2023/sessions/ready-for-brain -transparency.

66. Thompson and Farahany, "Ready for Brain Transparency?."

67. "Captain America: The Winter Soldier/Transcript," Fandom, accessed May 30, 2023, https://movies.fandom.com/wiki/Captain_America:_The_Winter_Soldier /Transcript.

68. "Captain America: The Winter Soldier/Transcript," Fandom.

69. Nico Grant and Cade Metz, "New Chatbot Is a 'Code Red' for Google's Search Business," *New York Times*, December 12, 2021, https://www.nytimes.com/2022 /12/21/technology/ai-chatgpt-google-search.html.

70. Tomas Chamorro-Premuzic, *I, Human: AI, Automation, and the Quest to Reclaim What Makes Us Unique* (Boston: Harvard Business Review Press, 2023).

CHAPTER 4

1. "What Is Evidence-Based Management?," Center for Evidence-Based Management, accessed May 30, 2023, https://cebma.org/faq/evidence-based-management/.

2. Jeffrey Pfeffer and Robert I. Sutton, *Hard Facts, Dangerous Half-Truths, and Total Nonsense: Profiting from Evidence-Based Management* (Boston: Harvard Business School Press, 2006).

3. Rob Briner, "Evidence-Based Human Resource Management," in *Evidence-Based Practice: A Critical Appraisal*, eds. Liz Trinder and Shirley Reynolds (London: Blackwell Science, 2000), 184–211; Wayne F. Cascio, "Evidence-Based Management and the Marketplace for Ideas," *Academy of Management Journal* 50, no. 5 (2007): 1009–1012; Edward E. Lawler III, "Why HR Practices Are Not Evidence-Based," *Academy of Management Journal* 50, no. 5 (2007): 1033–1036; Rob B. Briner and Eric Barends, "The Role of Scientific Findings in Evidence-Based HR," *People and Strategy* 39, no. 2 (2016): 16–20.

4. Eric Barends and Denise M. Rousseau, *Evidence-Based Management: How to Use Evidence to Make Better Organizational Decisions* (London, Kogan Page, 2018).

5. Rob B. Briner, "The Basics of Evidence-Based Practice," *People & Strategy* 42, no. 1 (2019): 1–7.

6. Steven McCartney and Na Fu, "Bridging the Gap: Why, How, and When HR Analytics Can Impact Organizational Performance," *Management Decision* 60, no. 13 (2022): 25–47.

7. John W. Boudreau and Steven Rice, "Bright, Shiny Objects and the Future of HR," *Harvard Business Review* 93 (2015): 72–78; Sergey Gorbatov and Angela Lane, "Is HR Missing the Point on Performance Feedback?," *MIT Sloan Management Review*, April 4, 2018, https://sloanreview.mit.edu/article/is-hr-missing-the-point-on-performance-feedback/.

8. Sean R. McMahon and Laura A. Orr, "Pop Psychology? Searching for Evidence, Real or Perceived, in Bestselling Business Books," *Organizational Dynamics* 46, no. 4 (2017): 195–201.

9. Edward E. Lawler III and George S. Benson, "The Practitioner-Academic Gap: A View from the Middle," *Human Resource Management Review* 32, no. 1, https://doi.org/10.1016/j.hrmr.2020.100748.

10. Pfeffer and Sutton, *Hard Facts, Dangerous Half-Truths, and Total Nonsense*.

11. Rob B. Briner and Neil D. Walshe, "Evidence-Based Management and Leadership" in *The Wiley-Blackwell Handbook of the Psychology of Leadership, Change, and Organizational Development*, eds. H. Skipton Leonard, Rachel Lewis, Arthur M. Freedman, and Jonathan Passmore (UK, Wiley Blackwell, 2013), 49–64.

12. Briner and Walshe, "Evidence-Based Management and Leadership."

13. Briner and Barends, "The Role of Scientific Findings in Evidence-Based HR."

14. Pfeffer and Sutton, *Hard Facts, Dangerous Half-Truths, and Total Nonsense*.

15. Rob B. Briner and Denise M. Rousseau, "Evidence-Based I-O Psychology: Not There Yet," *Industrial and Organizational Psychology* 4, no. 1 (2011): 3–22.

16. Denise M. Rousseau, "Envisioning Evidence-Based Management?," in *The Oxford Handbook of Evidence-Based Management*, ed. Denise M. Rousseau (New York, Oxford University Press, 2012), 3–24.

17. Martin R. Edwards, Andy Charlwood, Nigel Guenole, and Janet Marler, "HR Analytics: An Emerging Field Finding Its Place in the World Alongside Simmering Ethical Challenges," *Human Resource Management Journal* 1, (2022): 1–11, https://doi.org/10.1111/1748-8583.12435.

18. Laurie Bassi, "Raging Debates in HR Analytics," *People & Strategy* 34, no. 2 (2011): 14–18.

19. David Green, "Don't Forget the 'H' in HR: Ethics & People Analytics," *LinkedIn Pulse*, March 19, 2018, https://www.linkedin.com/pulse/dont-forget-h-hr-ethics-people-analytics-david-green/.

20. Jonathan Ferrar and David Green, *Excellence in People Analytics: How to Use Workforce Data to Create Business Value* (London: Kogan Page, 2021).
21. Amber Stark, "SIOP Issues Statement on AI-Based Personnel Assessment and Prediction," Society for Industrial and Organizational Psychology, March 1, 2022, https://www.siop.org/Research-Publications/Items-of-Interest/ArtMID/19366/ArticleID/5651/SIOP-Issues-Statement-on-AI-Based-Personnel-Assessment-and-Prediction.
22. "EEOC Hearing Explores Potential Benefits and Harms of Artificial Intelligence and Other Automated Systems in Employment Decisions," U.S. Equal Employment Commission, January 31, 2023, https://www.eeoc.gov/newsroom/eeoc-hearing-explores-potential-benefits-and-harms-artificial-intelligence-and-other.
23. John Simons, "The Creator of ChatGPT Thinks AI Should Be Regulated," *Time* magazine, February 5, 2023, https://time.com/6252404/mira-murati-chatgpt-openai-interview/.
24. Ferrar and Green, *Excellence in People Analytics*.
25. Dirk Petersen, "6 Steps to Ethically Sound People Analytics," myHRfuture, Insight222, October 20, 2020, https://www.myhrfuture.com/blog/2018/11/19/six-steps-to-ethically-sound-people-analytics.
26. "Technology Trust Ethics Framework," Deloitte, accessed May 23, 2023, https://www2.deloitte.com/us/en/pages/about-deloitte/articles/technology-trust-ethics-framework.html.
27. "Trustworthy AI Framework," Deloitte, accessed May 23, 2023, https://www2.deloitte.com/us/en/pages/deloitte-analytics/solutions/ethics-of-ai-framework.html.
28. Al Adamsen, "People Analytics and Future of Work," accessed May 23, 2023, https://pafow.net/.
29. Al Adamsen, *People Data for Good* podcast, accessed May 23, 2023, https://pafow.net/podcast.
30. Salvatore V. Falletta and Wendy L. Combs, "The HR Analytics Cycle: A Seven-Step Process for Building Evidence-Based and Ethical HR Analytics Capabilities," *Journal of Work-Applied Management* 13, no. 1 (2021): 51–68, https://doi.org/10.1108/JWAM-03-2020-0020.
31. Sam Adler-Bell and Michelle Miller, "The Datafication of Employment: How Surveillance and Capitalism Are Shaping Workers' Futures Without Their Knowledge," The Century Foundation, December 19, 2018, https://tcf.org/content/report/datafication-employment-surveillance-capitalism-shaping-workers-futures-without-knowledge/.
32. Ferrar and Green, *Excellence in People Analytics*.

CHAPTER 5

1. Mike Clayton, *The Influence Agenda: A Systematic Approach to Aligning Stakeholders in Times of Change* (New York: Palgrave Macmillan, 2014).
2. Eric Barends and Denise M. Rousseau, *Evidence-Based Management: How to Use Evidence to Make Better Organizational Decisions* (London, Kogan Page, 2018).
3. Alec Levenson, *Strategic Analytics: Advancing Strategy Execution and Organizational Effectiveness* (Oakland: Berrett-Koehler Publishers, 2015).
4. Levenson, *Strategic Analytics*.
5. Levenson, *Strategic Analytics*.

6. Jonathan Ferrar and David Green, *Excellence in People Analytics: How to Use Workforce Data to Create Business Value* (London: Kogan Page, 2021), 37.

7. Ferrar and Green, *Excellence in People Analytics*.

8. Ferrar and Green, *Excellence in People Analytics*.

9. Robert Prentice, "Being Your Best Self, Part 3: Moral Intent," Ethics Unwrapped, McCombs School of Business, University of Texas at Austin, video, https://ethicsunwrapped.utexas.edu/video/best-self-part-3-moral-intent.

10. Carl Sagan, *The Demon-Haunted World: Science as a Candle in the Dark* (New York: Ballantine Books, 1996).

11. Max Blumberg, LinkedIn message to the author, February 17, 2023.

12. Peter Cappelli and Martine J. Conyon, "What Do Performance Appraisals Do?," *ILR Review* 71, no 1 (2018): 88–116.

13. Jackie Wiles, "The Real Impact on Employees of Removing Performance Ratings," *Gartner*, August 15, 2019, https://www.gartner.com/smarterwithgartner/corporate-hr-removing-performance-ratings-is-unlikely-to-improve-performance.

14. Elaine D. Pulakos, Rose Mueller-Hanson, Sharon Arad, and Neta Moye, "Performance Management Can Be Fixed: An On-the-Job Experiential Learning Approach for Complex Behavior Change," *Industrial and Organizational Psychology: Perspectives on Science and Practice* 8, no. 1 (2015): 51–76.

CHAPTER 6

1. Jean Paul Isson and Jesse S. Harriott, *People Analytics in the Era of Big Data: Changing the Way You Attract, Acquire, Develop, and Retain Talent* (Hoboken: Wiley, 2016).

2. Nigel Guenole, Jonathan Ferrar, and Sheri Feinzig, *The Power of People: Learn How Successful Organizations Use Workforce Analytics to Improve Business Performance* (Pearson Education, 2017).

3. Alexis A. Fink, "Getting Results with Talent Analytics," *People & Strategy* 40, no. 3 (2017): 36–40.

4. Neil W. Schmitt and Richard J. Klimoski, *Research Methods in Human Resource Management* (Cincinnati: South-Western Publishing, 1991).

5. Elaine D. Pulakos, Rose Mueller-Hanson, Sharon Arad, and Neta Moye, "Performance Management Can Be Fixed: An On-the-Job Experiential Learning Approach for Complex Behavior Change," *Industrial and Organizational Psychology: Perspectives on Science and Practice* 8, no. 1 (2015): 51–76.

6. Schmitt and Klimoski, *Research Methods in Human Resource Management*.

7. Salvatore V. Falletta, "In Search of HR Intelligence: Evidence-Based HR Analytics Practices in High Performing Companies," *People & Strategy* 36, no. 4 (2014): 28–37.

CHAPTER 7

1. IBM, "Structured vs. Unstructured Data: What's the Difference?," IBM Cloud Education, June 29, 2021, https://www.ibm.com/cloud/blog/structured-vs-unstructured-data.

2. IBM, "Structured vs. Unstructured Data: What's the Difference?."

3. William H. Macey and Alexis A. Fink, eds., *Employee Surveys and Sensing: Challenges and Opportunities* (New York: SIOP Professional Practice Series, Oxford University Press, 2020).

4. Allan H. Church and Janine Waclawski, *Designing and Using Organizational Surveys: A Seven-Step Process* (San Franciso: Jossey-Bass, 2001).

5. Jack E. Edwards, John C. Scott, and Nambury S. Raju, *Evaluating Human Resources Programs: A 6-Phase Approach for Optimizing Performance* (San Franciso: Pfeiffer, 2007).

6. Seung Youn (Yonnie) Chyung, *10-Step Evaluation for Training and Performance Improvement* (Los Angeles: Sage, 2019).

7. Wendy L. Combs and Salvatore V. Falletta, *The Targeted Evaluation Process: A Performance Consultant Guide to Asking the Right Questions and Getting the Results You Trust* (Alexandria: ASTD, 2000).

8. Annie Murphy Paul, *The Cult of Personality: How Personality Tests Are Leading Us to Miseducate Our Children, Mismanage Our Companies, and Misunderstand Ourselves* (New York: Free Press, 2004).

9. Jack Phillips and Patti Phillips, ROI Institute, accessed June 23, 2023, https://roiinstitute.net.

10. Eric Barends and Denise M. Rousseau, *Evidence-Based Management: How to Use Evidence to Make Better Organizational Decisions* (London, Kogan Page, 2018).

11. Thomas H. Davenport, Jeanne Harris, and Jeremy Shapiro, "Competing on Talent Analytics," *Harvard Business Review* 88, no. 10 (2010): 52–58.

12. Alec Levenson, *Employee Surveys That Work: Improving Design, Use, and Organizational Impact* (San Francisco: Berrett-Koehler, 2014).

13. Dave Angrave, Andy Charlwood, Ian Kirkpatrick, Mark Lawrence, and Mark Stuart, "HR and Analytics: Why HR Is Set to Fail the Big Data Challenge," *Human Resource Management Journal* 26, no. 1 (2016): 1–11, https://doi.org/10.1111/1748-8583.12090.

14. Nate Silver, *The Signal and the Noise: Why So Many Predictions Fail—but Some Don't* (New York: Penguin Books, 2012).

CHAPTER 8

1. Madhura Chakrabarti and Elizabeth A. McCune, "Is the Engagement Survey the Only Way? Alternative Sources for Employee Sensing," in *Employee Surveys and Sensing: Challenges and Opportunities*, eds. William H. Macey and Alexis A. Fink (New York: SIOP Professional Practice Series, Oxford University Press, 2020), 219–235.

2. Roger Tourangeau and Ting Yan, "Sensitive Questions in Surveys," *Psychological Bulletin* 133, no. 5 (2007): 859–883.

3. R. Michael Furr, *Methods for Behavioral Research: A Systematic Approach* (Los Angeles: Sage, 2011).

4. Chakrabarti and McCune, "Is the Engagement Survey the Only Way?."

5. Arlene Fink, *How to Conduct Surveys: A Step-by-Step Guide* (Los Angeles: Sage, 2017).

6. Wendy L. Combs and Salvatore V. Falletta, *The Targeted Evaluation Process: A Performance Consultant Guide to Asking the Right Questions and Getting the Results You Trust* (Alexandria: ASTD, 2000).

7. Allan H. Church and Janine Waclawski, *Designing and Using Organizational Surveys: A Seven-Step Process* (San Franciso: Jossey-Bass, 2001).

8. Subhadra Dutta and Eric M. O'Rourke, "Open-Ended Questions: The Role of Natural Language Processing and Text Analytics," in *Employee Surveys and Sensing:*

Challenges and Opportunities, eds. William H. Macey and Alexis A. Fink (New York: SIOP Professional Practice Series, Oxford University, 2020), 202–218.

9. Combs and Falletta, *The Targeted Evaluation Process*.
10. Fink, *How to Conduct Surveys*.
11. Jen Katz-Buonincontro, *How to Interview and Conduct Focus Groups* (Washington, DC: American Psychological Association).
12. Katz-Buonincontro, *How to Interview and Conduct Focus Groups*.
13. Katz-Buonincontro, *How to Interview and Conduct Focus Groups*.
14. Katz-Buonincontro, *How to Interview and Conduct Focus Groups*.
15. Katz-Buonincontro, *How to Interview and Conduct Focus Groups*.
16. Combs and Falletta, *The Targeted Evaluation Process*.
17. Combs and Falletta, *The Targeted Evaluation Process*.
18. Anne Anastasi and Susana Urbina, *Psychological Testing*, 7th ed. (New York: Prentice Hall/Pearson Education, 1997); Richard Jeanneret and Rob Silzer, eds., *Individual Psychological Assessment: Predicting Behavior in Organizational Settings* (San Francisco: SIOP Professional Practice Series, Jossey-Bass, 1998); Tomas Chamorro-Premuzic, *Personality and Individual Differences*, 3rd ed. (UK: British Psychological Society and John Wiley & Sons, 2015).
19. Cecil R. Reynolds and Lisa A. Suzuki, "Bias in Psychological Assessment: An Empirical Review and Recommendations," in *Handbook of Psychology*, 2d ed., ed. Irvin B. Weiner (New York: John Wiley & Sons, 2013), 82–113.
20. "Best Buy and EEOC Reach Agreement to Resolve Discrimination Charge," U.S. Equal Employment Commission, June 6, 2018, https://www.eeoc.gov/newsroom/best-buy-and-eeoc-reach-agreement-resolve-discrimination-charge.
21. Dail L. Fields, *Taking the Measure of Work: A Guide to Validated Scales for Organizational Research and Diagnosis* (Thousand Oaks: Sage, 2002).
22. Eben Harrell, "A Brief History of Personality Tests," *Harvard Business Review*, March-April, 2017, https://hbr.org/2017/03/a-brief-history-of-personality-tests.
23. "HR Metrics Library," *McLean & Company*, accessed June 24, 2023, https://hr.mcleanco.com/research/hr-metrics-library.
24. Susan Cantrell and David Smith, *Workforce of One: Revolutionizing Talent Management Through Customization* (Boston: Harvard Business Press, 2010).
25. Neil J. Salkind, *100 Questions (and Answers) About Research Methods* (Los Angeles: Sage, 2012).
26. Salkind, *100 Questions (and Answers) About Research Methods*.
27. Donald T. Campbell and Julian C. Stanley, *Experimental and Quasi-Experimental Designs for Research* (Boston: Houghton Mifflin Company, 1963).
28. Campbell and Stanley, *Experimental and Quasi-Experimental Designs for Research*.
29. Stephen Few, *Signal: Understanding What Matters in a World of Noise* (Burlingame: Analytics Press, 2015).
30. Salkind, *100 Questions (and Answers) About Research Methods*.
31. Neil J. Salkind and Bruce B. Frey, *Statistics for People Who (Think They) Hate Statistics* (Los Angeles: Sage, 2020).
32. Salkind and Frey, *Statistics for People Who (Think They) Hate Statistics*.
33. Salkind and Frey, *Statistics for People Who (Think They) Hate Statistics*.
34. Salkind and Frey, *Statistics for People Who (Think They) Hate Statistics*.
35. Salkind and Frey, *Statistics for People Who (Think They) Hate Statistics*.
36. Salkind and Frey, *Statistics for People Who (Think They) Hate Statistics*.

37. Salkind and Frey, *Statistics for People Who (Think They) Hate Statistics.*
38. Combs and Falletta, *The Targeted Evaluation Process.*
39. Salkind and Frey, *Statistics for People Who (Think They) Hate Statistics.*
40. Bruce B. Frey, *100 Questions (and Answers) About Tests and Measurement* (Los Angeles: Sage, 2015).
41. Frey, *100 Questions (and Answers) About Tests and Measurement.*

CHAPTER 9

1. Erik van Vulpen, *The Basic Principles of People Analytics* (AnalyticsinHR.com, 2016).
2. Neil J. Salkind, *100 Questions (and Answers) About Statistics* (Los Angeles: Sage, 2015).
3. Neil J. Salkind and Bruce B. Frey, *Statistics for People Who (Think They) Hate Statistics* (Los Angeles: Sage, 2020).
4. Lei Chang, "Dependability of Anchoring Labels of Likert-Type Scales," *Educational and Psychological Measurement* 57, no. 5 (1997): 800–807.
5. Salkind and Frey, *Statistics for People Who (Think They) Hate Statistics.*
6. Salkind and Frey, *Statistics for People Who (Think They) Hate Statistics.*
7. Salkind and Frey, *Statistics for People Who (Think They) Hate Statistics.*
8. Fred B. Bryant and Paul R. Yarnold, "Principal-Components Analysis and Exploratory and Confirmatory Factor Analysis," in *Reading and Understanding Multivariate Statistics*, eds. Laurence G. Grimm and Paul R. Yarnold (Washington, DC: American Psychological Association, 1995), 99–136.
9. Salkind and Frey, *Statistics for People Who (Think They) Hate Statistics.*
10. Salkind and Frey, *Statistics for People Who (Think They) Hate Statistics.*
11. Salkind and Frey, *Statistics for People Who (Think They) Hate Statistics.*
12. Fredrick L. Oswald, Tara S. Behrend, Dan J. Putka, and Evan Sinar, "Big Data in Industrial-Organizational Psychology and Human Resource Management: Forward Progress for Organizational Research and Practice, *Annual Review of Organizational Psychology and Behavior* 7, no. 1 (2020): 505–533.
13. IBM, "What Is Data Science?" accessed June 24, 2023, https://www.ibm.com/topics /data-science.
14. Oswald et al., "Big Data in Industrial-Organizational Psychology and Human Resource Management."
15. Oswald et al., "Big Data in Industrial-Organizational Psychology and Human Resource Management."
16. Jure Leskovec, Anand Rajaraman, and Jeffrey David Ullman, *Mining of Massive Datasets* (UK: Cambridge University Press, 2020).
17. Eric Barends and Denise M. Rousseau, *Evidence-Based Management: How to Use Evidence to Make Better Organizational Decisions* (London, Kogan Page, 2018).
18. Oracle Cloud Infrastructure, "What Is a Data Warehouse?," accessed June 24, 2023, https://www.oracle.com/database/what-is-a-data-warehouse/.

CHAPTER 10

1. Gary Cokins, *Performance Management: Integrating Strategy Execution, Methodologies, Risk, and Analytics* (Hoboken, John Wiley & Sons, 2009).
2. Cokins, *Performance Management.*

3. Dana B. Minbaeva, "Building Credible Human Capital Analytics for Organizational Competitive Advantage," *Human Resource Management* 57, no. 3 (2018): 701–713.

4. Shonna D. Waters, Valerie N. Streets, Lindsay A. McFarlane, and Rachael Johnson-Murray, *The Practical Guide to HR Analytics: Using Data to Inform, Transform, and Empower HR Decisions* (Alexandria: SHRM, 2018); Theresa M. Welbourne, "Data-Driven Storytelling: The Missing Link in HR Data Analytics," *Employment Relations Today* 41, no. 4 (2015): 27–33.

5. Cole Nussbaumer Knaflic, *Storytelling with Data: A Data Visualization Guide for Business Professionals* (Hoboken: Wiley, 2015).

6. Brent Dykes, *Effective Data Storytelling: How to Drive Change with Data, Narrative, and Visuals* (Hoboken: Wiley, 2020).

7. Dykes, *Effective Data Storytelling.*

8. Thomas Rasmussen and Dave Ulrich, "Learning from Practice: How HR Analytics Avoids Being a Management Fad," *Organizational Dynamics* 44, no. 3 (2015): 236–242, https://doi.org/10.1016/j.orgdyn.2015.05.008.

9. Christopher T. Rotolo and Allan H. Church, "Big Data Recommendation for Industrial-Organizational Psychology: Are We in Whoville?," *Industrial and Organizational Psychology: Perspectives on Science and Practice* 8, no. 4 (2015): 515–520.

CHAPTER 11

1. *House*, Season 7, episode 708, "Small Sacrifices."

2. Henry Mintzberg, Bruce Ahlstrand, and Joseph Lampel, *Strategy Bites Back: It Is Far More and Less Than You Ever Imagined* (Upper Saddle River: Pearson Prentice Hall, 2005).

3. Mintzberg, Ahlstrand, and Lampel, *Strategy Bites Back.*

4. Wayne Cascio and John Boudreau, "HR Strategy: Optimizing Risks, Optimizing Rewards," *Journal of Organizational Effectiveness: People and Performance* 1, no. 1 (2014): 77–97.

5. Nadeem Kahn and Dave Millner, *Introduction to People Analytics: A Practical Guide to Data-Driven HR* (London: Kogan Page, 2020).

6. Lynda Gratton, *Living Strategy: Putting People at the Heart of Corporate Purpose* (London: Prentice Hall-FT, 2000).

7. Gratton, *Living Strategy.*

8. Gratton, *Living Strategy.*

9. Gratton, *Living Strategy.*

10. Gratton, *Living Strategy.*

11. Brian E. Becker, Mark A, Huselid, and Richard W. Beatty, *The Differentiated Workforce: Transforming Talent into Strategic Impact* (Boston: Harvard Business Press, 2009).

12. Becker, Huselid, and Beatty, *The Differentiated Workforce.*

13. Graeme Salaman and David Asch, *Strategy and Capability: Sustaining Organizational Change* (Malden: Blackwell Publishing, 2003).

14. Becker, Huselid, and Beatty, *The Differentiated Workforce.*

15. Dave Ulrich, *Human Resource Champions: The Next Agenda for Adding Value and Delivering Results* (Boston: Harvard Business School Press, 1997).

16. Wayne F. Cascio and John W. Boudreau, *Investing in People: Financial Impact of Human Resource Initiatives* (Upper Saddle River, NJ: Pearson, FT Press, 2008).
17. James L. Heskett, W. Earl Sasser Jr., and Leonard A. Schlesinger, *The Service Profit Chain: How Leading Companies Link Profit and Growth to Loyalty, Satisfaction, and Value* (New York, The Free Press, 1997).
18. John W. Boudreau and Peter M. Ramstad, *Beyond HR: The New Science of Human Capital* (Boston: Harvard Business School Press, 2007).
19. Rob B. Briner and Eric Barends, "The Role of Scientific Findings in Evidence-Based HR," *People and Strategy* 39, no. 2 (2016): 16–20.
20. List adapted from Sandra Durth, Neel Gandhi, Asmus Komm, and Florian Poll-ner, "HR's New Operating Model," McKinsey and Company, December 22, 2022, https://www.mckinsey.com/capabilities/people-and-organizational-performance/our-insights/hrs-new-operating-model.
21. Josh Bersin, "Redesigning HR: An Operating System, Not an Operating Model," Josh Bersin: Insights on Corporate Talent, Learning, and HR Technology, March 10, 2023, https://joshbersin.com/2023/03/redesigning-hr-an-operating-system-not-an-operating-model/.
22. John W. Boudreau and Edward E. Lawler III, "Stubborn Traditionalism in HRM: Causes and Consequences," *Human Resource Management Review* 24, no. 3 (2014): 232–244.
23. Cascio and Boudreau, "HR Strategy: Optimizing Risks, Optimizing Rewards."
24. Salvatore V. Falletta, "In Search of HR Intelligence: Evidence-Based HR Analytics Practices in High Performing Companies," *People & Strategy* 36, no. 4 (2014): 28–37.
25. Jeffrey Pfeffer and Robert I. Sutton, *Hard Facts, Dangerous Half-Truths, and Total Nonsense: Profiting from Evidence-Based Management* (Boston: Harvard Business School Press, 2006).
26. James C. Sesil, *Applying Advanced Analytics to HR Management Decisions: Methods for Selection, Developing Incentives, and Improving Collaboration* (Saddle River: Pearson, 2014).
27. Sesil, *Applying Advanced Analytics to HR Management Decisions.*
28. Thomas H. Davenport, Jeanne G. Harris, and Robert Morison, *Analytics at Work: Smarter Decisions, Better Results* (Boston: Harvard Business School Press, 2010).

CHAPTER 12

1. Thomas Rasmussen and Dave Ulrich, "Learning from Practice: How HR Analytics Avoids Being a Management Fad," *Organizational Dynamics* 44, no. 3 (2015): 236–242, https://doi.org/10.1016/j.orgdyn.2015.05.008; Dave Ulrich and John H. Dulebohn, "Are We There Yet? What Next for HR?," *Human Resource Management Review* 25, (2015): 188–204.
2. Salvatore V. Falletta, "In Search of HR Intelligence: Evidence-Based HR Analytics Practices in High Performing Companies," *People & Strategy* 36, no. 4 (2014): 28–37.
3. Naomi Verghese, "How Has People Analytics Grown in Importance?," myHRfuture, Insight222, March 2023, https://www.myhrfuture.com/blog/how-has-people-analytics-grown-in-importance.
4. Richard Rosenow, "Find Your Next HR Technology and People Analytics Role," accessed May 30, 2023, https://www.onemodel.co/roles-in-people-analytics-hr-technology.

5. Richard Rosenow, VP people analytics strategy, One Model, interview by Salvatore Falletta, May 5, 2023.

6. Christopher T. Rotolo and Allan H. Church, "Big Data Recommendation for Industrial-Organizational Psychology: Are We in Whoville?," *Industrial and Organizational Psychology: Perspectives on Science and Practice* 8, no. 4 (2015): 515–520.

7. "Ethical Principles of Psychologists and Code of Conduct," American Psychological Association, January 1, 2017, https://www.apa.org/ethics/code.

8. Logan L. Watts, Joel Lefkowitz, Manuel F. Gonzalez, and Sampoorna Nandi, "How Relevant Is the APA Ethics Code to Industrial-Organizational Psychology? Applicability, Deficiency, and Recommendations," *Industrial and Organizational Psychology* 16 (2023): 143–165, doi:10.1017/iop.2022.112.

9. "Ethics Code Task Force: Drafting a Transformational APA Ethics Code," American Psychological Association, accessed June 21, 2023, https://www.apa.org/ethics/task-force.

10. Lyle M. Spencer and Signe M. Spencer, *Competence at Work: Models for Superior Performance* (New York: John Wiley & Sons, 1993).

11. Spencer and Spencer, *Competence at Work.*

12. Nigel Guenole, Jonathan Ferrar, and Sheri Feinzig, *The Power of People: Learn How Successful Organizations Use Workforce Analytics to Improve Business Performance* (Pearson Education, 2017).

13. Rob Maurer, "HR Roles Among the Fastest Growing in US," February 6, 2023, https://www.shrm.org/resourcesandtools/hr-topics/talent-acquisition/pages/hr-roles-among-fastest-growing-us-linkedin.aspx.

14. List adapted from Nicholas Garbis, "Blueprint for Building a People Analytics Team," One Model, 2022, https://www.onemodel.co/whitepapers/blueprint-pa-team.

CHAPTER 13

1. Salvatore V. Falletta, "Organizational Intelligence Surveys," *Training & Development*, June 2008, 52–58; Salvatore V. Falletta and Wendy L. Combs, "The Organizational Intelligence Model in Context: A Comparative Analysis Case Study," *OD Practitioner* 50, no. 1 (2018): 22–29.

2. Falletta and Combs, "The Organizational Intelligence Model in Context."

3. Jose M. Cortina, "What Is Coefficient Alpha? An Examination of Theory and Applications," *Journal of Applied Psychology* 78, no. 1 (1993): 98–104.

4. Jim Clifton and Jim Harter, *It's The Manager: Moving from Boss to Coach* (New York: Gallup Press, 2019).

5. HRCI, accessed June 10, 2023, https://www.hrci.org/.

6. Jim Harter, "U.S Employee Engagement Slump Continues," *Gallup Workplace*, April 25, 2022, https://www.gallup.com/workplace/391922/employee-engagement-slump-continues.aspx.

7. Katheryn Brekken, Kevin Oakes, and Kevin Martin, "The Talent Imperative: A Fortune/i4CP Report," Institute of Corporate Productivity, 2022, www.i4cp.org.

8. Falletta and Combs, "The Organizational Intelligence Model in Context"; Jae Young Lee, Tonette S. Rocco, and Brad Shuck, "What Is a Resource: Toward a Taxonomy of Resources for Employee Engagement," *Human Resource Development Review* 19, no. 1 (2020): 5–38, doi: 10.1177/1534484319853100.

9. Salvatore V. Falletta and Wendy L. Combs, "The HR Analytics Cycle: A Seven-Step Process for Building Evidence-Based and Ethical HR Analytics Capabilities," *Journal of Work-Applied Management* 13, no. 1 (2021): 51–68, https://doi.org/10.1108/JWAM-03-2020-0020.

10. Susan Ladika, "Burnout Is a Problem for HR Professionals, *HR Magazine*, March 14, 2022, https://www.shrm.org/hr-today/news/hr-magazine/spring2022/pages/hr-practitioners-are-coping-with-burnout.aspx; Cory J. Wicker, "Where Is the Engagement of HRD Practitioners?," *New Horizons in Adult Education and Human Resource Development* 34, no. 1 (2022): 1–2, https://doi.org/10.1002/nha3.20353.

11. "State of HR Report: How the Great Resignation Is Impacting HR," *GoCo*, November 8, 2021, https://www.goco.io/blog/state-of-hr-the-great-resignation.

12. Brad Shuck, Jill L. Adelson, and Thomas G. Reio, "The Employee Engagement Scale: Initial Evidence for Construct Validity and Implications for Theory and Practice," *Human Resource Management* 56, no. 6 (2017): 953–977, https://doi.org/10.1002/hrm.21811.

13. Brad Shuck, *The Employee Engagement Scale (6 questions)*, Washington, DC: U.S. Copyright Office (1-7762123109).

14. Harter, "U.S Employee Engagement Slump Continues."

15. Ian Cook, Who Is Driving the Great Resignation? *Harvard Business Review,* September 15, 2021, https://hbr.org/2021/09/who-is-driving-the-great-resignation.

16. Jim Harter, "If Your Managers Aren't Engaged, Your Employees Won't Be Either," *Harvard Business Review,* June 6, 2019, https://hbr.org/2019/06/if-your-managers-arent-engaged-your-employees-wont-be-either.

17. Rebecca L. Ray, Peter Stathatos, and Brian Powers, "Employee Engagement: What Works Now?," The Conference Board, Report No. R-1504-12-RR, December 17, 2012, https://www.conference-board.org/publications/publicationdetail.cfm?publicationid=2382.

18. Kris Kitto, "What Are the Drivers of Employee Engagement?," *Glint*, April 21, 2020, https://www.glintinc.com/blog/drivers-of-employee-engagement/.

19. Clifton and Harter, *It's the Manager.*

20. Angela L. Duckworth, Christopher Peterson, Michael D. Matthews, and Dennis Kelly, "Grit: Perseverance and Passion for Long-Term Goals," *Journal of Personality and Social Psychology* 9, no. 6 (2007): 1087–1101.

21. Susan Cantrell and David Smith, *Workforce of One: Revolutionizing Talent Management Through Customization* (Boston: Harvard Business Press, 2010).

22. Dawn Klinghoffer and Elizabeth McCune, "Why Microsoft Measures Employee Thriving, Not Engagement," *Harvard Business Review,* June 24, 2022, https://hbr.org/2022/06/why-microsoft-measures-employee-thriving-not-engagement.

23. Lorrie Lykins, "Research Confirms It: Your Employees Are Fried," *The I4CP Productivity Blog*, I4CP, May 20, 2021, https://www.i4cp.com/productivity-blog/research-confirms-it-your-employees-are-fried.

INDEX

ABOUT THE AUTHOR

Dr. Salvatore Falletta is a director and professor of human resource leadership and organizational science at Drexel University. He also serves as a distinguished principal research fellow for The Conference Board. Additionally, he is the founder and president of HR Intelligence, an educational advisory and consulting group specializing in human capital research, HR analytics and strategy, workforce surveys, organizational diagnosis, employee engagement, talent management, learning and performance improvement evaluation, organizational effectiveness, workplace culture, and the future of work.

Dr. Falletta has authored or coauthored over 30 publications, including books, book chapters, articles, and reports in scientific and practitioner outlets. He is a highly sought-after speaker and frequently presents at national and international conferences and events. Over the past 20 years, Dr. Falletta has provided consulting and advisory services to a wide range of organizations, including FedEx, Hitachi, Meta, Oracle, SAP, Stanford University, and the State of California, among others.

Before embarking on his academic and consulting career, Dr. Falletta held the position of vice president and chief HR officer for a Fortune 1000 firm based in Silicon Valley, California. He has also held leadership positions in human resources at several well-known companies, including Nortel Networks, Alltel, Intel, SAP, and Sun Microsystems. During his time at Intel, he served as the head of global HR research and analytics and was a board member for the IT Survey Group, an industry consortium dedicated to employee and organizational surveys.

Dr. Falletta holds a doctoral degree in human resource development with specialized coursework in organizational behavior and psychology from North Carolina State University. Additionally, he has completed advanced people analytics courses at the University of Pennsylvania's Wharton School and the University of Cambridge. He is an active member of several academic and professional associations, including the Society for Industrial and Organizational Psychology, Academy of Management, Academy of Human Resource Development, Organization Development Network, Society for Human Resource Management, and Association for Talent Development.